PUBLIC ENGAGEMENT AND EDUCATION

Public Engagement and Education

Developing and Fostering Stewardship for an Archaeological Future

Edited by
Katherine M. Erdman

berghahn
NEW YORK • OXFORD
www.berghahnbooks.com

First published in 2019 by
Berghahn Books
www.berghahnbooks.com

© 2019, 2022 Katherine M. Erdman
First paperback edition published in 2022

All rights reserved. Except for the quotation of short passages for the purposes of criticism and review, no part of this book may be reproduced in any form or by any means, electronic or mechanical, including photocopying, recording, or any information storage and retrieval system now known or to be invented, without written permission of the publisher.

Library of Congress Cataloging-in-Publication Data

Names: Erdman, Katherine M., editor.
Title: Public Engagement and Education: Developing and Fostering Stewardship for an Archaeological Future / edited by Katherine M. Erdman.
Description: New York: Berghahn Books, 2019. | Includes bibliographical references and index.
Identifiers: LCCN 2018054497 (print) | LCCN 2018058638 (ebook) | ISBN 9781789201451 (ebook) | ISBN 9781789201444 (hardback: alk. paper)
Subjects: LCSH: Community archaeology. | Archaeology—Study and teaching. | Cultural property—Protection—Study and teaching.
Classification: LCC CC77.C66 (ebook) | LCC CC77.C66 P83 2019 (print) | DDC 930.107—dc23
LC record available at https://lccn.loc.gov/2018054497

British Library Cataloguing in Publication Data

A catalogue record for this book is available from the British Library

ISBN 978-1-78920-144-4 hardback
ISBN 978-1-80073-436-4 paperback
ISBN 978-1-78920-145-1 ebook

Contents

List of Tables and Figures   vii

List of Abbreviations   xi

Introduction. Opening a Dialog: Bringing Archaeology to
the Public   1
    Katherine M. Erdman

Part I. Inspiring and Developing an Interest in the Past

Chapter 1. Schools and Public Archaeology: Igniting
a Commitment to Heritage Preservation   21
    Charles S. White

Chapter 2. Science and Social Studies Adventures: Using
an Interdisciplinary Approach to Inspire School-Age Children
to Become Knowledge Producers   45
    Katrina Yezzi-Woodley, Chris Kestly, Beth Albrecht,
    Paul Creager, Joel Abdella, and Katherine Hayes

Chapter 3. Strengthening a Place-Based Curriculum through
the Integration of Archaeology and Environmental Education   74
    Appendix: Questionnaire Designed to Assess Student
    Understanding of the People and the Land Unit at School
    of the Wild   105
    Elizabeth C. Reetz, Chérie Haury-Artz, and Jay A. Gorsh

Chapter 4. Engaging with the Past through Writing
Accountable First-Person Creative Fiction: BACAB CAAS   109
    Appendix: BACAB CAAS Final Draft Evaluation Form
    Used in North American Archaeology Class   131
    Lewis C. Messenger, Jr.

Part II. Fostering a Deeper Respect for Archaeological Heritage

Chapter 5. Archaeologists and the Pedagogy of Heritage: Preparing Graduate Students for Tomorrow's Interdisciplinary, Engaged Work in Heritage   137
   Phyllis Mauch Messenger

Chapter 6. Gathering Public Opinions about Archaeology and Heritage in Belize: A Drive toward Better Local Access and Programming   157
   Geralyn Ducady

Chapter 7. Archaeology for a Lifetime: Reaching Older Generations through Adult Education Programs   186
   Appendix: Archaeological Heritage Survey 2015   207
   Katherine M. Erdman

Part III. The Future of Archaeology, Education, and Preservation

Chapter 8. Best Practices in Archaeology Education: Successes, Shortcomings, and the Future   215
   Jeanne M. Moe

Chapter 9. Navigating Heritage Stewardship in the Digital Age   237
   Jodi Reeves Eyre and Leigh Anne Ellison

Glossary   255

Index   263

Tables and Figures

Tables

2.1. Maple Grove Middle School program budget for years one and two. Courtesy of the authors.   59

3.1. The categories of environmental education objectives, as outlined in the Tbilisi Declaration. Source: UNESCO 1978; author-generated table.   76

3.2. Students' responses to People and the Land questions, showing the percentage of students who chose each response and the percentage of increase or decrease between the pre- and post-tests. Courtesy of the authors.   91

5.1. University of Minnesota Heritage Studies and Public History Graduate Program two-year curriculum and sample archaeology track. Courtesy of the author.   141

Figures

1.1. C3 Framework (National Council for the Social Studies 2013, 12; used with permission).   24

1.2. In touch with an ancient statue. Photo by Bananashake, "Touch for Memory," Dreamstime.com, used with permission.   28

1.3. Looking for artifacts. Photo by Amy Rowley, ThurstonTalk.com, used with permission.   33

2.1. Spear throwing at the Paleopicnic. Photo courtesy of Katrina Yezzi-Woodley. 46

2.2. Maple Grove Middle School students flintknapping at the University of Minnesota Anthropology Department–sponsored Paleopicnic. Photo courtesy of Katrina Yezzi-Woodley. 47

2.3. SASSA volunteer Sam Porter teaching Maple Grove Middle School students about flintknapping. Photo courtesy of Katrina Yezzi-Woodley. 51

2.4. SASSA volunteer Thomas Alberg teaching Maple Grove Middle School students about the anatomy of a flake. Photo courtesy of Katrina Yezzi-Woodley. 51

2.5. Maple Grove Middle School student learns about stone tool industries by refitting a magnetized, 3D puzzle. Photo courtesy of Katrina Yezzi-Woodley. 52

2.6. Dr. Kat Hayes and SASSA volunteers Emily Briggs and Annie Melton teach Gordon Parks High School students how to work the GPR. Photo courtesy of the authors. 64

3.1. Teacher orientation. Archaeologist Chérie Haury-Artz works with sixth-grade teachers at the historic archaeological site. Photo courtesy of the University of Iowa Office of the State Archaeologist. 83

3.2. Historical archaeological site 13JH1479 and adjacent Iowa River. Photo courtesy of the University of Iowa Office of the State Archaeologist. 84

3.3. Chéric Haury-Artz works with Johnathan Buffalo and Suzanne Wanatee Buffalo to build the wickiup frame in the fall of 2016. Photo courtesy of the University of Iowa Office of the State Archaeologist. 85

3.4. Elizabeth Reetz and students listen as Suzanne Wanatee Buffalo and Johnathan Buffalo explain Meskwaki traditions associated with wickiups. Photo courtesy of the University of Iowa Office of the State Archaeologist. 86

3.5. Students stand around the hearth in the completed wickiup frame. Photo courtesy of the University of Iowa Office of the State Archaeologist. 87

Tables and Figures   ix

3.6. Expedient, temporary shelters built by School of the Wild students. Photo courtesy of the University of Iowa Office of the State Archaeologist.   87

4.1. Title page of "Rainforest Adventure . . . involving Silvery Gibbons and Jambu Fruit Doves" by Emma Swank (2006). Courtesy of Emma Swank.   120

4.2. Colorful apes and the Stone Mountain—Borobudur. From "Rainforest Adventure . . . involving Silvery Gibbons and Jambu Fruit Doves" by Emma Swank (2006, 15). Courtesy of Emma Swank.   121

4.3. Final page of explanation section for parents from "Rainforest Adventure . . . involving Silvery Gibbons and Jambu Fruit Doves" by Emma Swank (2006, 25). Courtesy of Emma Swank.   122

4.4. Title page of "Suchin and the Prince in Angkor Thom" by Bonnie Wetherby (2006). Courtesy of Bonnie Wetherby.   123

4.5. Text and images introducing Angkor Thom, the Prince, and Suchin. From "Suchin and the Prince in Angkor Thom" by Bonnie Wetherby (2006, 5–6). Courtesy of Bonnie Wetherby.   123

4.6. Suchin runs through Angkor Thom's market. From "Suchin and the Prince in Angkor Thom" by Bonnie Wetherby (2006, 12–13). Courtesy of Bonnie Wetherby.   124

5.1. The *Remembering the Bohemian Flats: One Place, Many Voices* exhibit was visited by descendants of families who had lived there. The exhibit was held in the central lobby of the Mill City Museum on the Mississippi River in Minneapolis. Exhibit developers used QR codes for each panel to provide access to additional research done by students in a spring 2014 archival research class. Photo by David Stevens, courtesy of the Minnesota Historical Society.   147

5.2. University of Minnesota students participated in collaborative research on Historic Fort Snelling as part of the MNHS–UMN Heritage Partnership. Graduate research assistant Kelly Wolf (*top center*) and undergraduate Meron Tebeje (*lower right*) inventory artifacts from the Fort Snelling Collection. Photo by Nancy Buck Hoffman, courtesy of the Minnesota Historical Society.   149

5.3.	The Museum Fellows group from the University of Minnesota toured museums in Washington, DC, and met with Lonnie Bunch, Founding Director of the National Museum of African American History and Culture. Photo by Chris Taylor, courtesy of the Minnesota Historical Society.	152
6.1.	Map of the districts of Belize. Wikimedia Commons.	160
6.2.	Community children look closely at a feature at Kaq Ru Ha. Photo courtesy of the author.	163
6.3.	Artifact "display" at the Marco Gonzalez archaeological site. Photo courtesy of the author.	169
6.4.	The author at Cahal Pech archaeological site. Photo by Angela Dion, used with permission.	170
6.5.	Percentage of surveys from each district. Courtesy of the author.	172
6.6.	Survey result: How have you learned about the past cultures of Belize? Courtesy of the author.	176
6.7.	Survey result: How have you learned about new archaeological discoveries in Belize? Courtesy of the author.	176
6.8.	Survey result: What kind of outreach programs about history or archaeology would you be likely to participate in? Courtesy of the author.	177

Abbreviations

ADS – Archaeology Data Service
AIA – Archaeological Institute of America
AMLE – Association of Middle Level Education
ARPA – Archaeological Resources Protection Act
ARRA – American Revitalization and Recovery Act
ATM – Actun Tunichil Muknal
BACAB CAAS – Bringing Ancient Cultures Alive by Creating Archaeologically Accountable Stories
BLM – Bureau of Land Management
C3 – College, Career, and Civic Life Framework for Social Studies State Standards
CCSS – Common Core State Standards
CDES – College of Design (University of Minnesota, Twin Cities)
CEDS – Civic Engaged Digital Storytelling
CLA – College of Liberal Arts
DNR – Department of Natural Resources
EE – Environmental education
EPA – Environmental Protection Agency
EXARC – The International Council of Museums (ICOM) Affiliated Organization, representing archaeological open-air museums, experimental archaeology, ancient technology, and interpretation.
FADGI – Federal Agencies Digital Guidelines Initiative
GIS – geographic information systems
GPHS – Gordon Parks High School

GPMP – Guantánamo Public Memory Project
GPR – ground-penetrating radar
HAL – Humanities Action Lab
HSPH – Heritage Studies and Public History
IA – Belize Institute of Archaeology
IAS – Institute for Advanced Study (University of Minnesota)
ICCSD – Iowa City Community School District
ICOM – International Council of Museums
IES – Institute of Educational Sciences
ISD – intermediate school district
ISIS – Islamic State of Iraq and Syria
LiDAR – Light Detection and Ranging
MACHI – Maya Area Cultural Heritage Initiative
MGMS – Maple Grove Middle School
MNHS – Minnesota Historical Society
MNRA – Macbride Nature Recreation Area
MOU – Memorandum of Understanding
MSU – Montana State University
NAAEE – North American Association for Environmental Education
NAGPRA – Native American Graves Protection and Repatriation Act
NCA – North Central Association
NEH – National Endowment for the Humanities
NHPA – National Historic Preservation Act
NICH – Belize National Institute of Culture and History
NPS – National Parks Service
NRHP – National Register of Historic Places
NTHP – National Trust for Historic Preservation
OLLI – Osher Lifelong Learning Institute
OSA – Office of the State Archaeologist
Outdoors Program – University of Iowa Recreational Services Outdoors Program
PBL – problem-based learning
PEC – Public Education Committee
PKEMRA – Post–Katrina Emergency Management Reform Act

REAP–CEP – Resource Enhancement and Protection Conservation Education Program
SAA – Society for American Archaeology
SASSA – Science and Social Studies Adventures
SBG – standards-based grading
SLE – significant life experiences
SoW – School of the Wild
STEAM – Science, Technology, Engineering, Arts, and Mathematics
STEM – Science, Technology, Engineering, and Mathematics
tDAR – the Digital Archaeological Record
THEN – The Heritage Education Network
TWHP – Teaching with Historic Places
UbD – Understanding by Design
UMN – University of Minnesota, Twin Cities
UNESCO – United Nations Educational, Scientific, and Cultural Organization
XARP – Xibun Archaeological Research Project

INTRODUCTION

Opening a Dialog
Bringing Archaeology to the Public

Katherine M. Erdman

The Challenge(s) Facing Archaeology

It is a challenging time to be an archaeologist. The world's collective archaeological heritage is threatened on multiple fronts by both anthropogenic and natural causes (Pace 2012), many of which seem beyond our ability to aid or influence. Necessities for human survival, such as infrastructure development or agriculture, pose threats to the preservation of archaeological materials. As areas of the world continue to experience rapid periods of urbanization or develop their infrastructure to meet the needs of their citizens, as seen in Palestine or Turkey, more cultural and archaeological heritage sites are at risk for destruction from new construction projects (Al-Houdalieh and Sauders 2009; Özdoğan 2013). With limited real estate available, it is hard to justify preserving plots of land with unusable ruins when residents need housing and services. Agricultural cultivation contributes to soil loss and is likely only to increase damage to sites in coming years with the development of new technologies and more efficient machinery (Wilkinson et al. 2006). Even unchecked invasive species, such as feral pigs in Florida, are known to disrupt undiscovered sites by causing soil disturbance and subsequent erosion while burrowing (Engeman et al. 2013).

Black-market sales, economic disparities, and war affect the security and preservation of sites globally (Brodie, Doole, and Renfrew 2001; Proulx 2013). Wealthy collectors of antiquities continue to drive the illicit market and prey upon people in economically depressed or war-torn areas, such as Afghanistan or across Central and South America, who have turned to looting in order to survive and provide for their families (Mackenzie 2011, 134; Campbell 2013, 120; Matsuda 1998). Digging fortifications, combat, occupation, and other side effects of violent conflicts have destroyed or damaged over seven hundred archaeological and cultural heritage sites across Syria and Iraq illustrating the effects of modern war on the past (Danti 2015). We may hear about only some of these events because they make it into mainstream media, but the loss of archaeological sites, artifacts, and the knowledge they stand to share, is a worldwide problem (e.g., Chippindale and Gill 2000; Davis 2011; Goddard 2011; K. L. Smith 2005).

Additionally, climate and environmental changes are increasingly affecting the dignity of sites around the world. Countries rich with ice, such as Norway, are now centers for "ice melt archaeology" with rates of thaw that do not allow archaeologists to keep up with documenting, gathering, and preserving the quantities of artifacts being revealed (Curry 2014). Such situations represent significant losses of knowledge since many of the artifacts are organic, such as textiles, and would normally not have been preserved in the first place. Coastal and underwater sites are similarly affected by changes in climate and environment. Increased rates of erosion and the decline of protective aquatic vegetation (Milner 2012), increases in damaging storms and ocean acidity (Wright 2016), and increased flooding and ground instability (Bickler, Clough, and Macready 2013) all affect the preservation of artifacts and known and yet unrecorded archaeological sites.

Many of these issues are rooted in complex regional or nation-specific social, political, historic, and economic systems (Contreras 2010; Davis 2011; Matsuda 1998; K. L. Smith 2005; Wright 2016); meaning there is no cure-all solution. There is, however, one challenge not listed above which we can address—the lack of understanding of our discipline. Who among us has not been mistaken for a paleontologist at some point (Moe, Chapter 8), or has had questions about keeping the "treasure" we find (Ducady, Chapter 6)? There is a fundamental misunderstanding amongst much of the public about what archaeologists do, how we do it, and why. We cannot begin to address the importance of archaeological context, preservation and stewardship, and the value of archaeology as a lens through which to see the world if we do not first clearly communicate the basics of the discipline and the role of professionals in it. By laying a strong foundation in archaeology education at a young age, and then fostering it over time, we will begin to see ripples of change as they affect some of the more complex threats to our collective heritage, for, as Franklin and Moe observe, "An archaeologically literate citizenry concerns itself with saving the past for the future. It understands that history matters and, more importantly, that everybody's history matters" (2012, 570).

Opening a Dialog with Public Audiences Is Worth the Effort

There are many reasons why we must open engaging and educational dialogs with the public. I focus here on two points: archaeology is a valuable tool for understanding the world and learning about other disciplines, and we need allies.

The Value of Archaeology

The public deserves to have a clear grasp of what archaeology is and why it is worth preserving. Archaeology appeals to many of us because we recognize the deep perspective it offers in understanding the role past events and relationships play in shaping the social and political realities of the present (Little 2012). As Little and Shackel (2014) have shown, archaeology can be a tool for social justice and peacebuilding by bringing together multiple histories and narratives; it can unite people and transcend boundaries. It is a way of teaching cultural sensitivity and fosters cross-cultural empathy (L. Messenger, Chapter 4).

In addition to the value inherent within the discipline itself, it is also special because it is one of the few that can unite social science, humanities, the hard sciences, environmental studies, and technology (Yezzi-Woodley et al., Chapter 2; Reetz, Haury-Artz, and Gorsh, Chapter 3). For this reason, archaeology illustrates the value of interdisciplinary approaches to solving multifaceted problems, working across perceived boundaries, and the application of skills in other contexts.

Archaeology possesses fascinating and unique values and capabilities that are readily apparent to those exposed to the field and, consequently, become something worth saving and protecting. When the significance of archaeology is recognized by those outside of the discipline, we can begin to create archaeology allies. It is at this point that we can tackle some of the other problems, such as the looting and illicit trade of antiquities, which threaten sites and materials. If people see that objects are more than their monetary worth or items of prestige, we can begin to make progress in the protection of the past. As Campbell observes, "By challenging collectors' desire for status symbols, a culture change would prevent the trafficking from the top down . . . Educating the public about the quantitative and qualitative impact of antiquities trafficking should help promote a culture change" (2013, 137–38). But to promote change, even in one area, we have to ensure the public understands and appreciates what archaeology is and what is at stake.

Strength in Numbers

If there is any chance for preserving the past for future generations to come, it will require teamwork and the collective skills and passion of both professionals and nonprofessionals. Through meaningful and engaging educational experiences where participants can both learn and construct knowledge, the value of archaeology and its ability to enrich one's understanding of the world becomes evident and meaningful (Franklin and Moe 2012, 569). When something is meaningful, a person is more likely to fight for it; this is how we build stewardship allies.

The term "stewardship" has been problematic at times in archaeological discourse (L. Smith and Waterton 2012, 157; Jeppson 2012, 592–93), and is necessary to clarify what we mean by it in this volume. Pace describes stewardship as "the care and prudent use of something or resources entrusted to one's care . . . to care means to look after and provide for; to entrust means to confide the care or responsibility over something or a task outside one's ownership. Entrustment therefore implies guardianship" (2012, 290). The contributors to this volume maintain a similar understanding. When discussing stewards or stewardship, we are referring to the collective responsibility and effort by professionals and nonprofessionals to maintain and conserve existing archaeological sites and materials for all peoples so that we may continue to learn and expand our knowledge of human experiences in the past. As guardians, not owners, of these resources, we are ensuring that generations to come have the opportunity to contribute their voices and experiences to develop a more inclusive understanding of human history.

To build stewardship networks to help us with this undertaking, we should appeal to the young and old alike. Developing a love of, or at least a respect for, archaeology at a young age will ensure we have allies for the future. Fostering an interest in older generations now will help us work toward more immediate preservation impacts, such as legislation to protect sites, voting for lawmakers who support heritage initiatives, or volunteers and donors to help with research. Creating allies of all ages can have positive effects when it comes to the protecting archaeological resources. Such solutions are not easy quick-fixes with instant results, but ones that, if implemented now, will have lasting effects for generations to come, and, as a result, will help us to more profoundly tackle some of the other challenges facing archaeological heritage.

Opening a Dialog Requires Engagement and Communication

In recent years, archaeologists have emphasized the importance of communicating our research to the public, how to do so effectively, and broader concerns for the future of archaeology (Corbishley 2014; Gransard-Desmond 2015; Harding 2007; Jameson and Baugher 2007; Little and Shackel 2014; Thomas and Lea 2014; Tully 2007; Watkins 2006). More than ever, there are seemingly endless options for dispersing information. To foster archaeological literacy successfully, it is necessary to outline the desired outcome of the educational outreach project, identify the learning objectives necessary to meet that outcome, and then determine the most appropriate method for executing it. There are three broad categories of communication available to archaeologists: traditional media, which includes print, audio, and visual forms; online digital content; and interpersonal or interactive learning experiences. Each has its strengths and weaknesses as venues for archaeological education, and it is critical to consider aspects of accuracy, access, and effectiveness.

Traditional Media

While grouped here as traditional media, print and audio/visual media have their own strengths and weaknesses for communicating archaeological information to non-specialist audiences.

Print media, which includes books, newspapers, and magazines, has been the preferred venue for disseminating archaeological research since the discipline's founding (Harding 2007). These are often viewed as the most credible sources of accurate information because they typically undergo extensive editing or peer review. However, while accurate at the time of publication, information can sometimes become outdated within a decade as new research changes our understanding of sites and cultures, as well as our theories for interpreting the past. Updated editions, if even produced, may take years to appear on the market.

The digitization of traditional media, both print and audio/visual, has made both forms more accessible than ever before. Printed materials remain physically available through bookstores, subscriptions, and libraries; however, electronic versions and digital subscriptions offer access anywhere and at any time. There are no limits or restrictions to sharing the information contained in physical books; they can be repeatedly accessed and easily distributed to others. Professional journals are the least publicly accessible print medium as they require hefty subscription fees. With the rise in popularity of sites like Academia.edu and ResearchGate, and a desire by researchers to share their work, even articles published in specialized journals are now accessible.

Books and other publications are effective for sharing varying degrees of knowledge. A short newspaper article offers highlights; a magazine, such as *Archaeology* or *National Geographic*, offers a more contextualized account of a site, artifact, or culture; and a book or professional journal may address a specific topic more in-depth. In each of these presentations, the reader can engage the material at their own pace offering them time to reflect on what they read, if desired. While in some ways reading is considered passive information transmission, since the reader is simply receiving it, books can spark more intensive active learning and lead to the pursuit of additional knowledge in other forms. However, print media transmit larger quantities of information and in greater detail, and can just as easily overwhelm and bore the reader by taking on a "telling," rather than "showing" approach to the past.

There is significant variation in the accuracy of audio and visual media (radio, film, and television). The BBC and British Museum's co-produced radio series *A History of the World in 100 Objects* (BBC 2010), for example, is well-researched and presents facts drawn directly from the objects to educate and inspire audiences. Other programs, such as *American Diggers* or *Ancient Aliens*, are sensationalized, viewership-driven productions that care nothing for actual archaeological methods or interpretations; the goal is entertainment, not accuracy or education (Pagán 2015). Despite the failings of some programs, others, such as PBS's *NOVA*, continue to present quality educational programs in engaging ways that often highlight some of the latest discoveries made by archaeologists and physical anthropologists (e.g., National Geographic Television and PBS's co-produced *NOVA* special, "Dawn of Humanity," which presented the *Homo naledi* discovery shortly after the professional publication appeared).

Audio and visual media, unlike print, are likely to reach a much greater audience (Pagán 2015). Traditionally, these media were limited to scheduled air dates and times, and for some, required paying for a cable subscription, thus limiting audiences to those who could afford both the time and money to watch them. Online distribution, however, is changing how people access these programs. Digital access to some programs may still require a subscription, such as through Netflix or Hulu, but others can be streamed directly from the producer's website or can be found on sites like YouTube. While online distribution means seemingly unlimited access for viewers, in some ways, the audience will likely be limited to those who have internet access and are actively searching for archaeology programs, whereas a cable viewer may stumble across one while casually channel surfing.

Listening to or viewing a program has the potential to spark greater interest in a subject because it is often presented in an engaging or entertaining manner (Carnes 1996, 9). Visual presentations of the past, in particular, make it easier for the audience to understand and connect; they literally show, rather than describes as print does, how scholars see past cultures and lifestyles. Even though the images presented are not directly tangible, they offer a physical point of reference for audiences who may not be familiar with archaeology. Such programs can be valuable, but like print media, they often represent a form of passive learning. Viewers and listeners receive information but have little time to reflect on it or must wait until the end of the program to do so. It may also be harder to follow up on certain details since it is unlikely that citations or additional information are offered, unless perhaps on a program website.

Online Digital Content

Digital content, i.e., those designed exclusively for the internet or as apps, have characteristics of both print and audio/visual media and the advantages and disadvantages of each. The greatest feature of digital media is accessibility. With a few key taps in a search browser, *anyone* interested in learning more about archaeology or a more specific aspect of it can find a plethora of multimedia resources. This content is also available *anywhere* one can access the internet—at home, the library, or on smartphones.

Professional archaeologists now have a relatively inexpensive and readily available method for bringing large audiences into archaeological discourse. Through excavation or research websites, professional blogs, social media, and online op-ed pieces, archaeologists can more easily share their accurate, up-to-date research in ways that will appeal to a variety of audiences. And unlike traditional media, digital media can be amended and easily updated as new information becomes available. Other platforms, such as GlobalXplorer, involve the public directly in the protection of sites from looting and further destruction while sharing educational materials about the archaeology of a particular country. Archaeology-specific news websites, websites with interactive artifact collections or 3D reconstructions of sites, podcasts of university lectures or archaeology-focused shows, videos on ArchaeologyChannel.org and other video platforms, apps such as Archaeology News, and educational games such as Dig Ventures, offer additional ways for professionals to maintain a dialog with the public and for someone to explore and learn more about archaeology.

Accessibility is also highly problematic. People untrained in archaeological methods and analysis can produce their own information or interpretations that may be wildly inaccurate or deliberately untruthful to further a specific agenda, and can easily be disguised in ways that are not apparent to other non-specialists. Sensational headlines, click bait, and "alternative facts" can spread across social media, like Facebook or Twitter, before professionals have time to respond. In some ways, even professional blogs or sites have the potential to be problematic if they represent only one opinion or side of a debate.

The incredible diversity found within digital media makes them effective teaching tools because they appeal to different styles of learning. As with print media, some forms of digital media, such as blogs or websites sharing large quantities of written information, represent passive learning in that the reader is receiving information, but not necessarily engaging or responding to it beyond the "comments" section. In other cases, online platforms may support active learning by offering space for the audience to interact with information or engage in discussions with others. Archaeology organizations using Facebook can easily share upcoming events or new research allowing for the public to respond and engage with professional organizations by "liking," commenting, or asking questions below the post (Huvila 2013, 28). Similarly, "ask-an-expert" type sessions on Reddit also offer the opportunity for the public to open a literal dialog with archaeologists. Websites with 3D models of artifacts and sites are also more likely to appeal to those who prefer active learning. The opportunity to look at the physical properties of ancient materials, to turn it in one's digital-hands, provides a powerful, more direct connection to the ancient world. Such connections with materials and professionals working with the past makes history come alive in a way traditional media is often unable to accomplish.

Interpersonal Approaches

Interacting directly with non-specialists through public lectures, museum and outreach programs, community education, community archaeology projects, etc., are examples of interpersonal approaches to archaeological education. Such programs disseminate current knowledge directly from an institution or professional to their audience, or offer the opportunity for the public to generate knowledge themselves. Events focused on knowledge-sharing are likely to disseminate well-researched information or information coming directly from an experienced professional in the field. The opportunity for continued participation through additional classes, distributed materials, hands-on workshops, or an online platform may also be available.

While providing accurate and contemporary information to diverse audiences, access to such programs may be limited. Not every town or city has an archaeologist, museum, or university to share information with the public or involve them in research. Having to travel to attend such events or, if available, having to pay for them, limits who can attend public talks, exhibitions, or projects. Even in cases where these are available, information about such types of programs may not be disseminated well or reach all members of the public who may be interested in attending.

Even though access may be a challenge, interpersonal approaches offer highly effective, active learning (White, Chapter 1). Unlike traditional media, and sometimes digital media, which reflect one-sided communication with viewers as passive recipients of information, interpersonal communication is dynamic. Interactions happen immediately and directly; no interface is needed to engage a professional. Real-time dialog is possible making the interaction more meaningful and constructive, especially if a participant has specific questions about the field or subject at hand. As White notes, for people to truly connect with history, they want to see it and touch it. Like artifacts or sites themselves, archaeologists represent a tangible link to the past because we are more connected to it than most; we experience it and work with it regularly. Our profession is unusual and exciting to the public and by engaging with us directly, in a way, they experience it too and connect with the past in more fulfilling and meaningful ways.

Traditional media, digital media, and interpersonal approaches each have strengths and weaknesses for opening dialogs about the past. In addition to access, accuracy, and effectiveness, there are other factors to consider, such as learning goals and the primary audience. The contributors to this volume primarily engage the public through interpersonal approaches in both formal and informal educational settings, however, digital media is increasingly playing a more integrated or supplementary role in their work. Employing a variety of communication methods ensures we reach diverse audiences and appeal to different types of learners.

Objectives of this Book

Across the United States and abroad, archaeologists have developed dozens of educational archaeology programs that incorporate interpersonal approaches with traditional and online media to inspire and communicate with nonprofessionals, such as the Peabody Museum's high school archaeology service learning program (Randall and Taylor 2016) or the STEAM-based professional development program out of the Oriental Institute of the University of Chicago (Ng-He and Makdisi 2016). Many of these were established after years of hard work perfecting learning objectives and the delivery of knowledge. Instead of trying to reinvent the wheel in archaeology education, we should start communicating with one another, learning from the other's contributions, and evaluating the effectiveness of our work (Franklin and Moe 2012, 568). Building on our collective successes or modifying them for one's own local educational programming is not uninventive or thoughtless; in fact, it is just the opposite. Like any other archaeological project, you do your background research, learn the established methods, and then implement them responsibly to ensure success in your own work. So much of archaeology overlaps at its roots that we can use the same framework and modify it for our individual regions, areas of study, or learning objectives; this offers a huge advantage as half of the work is completed already.

To ensure your success as you undertake public outreach to promote archaeology and heritage preservation, the contributions from this volume's authors include the following objectives.

Objective One: Inspiration and Getting Started

We hope after reading this book that you are inspired to get involved with existing programs in your community, or if educational archaeology programs are lacking, that you will consider opening a dialog in some manner. This undertaking does not have to be difficult; please, learn from these contributors' decades of combined experience. There is a desire from all ages to learn about archaeology; the subsequent chapters begin with K–12 education and end with senior learners to ensure all educational levels are addressed. Reaching out to even one demographic will have positive effects in the community and archaeology broadly. While some of the chapters represent specific case studies, the general outline and principles employed can be applied in different communities or countries using local, available resources.

Objective Two: Promote Sustainable Practices

The creation of the new *Journal of Archaeology and Education* indicates that there are many archaeologists interested in working within their communities and wish to succeed in their efforts. The examples presented in this volume focus on sustainable efforts for outreach and education. Contributors utilize existing resources, such as historic places or community education programs (Reetz et al., Chapter 3; Erdman, Chapter 7); construct their programs to fit within established educational practices, such as Common Core in K–12 education or university research assignments (White, Chapter 1; Yezzi-Woodley et al., Chapter 2; L. Messenger, Chapter 4); and look to the future of archaeology and education by discussing best practices or the role of digital archaeology (P. Messenger, Chapter 5; Ducady, Chapter 6; Moe, Chapter 8; Reeves Eyre and Ellison, Chapter 9). By working with existing resources, rather than starting from scratch, we hope that our readers will be able to build and maintain successful programs that do not diminish over time due to lack of funding or support.

Objective Three: Demonstrate How Engagement Efforts Will Lead to Archaeological Stewardship

Engaging educational experiences lead to an accurate and profound understanding of archaeology and many of the subtopics or other disciplines from which it draws—and we have the data to prove it. Several authors present survey data gathered from learners spanning all ages before and after their educational experiences or interactions with archaeologists and sites (Reetz et al., Chapter 3; L. Messenger, Chapter 4; Ducady, Chapter 6; Erdman, Chapter 7). While some responses illustrate room for improvement, most show positive views and a better understanding of archaeology and what heritage means for them and their communities following such programs. These data hint that such interest and acquired knowledge have the potential to develop into a sense of stewardship if fostered and maintained over time.

Develop, Foster, and Maintain for the Future

Meaningful interactions with our collective past should begin at a young age and be encouraged throughout one's life. To do this, we must make archaeology as accessible and vital to the public as other core disciplines since it introduces a new lens through which to see the world. Our methods for engaging the public must target specific audiences in intrinsically meaningful ways that bring archaeology into their everyday lives; it is here that a personal connection and passion for the past can develop. It is not enough to introduce archaeology and then hope for its advocacy, instead, the public must have opportunities to continue their archaeological curiosity and expand their foundational knowledge, which is accomplished by introducing more complicated archaeological and anthropological issues, such as who owns the past or how do we include multiple narratives when interpreting the past. The subtitle of this volume includes "developing" and "fostering," both of which reflect our overall approach—introduce archaeology as part of early childhood education and sustain a lifelong interest through formal and informal learning experiences.

Our holistic approach to archaeology education ensures we can maintain a steady dialog with all ages, one that emphasizes and reinforces the importance of archaeological heritage and its preservation. Additionally, we can nurture the interests of current and subsequent generations for whom the value of archaeology will be inherent and, therefore, should always be protected. We are reaching people who might not normally come into contact with archaeology, particularly after K–12 education, or may never have learned about archaeology. Developing and fostering that passion is how we will create stewards of archaeology and natural allies to help us preserve the past for generations to come.

This volume focuses on introducing all ages of the public to the fundamentals of archaeology and sustaining an interest over time. While we recognize the importance and significant contributions of informal settings to public engagement and education, our examples come from primarily formal or structured learning environments. Rather than creating completely new outreach programs from the ground up, which requires greater expense and resources, many of the contributors to this volume work within established education systems to reach the public. This has multiple advantages. For example, incorporating archaeology into K–12 Common Core curricula ensures it reaches every school-age child, as well as teachers and many parents, resulting in a very broad impact. Partnering with historical societies offers university students practical experience in heritage management. Working with community education programs offers vast resources, such as advertising and administrative support. Digitizing and publishing large quantities of archaeological data through online databases has the potential for global reach. Additionally, working within established systems is a naturally symbiotic relationship and one that encourages partnership, i.e., strength in numbers. Whether engaging an elementary classroom or partnering with local historical societies, such interactions promote a sense of community and cooperation where one side brings the expertise and the other provides an audience or participants.

There are several critical points addressed within that make this book indispensable for those interested in doing archaeology education. Not everybody learns the same, especially when we consider factors such as age, motivation to learn, language barriers, access, background interests, or learning environment. Each chapter in this volume accounts for such factors and presents models or suggestions for achieving best results. Secondly, our discipline does not exist in a vacuum; we should not teach it as such. Many of our contributors take an interdisciplinary approach to presenting archaeology and incorporate diverse voices from the community, which in turn, makes it accessible to audiences of all ages who can connect information and experiences to things they already know. Finally, we show how new programs can get started as well as how we can maintain and keep improving established, well-oiled machines. The latter is achieved by evaluating our teaching methods and measuring how and what the public learns from engaging with archaeologists both locally and abroad.

Organization of the Volume

The subsequent chapters of the text are organized into three parts to reflect our approach: develop, foster, and maintain for the future. Part I, "Inspiring and Developing an Interest in the Past," focuses on how we can spark an interest in archaeology amongst members of the public. Our examples focus primarily on K–12 and undergraduate formal learning situations. This is not to say a passion for archaeology cannot develop outside of these parameters, but rather, these offer direct and wide-reaching approaches for targeting our youngest demographic. Several themes stand out: the need for integrating archaeology education into existing teaching requirements, the impact of experiential learning, and the benefit of fostering empathy.

White (Chapter 1) sets the stage for K–12 classroom learning and how to ensure it is effective: work it into Common Core, or other standards, and make it come alive through relatable historical connections and hands-on activities. Yezzi-Woodley et al. (Chapter 2) present their successful application of effective learning, including how to work with teachers to implement archaeology education in the classroom and its value for students and teachers as a discipline that unites science and social studies. Reetz, Haury-Artz, and Gorsh (Chapter 3) foster an experiential approach to learning by pairing archaeology with environmental education and bring in Native voices to promote the connection between archaeological heritage and descendant communities. L. Messenger (Chapter 4) outlines an undergraduate research and creative writing project that promotes cross-cultural empathy as well as a better understanding of the complexity and challenges archaeologists face when interpreting the past.

Part II, "Fostering a Deeper Respect for Archaeological Heritage," explores how we can maintain and encourage a continued interest in the archaeological past and its future. Chapters in this section contain a mix of formal and informal educational experiences, aimed at adult audiences, that build on a basic understanding of archaeology by addressing more complicated issues such as ownership of the past, listening to the public's opinions about archaeology, and protection for future generations.

P. Messenger (Chapter 5), describes a collaborative effort to create a new Heritage Management graduate-level degree that will train a new generation of interdisciplinary scholars to engage with the public and ensure inclusive presentations and interpretations of the past. Ducady (Chapter 6) shares how archaeologists working in Belize include the public in their research and conversations about the past, and how Belizcans think about their heritage and the richness of the archaeological record in their country according to quantitative and qualitative data collected in a recent survey. Erdman (Chapter 7) suggests how archaeologists can utilize existing public education programs, such as community education or lifelong learning programs, to open a dialog with adults and senior learners who are interested in archaeology and the protection of world heritage.

Part III, "The Future of Archaeology, Education, and Preservation," looks at how to move forward with our efforts to educate and engage the public about archaeology. Moe (Chapter 8) reflects on lessons learned from over thirty years as an archaeology educator, shows the compatibility of archaeology education and Common Core standards, and outlines what the next generation of educators must do to be successful in the future. Reeves Eyre and Ellison (Chapter 9) present the value digital archaeology can offer preservation efforts, as well as how it serves as an educational tool to reach audiences in new and interactive ways.

Katherine M. Erdman, PhD, Visiting Scholar, University of Minnesota.

References

Al-Houdalieh, Salah H., and Robert R. Sauders. 2009. "Building Destruction: The Consequences of Rising Urbanization on Cultural Heritage in the Ramallah Province." *International Journal of Cultural Property* 16: 1–23. doi:10.1017/S0940739109090043.

BBC. 2010. "A History of the World in 100 Objects." *BBC Radio 4*. Accessed 23 May 2016. http://www.bbc.co.uk/programmes/b00nrtf5.

Bickler, Simon, Rod Clough, and Sarah Macready. 2013. "The Impact of Climate Change on the Archaeology of New Zealand's Coastline: A Case Study from the Whangarei District." *Science for Conservation* 322: 1–54. Accessed 24 September 2017. https://core.ac.uk/download/pdf/30676296.pdf.

Brodie, Neil, Jennifer Doole, and Colin Renfrew, eds. 2001. *Trade in Illicit Antiquities: The Destruction of the World's Archaeological Heritage.* Cambridge: McDonald Institute for Archaeological Research.

Campbell, Peter B. 2013. "The Illicit Antiquities Trade as a Transnational Criminal Network: Characterizing and Anticipating Trafficking of Cultural Heritage." *International Journal of Cultural Property* 20: 113–53. doi:10.1017/S0940739113000015.

Carnes, Mark C. 1996. *Past Imperfect: History According to the Movies.* New York: H. Holt.

Chippindale, Christopher, and David W. J. Gill. 2000. "Material Consequences of Contemporary Classical Collecting." *American Journal of Archaeology* 104(3): 463–511. doi: 10.2307/507226.

Contreras, Daniel A. 2010. "Huaqueros and Remote Sensing Imagery: Assessing Looting Damage in the Virú Valley, Peru." *Antiquity* 84(324): 544–55. http://works.bepress.com/daniel_contreras/10/.

Corbishley, Mike. 2014. *Pinning down the Past: Archaeology, Heritage, and Education Today.* Woodbridge, England: The Boydell Press.

Curry, Andrew. 2014. "Racing the Thaw." *Science* 346(6206): 157–59. doi: 10.1126/science.346.6206.157.

Danti, Michael D. 2015. "Ground-Based Observations of Cultural Heritage Incidents." *Near Eastern Archaeology* 78(3): 132–41. doi:10.1080/0143659042000231965.

Davis, Tess. 2011. "Supply and Demand: Exposing the Illicit Trade in Cambodian Antiquities through a Study of Sotheby's Auction House." *Crime, Law and Social Change* 56(2): 155–74. doi:10.1007/s10611-011-9321-6.

Engeman, Richard M., Kathy J. Couturier, Rodney K. Felix Jr., and Michael L. Avery. 2013. "Feral Swine Disturbance at Important Archaeological Sites."

Environmental Science and Pollution Research 20(6): 4093–98. doi:10.1007/s11356-012-1367-1.

Franklin, M. Elaine, and Jeanne M. Moe. 2012. "A Vision for Archaeological Literacy." In *The Oxford Handbook of Public Archaeology*, edited by Robin Skeates, Carol McDavid, and John Carman, 566–80. Oxford: Oxford University Press. doi:10.1093/oxfordhb/9780199237821.013.0030.

Goddard, Jennifer. 2011. "Anticipated Impact of the 2009 Four Corners Raid and Arrests." *Crime, Law and Social Change* 56: 175–88. doi:10.1007/s10611-011-9322-5.

Gransard-Desmond, Jean-Olivier. 2015. "Science Educators: Bridging the Gap between the Scientific Community and Society." *World Archaeology* 47(2): 299–316. doi:10.1080/00438243.2015.1020964.

Harding, Anthony. 2007. "Communication in Archaeology." *European Journal of Archaeology* 10(2–3): 119–33. doi:10.1177/1461957108095980.

Huvila, Isto. 2013. "Engagement Has Its Consequences: The Emergence of the Representations of Archaeology in Social Media." *Archäologische Informationen* 36(April): 21–30. doi: 10.11588/ai.2013.0.

Jameson, John H., and Sherene Baugher, eds. 2007. *Past Meets Present: Archaeologists Partnering with Museum Curators, Teachers, and Community Groups*. New York: Springer Science & Business Media.

Jeppson, Patrice L. 2012. "Public Archaeology and the US Culture Wars." In *The Oxford Handbook of Public Archaeology*, edited by Robin Skeates, Carol McDavid, and John Carman, 581–602. Oxford: Oxford University Press. doi:10.1093/oxfordhb/9780199237821.013.0031.

Little, Barbara J. 2012. "Public Benefits of Public Archaeology." In *The Oxford Handbook of Public Archaeology*, edited by Robin Skeates, Carol McDavid, and John Carman, 395–413. Oxford: Oxford University Press. doi:10.1093/oxfordhb/9780199237821.013.0021.

Little, Barbara J., and Paul A. Shackel. 2014. *Archaeology, Heritage, and Civic Engagement: Working Toward the Public Good*. Walnut Creek, CA: Left Coast Press.

Mackenzie, Simon. 2011. "Illicit Deals in Cultural Objects as Crimes of the Powerful." *Crime, Law and Social Change* 56(2): 133–53. doi:10.1007/s10611-011-9317-2.

Matsuda, David. 1998. "The Ethics of Archaeology, Subsistence Digging, and Artifact Looting in Latin America: Point, Muted Counterpoint." *International Journal of Cultural Property* 7(1): 87–97. doi: 10.1017/S0940739198770080.

Milner, Nicky. 2012. "Destructive Events and the Impact of Climate Change on Stone Age Coastal Archaeology in North West Europe: Past, Present and Future." *Journal of Coastal Conservation* 16(2): 223–31. doi:10.1007/s11852-012-0207-2.

Ng-He, Carol, and Leila Makdisi. 2016. "Public Education and Outreach." *Oriental Institute 2015–2016 Annual Report. Public Education and Outreach: Volunteers*. Accessed 14 October 2017. https://oi.uchicago.edu/sites/oi.uchicago.edu/files/uploads/shared/docs/ar/11-20/15-16/ar2016_Public_Education.pdf.

Özdoğan, Mehmet. 2013. "Dilemma in the Archaeology of Large Scale Development Projects: A View from Turkey." *Papers from the Institute of Archaeology* 23(1): 1–8. doi:http://dx.doi.org/10.5334/pia.444.

Pace, Anthony. 2012. "From Heritage to Stewardship: Defining the Sustainable Care of Archaeological Places." In *The Oxford Handbook of Public Archaeology*, edited by Robin Skeates, Carol McDavid, and John Carman, 275–95. Oxford: Oxford University Press. doi:10.1093/oxfordhb/9780199 237821.013.0015.

Pagán, Eduardo. 2015. "Digging for Ratings Gold: American Digger and the Challenge of Sustainability for Cable TV." *The SAA Archaeological Record* 15(2): 12–17.

Proulx, Blythe Bowman. 2013. "Archaeological Site Looting in 'Glocal' Perspective: Nature, Scope, and Frequency." *American Journal of Archaeology* 117(1): 111–25. doi:10.3764/aja.117.1.0111.

Randall, Lindsay, and Marla Taylor. 2016. "Uncommon Engagement: Integrating Archaeology into High School Education." Paper presented at the 81st Annual Society for American Archaeology Conference, Orlando, FL, 7 April 2016.

Smith, Kimbra L. 2005. "Looting and the Politics of Archaeological Knowledge in Northern Peru." *Ethnos* 70(2): 149–70. doi:10.1080/00141840500141139.

Smith, Laurajane, and Emma Waterton. 2012. "Constrained by Commonsense: The Authorized Heritage Discourse in Contemporary Debates." In *The Oxford Handbook of Public Archaeology*, edited by Robin Skeates, Carol McDavid, and John Carman, 153–71. Oxford: Oxford University Press. doi:10.1093/oxfordhb/9780199237821.013.0009.

Thomas, Suzie, and Joanne Lea. 2014. *Public Participation in Archaeology*. Woodbridge, England: Boydell & Brewer.

Tully, Gemma. 2007. "Community Archaeology: General Methods and Standards of Practice." *Public Archaeology* 6(3): 155–87. doi:10.1179/175355 307X243645.

Watkins, Joe E. 2006. "Communicating Archaeology: Words to the Wise." *Journal of Social Archaeology* 6(1): 100–18. doi:10.1177/1469605306060569.

Wilkinson, Keith, Andrew Tyler, Donald Davidson, and Ian Grieve. 2006. "Quantifying the Threat to Archaeological Sites from the Erosion of Cultivated Soil." *Antiquity* 80: 658–70. http://antiquity.ac.uk/ant/080/309/Default.htm.

Wright, Jeneva. 2016. "Maritime Archaeology and Climate Change: An Invitation." *Journal of Maritime Archaeology* 11(3): 255–70. doi:10.1007/s11457-016-9164-5.

PART I

INSPIRING AND DEVELOPING AN INTEREST IN THE PAST

CHAPTER 1

Schools and Public Archaeology
Igniting a Commitment to Heritage Preservation

Charles S. White

This chapter explores the potential for public schools to support and advance understanding of our heritage, embracing both common and diverse narratives, and to promote an appreciation for the need to preserve the touchstones of heritage that are historical and archaeological treasures. The route to seizing those opportunities requires, of course, that we can gain entry into the schools, no small challenge with an overcrowded curriculum and an emphasis on testing. Choosing productive curriculum entry and anchor points can increase the odds of success, building networks of like-minded scholars, educators, and communities that are connected physically and intellectually to heritage resources worthy of preservation.

Schools and Heritage Preservation: A Rationale

At the height of the "culture wars" in the 1980s and 1990s, scholars and opinion leaders expressed deep concern about the state of history teaching and learning in the United States. The issue spanned quantity, quality, and ideology. The Bradley Commission on History in the Schools published an influential book titled *Historical Literacy: The Case for History in American Education* (Gagnon and Bradley Commission on History in the Schools 1991). In that volume, historians articulated a rationale for history education that, I would suggest, animates our efforts to promote heritage preservation. One of the historians, William H. McNeil, observes:

> Historical knowledge is no more and no less than carefully and critically constructed collective memory. As such, it can make us both wiser in our public choices and more richly human in our private lives . . . Studying alien religious beliefs, strange customs, diverse family patterns, and vanished social structures show how differently various human groups have tried to cope with the world around them. Broadening our humanity and extending our sensibilities by recognizing sameness and difference throughout the recorded past is therefore an important reason for studying history, and especially the history of people far away and long ago. For we can know ourselves only by knowing how we resemble and how we differ from others. Acquaintance with the human past is the only way to such self-knowledge. (1991, 103, 110)

The institution of public schooling carries a special responsibility to help construct a collective memory, carefully and critically, as *pluribus* and *unum,* over years of serious study and exploration. This was clearly understood by leaders like Thomas Jefferson who worked earnestly in the eighteenth century to establish free, public education to fortify the new republic and its guiding principles: "History by apprising [youth] of the past will enable them to judge of the future" (Jefferson 1984, 274). Horace Mann and the common school movement advanced those efforts in Massachusetts and elsewhere in the nineteenth century (Tyack 1967). I should offer a clarification, however, concerning what historians typically reference as worthy sources of historical knowledge. The raw material for our collective memory need not be limited to the "written record"; rather, it should embrace a broad range of sources, both two-dimensional (maps, photographs, paintings) and three-dimensional (houses, landscapes, and the artifacts brought to light through the labors of archaeologists). Indeed, the products of archaeological research and outreach are the sparks that ignite our memories, as individuals and as a society. What a loss we bear, then, when we hear about archaeological sites and artifacts that are no longer available to us, whether through theft, deliberate destruction, or indifference and neglect.

Lest there be any doubt concerning the term "knowledge" in this chapter, let me add that I contemplate more than a collection of facts. The means of creating knowledge—cognitive skills and disciplinary procedures must be addressed as well. Particularly relevant for this chapter's topic is also the less tangible domain of values and moral commitments. These include an appreciation for history and its interpretation, as well as the need to preserve both heritage and the artifacts through which we come to learn about heritage. In schools, we aim to help students build habits of the head, hand, and heart, embracing the tri-partite dimensions of knowledge, skills, and dispositions. Fostering heritage and its preservation will require us to address this curricular triptych as we approach the schools.

Getting in the Door

For American schools today, scores of worthy goals far exceed the supply of time and resources. Since the days of Jefferson and Mann, we have expected schools to address more and more of society's needs, and schools are hard-pressed to keep pace with these demands. As a result, priorities are set and some demands are privileged over others. The accountability demands reflected in high-stakes testing and teacher evaluation tied to test scores often generate resistance to any "added" demands, however worthy. Successful initiatives in education help schools and teachers to fulfill these responsibilities in effective and compelling ways.

Entre to the School: Curriculum, Standards, and Accountability

For decades, waves of anxiety about the nation's competitiveness have been met with calls for greater mastery of subject matter by our students. Since *A Nation at Risk* (United States National Commission on Excellence in Education 1983) sounded an alarm about the decline of America's education system compared to other nations, national policy makers commissioned a collection of voluntary national content standards in the early 1990s. These influenced a parallel effort at the state level. Through a variety of carrot-and-stick federal financial incentives, the states also adopted testing programs to measure progress toward meeting rigorous benchmarks, primarily in reading, writing, and mathematics, as well as for developing higher-level thinking (inquiry/problem-solving and critical thinking). High-stakes tests administered in high school figure prominently in determining whether a student qualifies for a high school diploma.

Since 2010, the Common Core State Standards (CCSS) in mathematics and English language arts/literacy have guided changes in content and skill requirements (and testing programs) in more than forty states and the District of Columbia. The Council of Chief State School Officers and the National Governors Association Best Practices Center initiated CCSS development in 2009 and issued the final product the following year (National Governors Association Center for Best Practices and Council of Chief State School Officers 2010).[1] More recently, the National Council for the Social Studies released *The College, Career, and Civic Life (C3) Framework for Social Studies State Standards* (2013), which addresses Common Core expectations while maintaining focus on subject matter and thinking-skills goals in history/social science school curriculum. Most distinctively, though, the C3 standards are centered on an "inquiry arc" that spans the study of discipline-based subject matter (see Figure 1.1).

The implementation of standards and high-stakes testing has generated some unintended consequences for the nation's schools. The elementary curriculum has become so crowded and test driven that there is a growing backlash against reduced recess time and increased homework time (Bennett and Kalish 2006; Holland, Sisson, and Abeles 2015; Muto 2015). Tests that the government mandates as measures of student-teacher-school quality focus primarily on literacy and numeracy. For that reason, other subject areas beyond reading, writing, and mathematics have become marginalized with respect to instructional time and perceived value (Beddoes, Prusak, and Hall 2014; Cawelti 2006; NASBE Study Group on the Lost Curriculum 2003; Risinger 2012).

The good news is that subject matter that is aligned to curriculum and content standards and accountability demands has a good chance of being embraced by schools. Advocates for innovative subject matter should be seeking as many school curriculum connections as possible. Clearly, archaeology intersects with the sciences and should continue to seek opportunities to ally with the precollege science curriculum. At the secondary school level, these typically include physical/earth science, biology, chemistry, and physics; at the elementary level, general science. However, archaeology is also crucial to the humanities and

DIMENSION 1: DEVELOPING QUESTIONS AND PLANNING INQUIRIES	DIMENSION 2: APPLYING DISCIPLINARY TOOLS AND CONCEPTS	DIMENSION 3: EVALUATING SOURCES AND USING EVIDENCE	DIMENSION 4: COMMUNICATING CONCLUSIONS AND TAKING INFORMED ACTION
Developing Questions and Planning Inquiries	Civics	Gathering and Evaluating Sources	Communicating and Critiquing Conclusions
	Economics		
	Geography	Developing Claims and Using Evidence	Taking Informed Action
	History		

Figure 1.1. C3 Framework (National Council for the Social Studies 2013, 12; used with permission).

social sciences. Note, for example, how the National Council for the Social Studies defines its curriculum domain:

> Social studies is the integrated study of the social sciences and humanities to promote civic competence. Within the school program, social studies provides coordinated, systematic study drawing upon such disciplines as anthropology, archaeology, economics, geography, history, law, philosophy, political science, psychology, religion, and sociology, as well as appropriate content from the humanities, mathematics, and natural sciences. The primary purpose of social studies is to help young people develop the ability to make informed and reasoned decisions for the public good as citizens of a culturally diverse, democratic society in an interdependent world. (Anderson 1993, 2)

The discipline of archaeology is essential in acquiring well-grounded knowledge of the other disciplines that social studies draws together to foster historical and cultural understanding. Moreover, for the purposes of public archaeology and heritage preservation, the social studies curriculum is a kindred field.

Archaeological outreach efforts in the history and social studies curriculum, as with all school curriculum areas, must show that they attend to content and curriculum standards described earlier, particularly the C3 standards. Instructional material and projects must demonstrably support skillful reading, writing, and mathematics, and provide opportunities for students to learn and apply higher-level thinking skills relevant to the subject matter. I believe these criteria are well within the capacity of archaeology outreach initiatives. Once in the door, however, the success of public archaeology in the schools depends largely on the classroom teacher.

Partnering with Teachers: Goals and Practices

It is important to underscore that productive opportunities to engage with teachers involve more than parachuting into schools to show teachers how to do things or how they should embrace the scholar's preservation agenda. Zimmerman et al.'s (1994) reflections on their own work with teachers serve as a helpful guide:

> Few of us look beyond the goals of professional archaeology: preserving sites, preventing looting, and more public support for our efforts. . . . The point is not that our own goals are unreasonable, but rather that imposing them on students and their teachers might be. . . . Teachers have different goals from archaeologists. . . . Few archaeologists go beyond simply men-

tioning the broader educational goals.... Teachers are therefore forced to adapt our aims to their own, with little help from us.... Certainly we teach [teachers] the importance of site preservation, but do we give teachers a rationale for conveying this idea to students in a framework that is suitable to their own classroom agendas? (1994, 371)

The more we understand the goals, interests, and constraints of classroom teachers, the more likely we are to build a successful partnership.

In the elementary grades, each teacher is often responsible for teaching the full range of curriculum areas, making content mastery in any one field a daunting task. In contrast, secondary education teachers typically specialize in one content area. Even high school subjects, though, are expected to support achievement of literacy and numeracy goals that have traditionally been outside their content areas. The responsibility for broader educational goals will fall on teachers across the school curriculum, including history/social studies. In short, public archaeology and heritage advocates should make evident how they can help teachers meet the demands of more rigorous and all-encompassing standards and of rising school and community accountability expectations.

Teacher buy-in requires more than simply making an eloquent case and dropping off some instructional materials (or providing a few URLs). Curriculum alignment without classroom usability produces frustration and, inevitably, failure. Three questions can gauge the usability of classroom content and pedagogy. First, has the teacher had enough time, exposure, and support to understand the content, methodology, and intent of the material? This question is of particular import for elementary teachers, whose academic background (and, frankly, prime interest) lies outside history, social science, and the science of archaeology. Second, has the teacher had the chance to observe a model of best practice in implementing the material? Description only goes so far. Modeling takes one farther. Third, has the teacher been able to implement the material and receive feedback needed to mold the material to meet the needs of students? In short, one-time sessions at teachers' conferences or after school may be adequate for information dissemination but rarely produce robust and sustainable implementation (White and White 2000).

What makes a teacher persist in trying something new, even if it takes a good deal of effort to align it with standards and shape it for the classroom? They persist because the innovation captured their interest, curiosity, and imagination; it tapped the learner in the teacher. Curriculum innovation is strewn with the remains of well-intentioned efforts to bring new methods or content into the precollege classroom. One can trace many of these casualties to a lack of teacher buy-in. Any effort of public archaeology to have a sustained impact on student knowledge and inclinations toward heritage preservation must attend to the needs and interests of teachers.

Addressing school priorities and gaining teacher buy-in are essential early steps. Teachers will persevere in implementing new ideas if they believe these ideas will also capture the interest, curiosity, and imagination of their students.

Connecting with Children and Youth

Narrative is a powerful gateway for young people to explore the past. Moreover, students can find their own place in the flow of narrative. Together, these possibilities constitute a recipe for deep cognitive and affective engagement with the artifacts of history and the means by which artifacts help us construct and refine narratives. The notion that history is not a given but is an interpretation is a revelation for many students (Levstik and Barton 2011; Wineburg 2001). So, too, is the idea that we may need to change a historical account in light of new evidence. Properly understood, history can come alive for those who study it, and archaeology adds to the reservoir of evidence upon which current and future interpretations of the past will be grounded. That young people themselves might engage in genuine, hands-on archaeological discovery completes the circuit that will spark long-term interest in archaeology, history, and preservation.

"Can I Touch It?" A First Connection to Historical Narrative

Over the years of preparing new teachers, I have recounted the story of my first encounter with the Coliseum in Rome. Years ago, my wife and I had an unexpected layover in Rome. We arranged for a hotel and made our way by bus into the city. It was still early enough in the day to cram in as much as we could see in the Eternal City, so we figured out the metro system and found the "Coliseum" stop. As we emerged from the underground station, there it was—the Coliseum. Now I ask my students, "What is the first thing I did?" The guesses usually range from "take a picture" to "buy a ticket to get inside." Rarely do they hit on the correct answer: "I touched it." They instantly understood the reason, because most had done the same thing (see Figure 1.2). Touch-

Figure 1.2. In touch with an ancient statue. Photo by Bananashake, "Touch for Memory," Dreamstime.com, used with permission.

ing connects us to the past in a unique way, as we imagine people of the distant past placing their hands on the same spot. Touching a piece of moonrock at the Smithsonian's Air and Space Museum in Washington transports us beyond our own planet. Placing our hands into the preserved impression of a dinosaur's footprint connects us to that particular creature who roamed the planet more than sixty-five million years ago. Walking along the Appian Way in Rome or the Via Dolorosa in Jerusalem, we get the same sensation of "being there," walking paths we know were walked by kings and servants, saints and sinners—fellow humans like us.

When we step onto an archaeological site, we enter a stage upon which the lives of fellow humans played out in the past. How did they meet their basic needs? What did they value? What ideas occupied their minds? How did they think about the past? What did they wonder about the future? Answering these questions is not simply an intellectual exercise, because these questions occupy our thoughts and guide our lives. Using the evidence that archaeology uncovers, we can develop empathy for past peoples and their brief time on their stage (Baron 2012). We can ponder our own time on life's stage and the legacy we might leave behind.

Multiple Stories

As engaging as a story can be, though, it is still only *one* story. Across the stage of any place, many feet have trod. Crossing paths are many people who have their own stories—stories told in their own ways from their unique perspectives. In the ruins of Pompeii and Herculaneum, archaeologists have uncovered evidence of upper-class life as well as the lives of ordinary people. In the study of the antebellum American South, digs have unearthed artifacts left by both the plantation owners *and* by their slaves. As fieldwork continues, we expand the scope of historical interpretation beyond the traditional, dominant groups who have filled generations of school history books and embrace the stories of others of the same time and place. New stories add nuance and richness to our understanding of the past and cause historians to revise or overturn interpretations that are no longer supported by new evidence.

Archaeological sites do more than reveal a single time and place. They are three-dimensional spaces with layers upon layers of human activity—upper and lower stages, as it were, on which succeeding generations played out their lives, often without knowledge of what lies beneath. Archaeologists investigating the ruins of what is believed to be the site of ancient Troy have found no fewer than nine cities stacked on top of each other (Stiebing 1993). A single place, then, is a kind of time machine that stores evidence of human activity and, especially, human development over time. These multi-temporal stories also capture one's imagination, which explains the success of books like James Michener's 1974 novel *Centennial*, which portrays the stories of Colorado and its people across two centuries.

"My Story"

History is sometimes compared to a river, flowing past us standing on the shore. In the same way, students can observe the flow of history through the stories illuminated by historical and archaeological research. When it comes to time, though, we are not simply observers but participants. We are part of the flow, and we should invite young people to immerse themselves in their own place in history. Moreover, students should see themselves as makers of history, as were their own ancestors, recent and more distant.

Becoming part of a greater story is something that can begin in the home. With the clutter I have accumulated over the years, I sometimes kid about organizing a "dig" at my house to discover long-lost items. One's home often harbors cherished artifacts from a family's past, as well as precious items that represent our own achievements, interests, and aspirations. The former can link us to the near past; the latter might find their way into a time capsule for a future generation to ponder. Such was the case for the city of Boston in 2014, when workers removed for restoration the large statue of a lion from atop the Old State. Rumors of a time capsule from 1901 placed inside the statue proved true. Opening the box was a major city event covered by local and national media (Blessing 2014). Schools have also created time capsules (Rowell et al. 2007).

"Give Me a Mystery and Let Me Investigate!"

In their book, *Teaching US History as Mystery*, David Gerwin and Jack Zevin extol the virtues of viewing history as a puzzle:

> Human beings, particularly younger ones for whom experiences are fresh, have deep curiosity about themselves, their families and society, and why we behave or believe in certain ways. People also have a great need to play, to engage their minds and bodies in games that test their knowledge, skills, and cleverness. A mystery has many game-like features that challenge us to solve the problem, find the unknown . . . interpret clues, and so much more. In effect, a good mystery is a puzzle, a game, which beckons us to work out a solution. (2011, 8)

Drawing students to archaeology through unsolved mysteries provides an "itch that needs to be scratched."

Problem-Based Learning

The attraction of mystery is one of the reasons that C3 Standards developers employed an inquiry arc to organize the study and (especially) the application of disciplinary content. This may explain the growing interest in and student enthusiasm for problem-based learning (Bell 2010). Facts and principles of the disciplines are necessary but not sufficient for deep learning and long-term usefulness. Acquiring content for the purpose of solving problems gives meaning to content learning and agency to the learner. The discipline of archaeology aims to uncover and solve problems employing systematic inquiry and specialized methods and tools. Capitalizing on the investigative nature of the discipline, archaeological study is well suited to problem-based learning (Walker et al. 2015).

Problem-based learning (PBL) places the student at the center of inquiry and emphasizes the utility of deep knowledge in answering unresolved questions. PBL mirrors most of the C3 Standards' inquiry arc: students frame questions, plan their inquiry, apply knowledge and procedures from the disciplines to their research, and communicate their conclusions. At the university level, a growing number of fields, from medicine to engineering and beyond, are recognizing PBL's effectiveness—including archaeology (Kvapil 2009). Elementary and secondary schools have also embraced PBL-based instruction (Torp and Sage 2002; Wirkala and Kuhn 2011).[2]

Authentic Learning

PBL captures the interest of students, fosters historical empathy (Brush and Saye 2008), and helps them acquire powerful knowledge experience in collaboration with others. Solving novel problems or constructing compelling explanations are what professionals in the disciplines do, and so assigning similar tasks to students imbues their work with greater authenticity. Authentic learning tasks align as closely as is practicable to tasks carried out by professionals in the relevant field, in our case, archaeology. A sample task would involve students in an actual dig, at a real site. Short of that would be a simulated dig. An authentic school program, then, is designed to be more like life outside school (Brandt 1993, 3).[3]

Authentic learning goes beyond rousing student interest. According to King, Newmann, and Carmichael, "while some people may regard the term 'authentic' as equivalent to education that is 'relevant,' 'student-centered,' or 'hands-on,' we do not" (2009, 45). They describe the basis for authentic intellectual work as follows:

> We analyzed the kinds of mastery demonstrated by successful adults who continually work with knowledge—for example, scientists, musicians, childcare workers, construction contractors, healthcare providers, business entrepreneurs, repair technicians, teachers, lobbyists, and citizen activists. Adults in these diverse endeavors face common intellectual challenges that provide guidelines for an education that extends beyond basic skills to more complex academic work.
>
> Of course, we do not expect children to achieve the same level of mastery accomplished by skilled adults, but identifying the nature of intellectual work in these professions can help to define criteria for performance necessary for success in contemporary society. (43)

A school program that aims for authentic intellectual work addresses three overarching criteria. The program (instruction, assignments, and student tasks) must engage students in the construction of knowledge (not acquisition alone), in disciplined inquiry, and in work that has value beyond the classroom—that is connected to their own lives and to the world around them (King et al. 2009, 44).

As should be clear by now, aside from the seemingly trivial suggestion to "give students a mystery and let them investigate," there can and should be serious intellectual effort going on, including the opportunity for students to immerse themselves deeply in the discipline of archaeology. This, and engaging them with the fruits of archaeological research and narratives that emerge, improves the chances that students will develop a sense of responsibility over the sites and artifacts with which they interact. To foster personal connection and the excitement of investigation, however, we must find or construct hands-on experiences that tell a story, provoke curiosity, present a problem, and engage students in the kind of challenging intellectual work described by King and his colleagues.

Opportunities and Models

Fortunately, there are areas where archaeology has made its way beyond the site and research lab, including into schools. There are many more opportunities, I believe, that archaeologists should pursue within and beyond classrooms and in communities to broaden public awareness and support for heritage preservation. We also have a potentially useful model for developing learning resources in the work done by the National Register of Historic Places and their project *Teaching with Historic Places*. First, we will start at the beginning.

Sample Applications and Resources

The elementary classroom is often dismissed by serious scholars of the disciplines because they view young children as incapable of important intellectual work. That sentiment ignores the important foundational work that can catch the imagination of young people at an early age (see Figure 1.3). Moreover, elementary teachers take a more general approach to science instruction and are open to a range of science disciplines as long as fundamental scientific concepts and methods (and attitudes) are learned. Since archaeology also opens windows to history, anthropology, and allied disciplines, teachers can address learning goals across the school curriculum. One such example is an adaptation of a lesson developed by the Archaeological Institute of America. The teacher, Beth Gryczewski, collaborated with a sixth grade English teacher to design a "history lab" that explores the *Mystery Cemetery* (Archaeological Institute of America 2016; Gryczewski 2013). Fourth and fifth grade students can help solve *The Mystery of Quick Gulch,* a simulation of American Great Plains salvage archaeology produced by Looking-Glass Science (2013).

Figure 1.3. Looking for artifacts. Photo by Amy Rowley, ThurstonTalk.com, used with permission.

For both elementary and secondary education, national archaeological associations, such as the Society for American Archaeology and the Archaeological Institute of America, have taken steps to reach out to classrooms, from rationale-building and general guidance (Smardz and Smith 2000) to collections of specific lesson plans (Society for American Archaeology 2016). The National Endowment for the Humanities evaluates websites for instructional and content quality (National Endowment for the Humanities 2016b) and is another useful source for archaeology-related lessons. Using the search term "archaeology" yielded eighty-two lessons in history and social studies, seventy-two in art and culture, forty-one in literature and language arts, and thirty-seven in foreign language (National Endowment for the Humanities 2016a).

As argued earlier, though, the extent to which any of these applications succeed in the classroom will depend on the how they address teachers' interests and needs, as well as factors that foster student motivation, including a meaningful connection, mystery, and intellectual engagement. Using these elements as development criteria can guide more comprehensive projects that developers and professional organizations might pursue. The National Park Service provides an instructive model that others might wish to emulate and perhaps enhance.

A Comprehensive Model: Teaching with Historic Places

In the early 1990s, the National Register of Historic Places (NRHP), a department within the National Park Service, recognized that they possessed a largely untapped repository of historic places rich in source material generated as part of their nomination process. The National Trust for Historic Preservation (NTHP) serves as a steward for historic places that are often overlooked and under-appreciated by the public at large. Under the leadership of Carol Shull, Chief of Registration at NRHP, and Kathleen Hunter, Director of Education Initiatives at NTHP, the two organizations collaborated on a new project called Teaching with Historic Places (TWHP) (Shull and Hunter 1992). As Boland observed, the partnership sought to capitalize on their collective treasure of resources under the umbrella of "place" and on the power of place to inform and move people:

> Teachers searching for ways to capture student interest and spark learning.... Historians eager to instill enthusiastic, yet critical understanding of the stories and lessons from the past.... Historic places form common ground where educators and content specialists can reach out with great advantage to each other and to the students they both care about.... As authentic remnants of the past, historic places provide both an emo-

tional link, which generates interest and excitement, and an intellectual gateway into investigating and understanding people and events in history. And the best part is that we can find these places all around us in the communities where we live. (Boland 2002, 19)

Given the rich database at their disposal, the most logical initial foray into the classroom for both organizations was to develop lesson plans (National Park Service 2016d) based on a template that tapped the empathetic and inquiry potential of places. The earlier commentary on teachers and students in this article should inform the design of material for the field of archaeology as well.

What makes the TWHP program a useful model for archaeology, however, is the addition of elements beyond a disconnected array of lessons. Appreciating the need to engage teachers as partners and to better address their accountability responsibilities, the project commissioned *Teaching with Historic Places: A Curriculum Framework for Professional Training and Development of Teachers, Preservationists, and Museum and Site Interpreters* (White and Hunter 1995). The publication aimed to bring together these varied constituencies to improve links to schools.

Recognizing the centrality of the teacher in successful integration of historic places in the curriculum, the TWHP website provides resources to support professional development for teachers, offering sample workshop agendas (National Park Service 2016c). The project recognizes the importance of encouraging new teachers to explore historic places (White and White 2000) as part of their teaching repertoire, through their elementary (Yeşilbursa and Barton 2011) or secondary level methods course (National Park Service 2016a). In short, forming partnerships with schools and teacher education institutions can magnify the likelihood of successful outreach to the classrooms.

Scholars, Schools, and Communities: Partners in Preserving Heritage

Thus far, I have focused primarily on outreach to schools to foster interest in and appreciation for archaeology. Professionals in the field can magnify their influence in preserving archaeological heritage by forging partnerships with communities, especially in linking archaeology-based school initiatives to experiences out in their communities.

Many urban areas employ their own city archaeologist, who can raise the visibility of efforts to learn from and preserve valuable cultural sites. Where no such position exists, though, outreach to local historical societies can serve to forge useful partnerships. In Boston,

Massachusetts, city archaeologist Joe Bagley initiated projects that have tapped the imagination of students and the pride of neighborhoods and the broader community. One example that received a good deal of media coverage was a 2016 dig at the site of Malcolm X's teenage and young adult home in the Roxbury section of the city. A middle school humanities teacher, Nathan Sokol-Margolis, brought his students to the site. As you read his commentary below, refer back to the discussion on schools, teachers, and student engagement and consider what elements are found in this teacher's experience:

> Because it was such a powerful experience for me, I especially enjoy reading [*The Autobiography of Malcolm X*] with students in our American Historiography class. However, this class focuses not only on X's racial struggle, but also on the truthfulness of his account. . . . With all of this in mind, one can imagine my excitement upon hearing that the city of Boston planned to conduct an archeological dig at Ella Little's house. . . . Here was an opportunity for students to see how historical truth is formed at the foundation of a story (pun intended). I contacted Joe Bagley, Boston's resident archeologist, and he kindly invited us to the dig. During our afternoon there, we were not only able to speak with X's nephew and grand niece [*sic*], but we also had the opportunity to pull up the ground, sift through the dirt, and examine the shards of ceramics, glass, and other material that we found. The archaeologists explained that much of this came from far before Malcolm X's time. This was perhaps the most exciting part: we got to be agents of history. Instead of the importance of a single house and its connection with a single historical figure, we were given the opportunity to understand the scope of history. Malcolm X's story was only the first few inches of dirt in the yard; beneath were many others waiting to be explored, discussed, and told. (2016)

In this brief reflection, Mr. Sokol-Margolis notes the power of connecting students to real people and those people's connection to the past. Even more, the students had a chance to get their hands dirty—to "do" a bit of archaeology and to inquire about the meaning of some unexpected discoveries. For his part, the teacher had already thought through the connection to his instructional goals and recognized what a "value-added" opportunity a site visit represented. The mayor of Boston, Martin J. Walsh, extended the significance of the project by referring to it as a "community dig" where residents could uncover *their* history ("Malcolm X's former home . . ." 2016).

Preserving Our Identities

On display or tucked away, we all have memorabilia of people and times past—a piece of jewelry, a medal from a family member who fell in battle, an autographed photo. These are parts of history that adhere to our identities; we preserve them both to spark our own memories and to pass on those memories to those who come after us. We bequeath artifacts with the hope and expectation that the preservation will extend into the future. This is why it is so important for the preservation of cultural artifacts that we foster a kind of personal and communal historical responsibility. This is part of what Boston's mayor meant by in his reference to a "community" dig. Archaeologists and their various institutions cannot be the sole interpreters of history, in part because they alone cannot preserve the fruits of their labors. A shared embrace of and responsibility for heritage is not without its challenges (Boyer 1996; Symcox 2002), but reaching out to youth and their communities can create a rich dialog and a commitment to stewardship.

Examples abound of local archaeology organizations—large and small—working to promote a sense of responsibility of cultural resources, and not only in the United States. To engage community residents in local archaeology, the county council of Warwickshire, England, sponsored an Archaeology Taster Day ("Budding archaeologists . . ." 2014). They invited locals of all ages to participate in a dig at a local site. Brits interested in excavations elsewhere around the country can consult the Facebook page *British Archaeological Excavations* (2016). For northern Virginia residents, the City of Alexandria's Archaeology Museum offers Family Dig Days for those interested in uncovering artifacts from the Shuter's Hill Site (City of Alexandria 2016). Beyond these efforts, though, the mission of public archaeology has broadened over time to embrace deeper engagement with the concerns of communities in which they work.

Taking Action: Public Archaeology and Civic Engagement

Looking back at the *College, Career, and Civic Life (C3) Framework for Social Studies State Standards* depicted in Figure 1.1, note that the inquiry arc does not end with "Communicating and Critiquing Conclusions," but with "Taking Informed Action." Fundamental to the civic grounding of the standards is a commitment to active engagement in one's community and beyond, and to addressing pressing social issues based on what one has learned. This sentiment of social responsibility has become increasingly important to public archaeology.

Public archaeology today seeks to deepen partnerships with communities, whether local, national, or global (Tuxill, Mitchell, and Clark 2009). As Marshall explains, it involves "relinquishing the right to total control over an archaeological project and allowing local communities to make critical decisions on research directions.... [Community archaeology] is the only way that indigenous people, descendant communities and other local interest groups will be able to own the pasts archaeologists are employed to create" (2002, 218). The field should respond to issues that divide some communities and silence others. In short, public archaeology, broadly understood, should be a tool of civic engagement (Little and Shackel 2007).

So conceived, public archaeology offers opportunities for service learning, a growing part of K–12 schools' civic mission. Service learning is one of six "proven practices" for civic learning and engagement (Gould et al. 2011, 29–32). A position statement issued by the National Council for the Social Studies offers a definition of service learning as it relates to the curriculum and elements that represent high-quality experiences:

> Service learning connects meaningful service in the school or community with academic learning and civic responsibility. Service learning is distinguished from community service or volunteerism in two ways. First, the service activity is integrated with academic skills and content. Second, students engage in structured reflection activities on their service experiences.... Effective service-learning projects go beyond simply using the community as a learning laboratory for student development. Of equal importance is the attempt to solve community problems, meet human and environmental needs, and advocate for changes in policies and laws to promote the common good. (2000)

Many current examples of precollege archaeology-related service learning promote heritage preservation, as a form of civic engagement (National Park Service 2016b). Occasionally, the lessons and activities recognize that heritage preservation can be a controversial issue. One example of the former involved a power company's plan to erect powerlines within sight of Jamestown Island, where English settlers establish the first permanent settlement in the New World. The issue raised several questions: "Should historic sites, and the views from those sights, be preserved? How will residents and businesses in the area have power if the high-rise towers are not allowed? What would be the ecological cost of various ways to power the region (e.g., an underground versus above-ground power line crossing)" (Butler and Burgin 2016)? Addressing passionate disputes about competing goods and contentious issues of social justice (Little 2009) can ignite a commitment to preservation at a time when there is a rising urgency to act.

Conclusion

The news is filled with stories of archaeological sites in peril. Sometimes, the cause is a failure to balance competing interests, as is the case of Recapture Canyon in Utah, where ATV access has damaged evidence of ancient Anasazi habitation ("An Illegal Trail" 2011). In other cases, neglect causes history to be washed away; along the coast of England, some seventy thousand archaeological sites are endangered by coastal erosion and rising sea levels (Kennedy 2015). Perhaps most troubling is the deliberate destruction of archaeological sites as a form of cultural "cleansing," exemplified by ISIS's destruction of Temple Bel in Syria (Westcott 2015). Representing a deep reservoir of stories, mysteries, and future discoveries, each of these places, and many more, will be lost unless more of us recognize that we all share in those histories—that we all have a responsibility for stewardship. These commitments take time to develop.

As archaeologists and teachers spark young people's curiosity and imagination, foster a sense of historical empathy, and give them agency in investigating and interpreting the past, students will realize that they are grasping a slice of history and that it has value. They will want to preserve it for themselves. They will discover that others have the right to embrace and preserve their own slices of history as well. They will discover that there is much history whose value should be shared and preserved for the public good. Schools are the place to ignite a shared commitment to heritage preservation.

Charles S. White, PhD, Executive Director, Social Science Education Consortium, Inc.

Notes

1. Despite its initial success, CCSS is now experiencing some pushback from individuals and groups opposed to the establishment of a de facto national curriculum. Historically, education policy in the United States has been a state responsibility.
2. The Buck Institute of Education (BIE), an excellent teaching resource, uses the term "project-based learning" to embrace a wide range of long-term, project-oriented experiences, a subset of which may be "problem-based" (Buck Institute of Education 2016).
3. The April 1993 issue of *Educational Leadership* (50: 7) focuses on authentic learning.

References

Anderson, Charlotte. 1993. "President's Message." *The Social Studies Professional* (January/February): 2.

"An Illegal Trail." 2011. *Salt Lake City Tribune*, 16 February. Accessed 11 August 2016. http://archive.sltrib.com/article.php?id=51215299&itype=CMSID.

Archaeological Institute of America. 2016. *Lesson Plans: Mystery Cemetery*. Accessed 1 August 2016. https://www.archaeological.org/education/lessons/cemetery.

Baron, Christine. 2012. "Understanding historical thinking at historic sites." *Journal of Educational Psychology* 104(3): 833–47.

Beddoes, Zack, Keven A. Prusak, and Amber Hall. 2014. "Overcoming Marginalization of Physical Education in America's Schools with Professional Learning Communities." *Journal of Physical Education, Recreation & Dance* 85(4): 21–27.

Bell, Stephanie. 2010. "Project-Based Learning for the 21st Century: Skills for the Future." *The Clearing House: A Journal of Educational Strategies, Issues and Ideas* 83(2): 39–43.

Bennett, S., and N. Kalish. 2006. *The Case against Homework: How Homework Is Hurting Our Children and What We Can Do*. New York: Crown Publishers.

Blessing, Kiera. 2014. "Contents of Old State House time capsule revealed." *Boston Globe*, 15 October. Accessed 19 July 2016. https://www.bostonglobe.com/metro/2014/10/15/old-state-house-time-capsule-opened-contents-fine-condition/vDq82PB75s3cHsjfml298M/story.html.

Boland, Beth M. 2002. "Historic Places: Common Ground for Teachers and Historians." *OAH Magazine of History* 16(2): 19–21.

Boyer, Paul. 1996. "Whose History is it Anyway? Memory, Politics, and Historical Scholarship." In *History wars: The Enola Gay and other battles for the American past*, ed. Edward T. Linenthal and Tom Englehardt, 115–39. New York: Henry Holt and Company.

Brandt, Ron. 1993. "Overview: More Like Life Outside." *Educational Leadership* 50(7): 3.

British Archaeological Excavations. 2016. Accessed 10 August 2016. https://www.facebook.com/britisharchaeologicalexcavations/home.

Brush, T., and J. Saye. 2008. "The Effects of Multimedia-Supported Problem-based Inquiry on Student Engagement, Empathy, and Assumptions about History." *Interdisciplinary Journal of Problem-Based Learning* 2(1). Accessed 15 August 2016. http://dx.doi.org/10.7771/1541-5015.1052.

Buck Institute of Education. 2016. "Project Based Learning vs. Problem Based Learning vs. XBL." Accessed 21 August 2016. http://www.bie.org/blog/project_based_learning_vs._problem_based_learning_vs._xbl.

"Budding archaeologists invited to join Warwick dig this weekend." 2014. *Coventry Telegraph*, 25 July. Accessed 10 August 2016. http://www.coventrytelegraph.net/news/coventry-news/archaeological-dig-st-johns-house-7506457.

Butler, B. M., and S. R. Burgin. 2016. "Jamestown and Power Lines: Teaching Controversy in an Inter-Disciplinary Manner." *Social Education* 80(1): 46–51.

Cawelti, Gordon. 2006. "The Side Effects of NCLB." *Educational Leadership* 64(3): 64–68.
City of Alexandria (VA). 2016. "Family Dig Days." Accessed 3 August 2016. https://www.alexandriava.gov/historic/archaeology/default.aspx?id=38960.
Gagnon, Paul, and Bradley Commission on History in the Schools, eds. 1991. *Historical literacy: The case for history in American education.* Boston, MA: Houghton Mifflin.
Gerwin, D., and J. Zevin. 2011. *Teaching US History as Mystery*, 2nd ed. New York: Routledge, Taylor and Francis e-Library.
Gould, Jonathan K., Kathleen Hall Jamieson, Peter Levine, Ted McConnell, and David B. Smith. 2011. "Guardian of democracy: The civic mission of schools." Philadelphia: Lenore Annenberg Institute for Civics of the Annenberg Public Policy Center and the Campaign for the Civic Mission of Schools. Accessed 10 August 2016. https://www.carnegie.org/media/filer_public/ab/dd/abdda62e-6e84-47a4-a043-348d2f2085ae/ccny_grantee_2011_guardian.pdf.
Gryczewski, Beth. 2013. "Labs in History? You Bet!" 3 February. Accessed 1 August 2016. http://teachersworkplace.net/2013/02/03/labs-in-history-you-bet.
Holland, Melissa, Hilary F. Sisson, and Vicki Abeles. 2015. "Academic Demands, Homework, and Social-Emotional Health." *Communique* (National Association of School Psychologists) 43(5): 12. Accessed 18 July 2016. http://search.proquest.com/docview/1675652302?accountid=9676.
Jefferson, Thomas. 1984. "Notes on the state of Virginia." In *Thomas Jefferson, Writings*, ed. Merrill D. Peterson, 123–325. New York: The Library of America.
Kennedy, Maev. 2015. "Volunteers and Drones to Survey Sites at Risk on British Coast." *The Guardian*, 4 August. Accessed 11 August 2016. https://www.theguardian.com/environment/2015/aug/03/drones-british-coast-volunteers.
King, M. Bruce, Fred M. Newmann, and Dana L. Carmichael. 2009. "Authentic Intellectual Work: Common Standards for Teaching Social Studies." *Social Education* 73(1): 43–49.
Kvapil, Lynne A. 2009. "Teaching Archaeological Pragmatism through Problem-Based Learning." *The Classical Journal* 105(1): 45–52.
Levstik, L. S., and K. C. Barton. 2011. *Doing history: Investigating with children in elementary and middle school.* New York: Routledge.
Little, Barbara J. 2009. "What Can Archaeology Do for Justice, Peace, Community, and the Earth?" *Historical Archaeology* 43(4): 115–19.
Little, J., and P. A. Shackel, eds. 2007. *Archaeology as tool of civic engagement.* Lanham, MD: Altamira Press.
Looking-Glass Science. 2013. "The Mystery of Quick Gulch: Plains Salvage Archaeology." Accessed 1 August 2016. http://www.lookingglassscience.com/elementary-science-curriculum/earth/archaeology-dig.html.
"Malcolm X's former home gets a closer look." 2016. *Boston Globe*, 29 March. Accessed 8 August 2016. https://www.bostonglobe.com/metro/2016/03/28/city-dig-for-artifacts-malcolm-former-home/gnrWFtydycKBGcpcP2Sb0H/story.html.

Marshall, Yvonne. 2002. "What is Community Archaeology?" *World Archaeology* 34(2): 211–19.
McNeil, William H. 1991. "Why Study History? Three Historians Respond." In *Historical literacy: The case for history in American education*, ed. Paul Gagnon and Bradley Commission on History in the Schools, 103–18. Boston, MA: Houghton Mifflin.
Michener, James A. 1974. *Centennial*. New York: Random House.
Muto, Jordan. 2015. "Too much homework? Study shows elementary kids get 3 times more than they should." Accessed 10 August 2016. http://www.today.com/parents/too-much-homework-study-shows-elementary-kids-get-3-times-t38491.
NASBE Study Group on the Lost Curriculum. 2003. *The Complete Curriculum: Ensuring a Place for the Arts and Foreign Languages in American Schools*. Alexandria, VA: National Association of State Boards of Education.
Nash, Gary B., Charlotte Antoinette Crabtree, and Ross E. Dunn. 2000. *History on trial: Culture wars and the teaching of the past*. New York: Vintage Books.
National Council for the Social Studies. 2000. *Service-Learning: An Essential Component of Citizenship Education. A Position Statement of the National Council for the Social Studies*. Accessed 3 August 2016. http://www.socialstudies.org/sites/default/files/publications/se/6504/650408.html.
———. 2013. *The College, Career, and Civic Life (C3) Framework for Social Studies State Standards: Guidance for Enhancing the Rigor of K–12 Civics, Economics, Geography, and History*. Silver Spring, MD: NCSS.
National Endowment for the Humanities. 2016a. "Content: Archaeology." Accessed 1 August 2016. https://edsitement.neh.gov/search?keywords=archaeology.
———. 2016b. "EDSITEment! The Best of the Humanities on the Web." Accessed 24 July 2016. https://edsitement.neh.gov/.
National Governors Association Center for Best Practices and Council of Chief State School Officers. 2010. *Common Core State Standards*. Washington, DC: National Governors Association Center for Best Practices and Council of Chief State School Officers.
National Park Service. 2016a. "A Social Studies Methods Course in the Power of Place." Accessed 10 August 2016. https://www.nps.gov/subjects/teachingwithhistoricplaces/prof-dev_methods-course_outline.htm.
———. 2016b. "Civic Engagement." Accessed 10 August 2016. https://www.nps.gov/civic/.
———. 2016c. "Professional Development." Accessed 31 March 2016. https://www.nps.gov/subjects/teachingwithhistoricplaces/professional-development.htm.
———. 2016d. "Teaching with Historic Places." Accessed 31 March 2016. https://www.nps.gov/subjects/teachingwithhistoricplaces/index.htm.
Risinger, C. Frederick. 2012. "What Social Studies Educators can do about the Marginalization of the Subject They Teach." *Social Education* 76(6): 299–300.
Rowell, C. Glennon, M. Gail Hickey, Kendall Gecsei, and Stacy Klein. 2007.

"A School-Wide Effort for Learning History via a Time Capsule." *Social Education* 71(5): 261–66, 271.
Shull, C. D., and K. Hunter. 1992. "Teaching with Historic Places." *Social Education* 56(5): 312.
Smardz, K., and S. J. Smith, eds. 2000. *The archaeology education handbook: Sharing the past with kids.* Walnut Creek, CA: AltaMira Press.
Society for American Archaeology. 2016. "Lesson plans and activities contributed by educators." Accessed 1 August 2016. http://www.saa.org/publicftp/public/resources/foredu_lessonplans.html.
Sokol-Margolis, Nathan. 2016. "Malcolm X: Digging Up Artifacts, Stories, and Questions about the Truth." Meridian Academy, 12 May. Accessed 8 August 2016. http://www.meridianacademy.org/news/2016/5/12/malcolm-x-digging-up-artifacts-stories-and-questions-about-the-truth.
Stiebing, William H. 1993. *Uncovering the past: A history of archaeology.* London: Oxford University.
Symcox, Linda. 2002. *Whose history? The struggle for national standards in American classrooms.* New York: Teachers College Press.
Torp, L., and S. Sage. 2002. *Problems as possibilities: Problem-based learning for K–16 Education,* 2nd ed. Alexandria, VA: Association for Supervision and Curriculum Development (ASCD).
Tuxill, Jacquelyn L., Nora J. Mitchell, and Delia Clark. 2009. "Stronger Together: A Manual on the Principles and Practices of Civic Engagement." *Conservation and Stewardship Publication no. 16.* Woodstock: Conservation Study Institute, National Park Service. Accessed 10 August 2016. https://www.nps.gov/civic/resources/CE_Manual.pdf.
Tyack, David B. 1967. *Turning points in American educational history.* Waltham, MA: Blaisdell.
United States National Commission on Excellence in Education. 1983. *A nation at risk: The imperative for educational reform. A report to the Nation and the Secretary of Education, United States Department of Education.* Washington, DC: The Commission.
Walker, Andrew, Heather Leary, Cindy E. Hmelo-Silver, and Peggy Ertmer, eds. 2015. *Essential readings in problem-based learning.* Lafayette, IN: Purdue University Press.
Westcott, Lucy. 2015. "What is Lost with Isis's Destruction of Syria's Temple of Bel." *Newsweek,* 1 September. Accessed 11 August 2016. http://www.newsweek.com/what-lost-isiss-destruction-syrias-temple-bel-367721.
White, C. S., and K. Hunter. 1995. *Teaching with historic places: A curriculum framework for professional training and development of teachers, preservationists, and museum and site interpreters.* Washington, DC: National Trust for Historic Preservation.
White, C. S., and D. J. D. White. 2000. "Preparing Teachers to Teach with Historic Places." *CRM* (National Park Service) 23(8): 28–30.
Wineburg, Sam. 2001. *Historical thinking and other unnatural acts: Charting the future of teaching the past.* Philadelphia: Temple University Press.
Wirkala, C., and D. Kuhn. 2011. "Problem-Based Learning in K–12 Education: Is it Effective and How Does it Achieve its Effects?" *American Educational Research Journal* 48(5): 1157–86.

Yeşilbursa, C. C., and K. C. Barton. 2011. "Preservice Teachers' Attitudes Toward the Inclusion of 'Heritage Education' in Elementary Social Studies." *Journal of Social Studies Education Research* 2(2): 1–21.

Zimmerman, Larry J., Steve Dasovich, Mary Engstrom, and Lawrence E. Bradley. 1994. "Listening to the Teachers: Warnings about the Use of Archaeological Agendas in Classrooms in the United States." In *The Presented Past: Heritage, Museums, and Education,* ed. Peter G. Stone and Brian Molyneaux, 359–71. New York: Routledge.

CHAPTER 2

Science and Social Studies Adventures
Using an Interdisciplinary Approach to Inspire School-Age Children to Become Knowledge Producers

Katrina Yezzi-Woodley, Chris Kestly, Beth Albrecht,
Paul Creager, Joel Abdella, and Katherine Hayes

Introduction

Educational outreach in K–12 schools can be an effective method for igniting participants' investment in their community, its heritage, and thus archaeology. Oftentimes efforts to gain a foothold in local schools have been stymied. Some have taken a top-down approach, reaching out to higher administrative offices at the district, and even the state level, and could not get buy-in. Others have entered the classroom but with a presentation that was ultimately seen as a one-time, isolated event, and, though interesting to the teacher and students, did not afford an opportunity to cultivate something of more lasting value. Still others have entered the classroom with the desire to share their passion for what they do in the hopes of invoking a similar passion in the students, without first reflecting on the needs of the students and school.

We posit that it is not enough to focus solely on archaeology; we have to contextualize it in the broader field of social science to meet the needs of the people we serve. We take the position that through a collaborative educational journey, participants are more likely to come to their own appreciation for archaeology and cultural heritage. In this chapter, we share how we meet the needs of students at two local schools, Maple Grove Middle School (MGMS) and Gordon Parks High School (GPHS), and how our approach creates meaning for students encouraging them to become stewards of cultural heritage.

Science and Social Studies Adventures (SASSA) began in 2015 with a couple photos (Figures 2.1 and 2.2). When Ms. Katrina Yezzi-Woodley, a parent and anthropologist, learned that her daughter was studying Native American history, she sent photos of her daughter participating in the University of Minnesota's Paleopicnic to Mr. Chris Kestly, her daughter's social studies teacher. The Anthropology Department–sponsored Paleopicnic introduces primarily college students to flintknapping, stone tool butchery, spear throwing with an atlatl, and archery. Kestly realized he wanted his social studies lesson to be more like the Paleopicnic—hands-on and interactive. So, Yezzi-Woodley, Kestly, and Ms. Beth Albrecht, a science teacher, began collaborating and founded Science and Social Studies Adventures, or SASSA.

When we came together, we wanted to find a way to bring archaeology to the classrooms at MGMS in order to enhance science and social studies lessons in a cross-curricular manner, recognizing that science and social studies are not isolated topics, but connected. We broadened our plans to include volunteer parents and graduate and undergraduate students from the University of Minnesota. By the year's end, we prepared three modules for which six-hundred sixth-grade students learned alongside dozens of volunteer parents. For many, these were

Figure 2.1. Spear throwing at the Paleopicnic. Photo courtesy of Katrina Yezzi-Woodley.

Figure 2.2. Maple Grove Middle School students flintknapping at the University of Minnesota Anthropology Department–sponsored Paleopicnic. Photo courtesy of Katrina Yezzi-Woodley.

the most memorable lessons of the year, and we agreed to continue our work with more modules, more grade levels, and more grants. In the next year, we expanded to seventh grade at MGMS and, through Dr. Katherine Hayes, we connected with GPHS. To be clear, this is framed as a collaborative educational project and not a research study of the schools.

Though this chapter is about the SASSA outreach program, it is really about the schools and community members we serve. Some of the authors of this chapter represent the schools (and districts) with which SASSA works and their contributions are essential in defining SASSA's vision and identity. When we use the term "we," it is done collectively as a community of individuals and collaborating organizations coming together to benefit local students and our shared community. In this chapter, we first describe our core values and the approach of our program. In the second half we provide examples of how we have implemented those values.

Our Methods and Approach

Our program is characterized by an interdisciplinary approach, hands-on learning, core-curricular support, collaboration, community involvement, and making lessons relevant to students. In addition to enhancing education, these key components bring participants together and we become invested in one another and in our community. This sense of shared investment is central to developing and fostering concern for heritage.

Soluri (2010) states that the learning process is the first of three components that comprise high-quality education. The second concern is retention, followed by later applications or transfer, where students demonstrate the ability to apply something learned in one context to another. Our approach to the learning process is based on constructivist (Blake and Pope 2008; Piaget 1970) and experiential (Jose, Patrick, and Moseley 2017; Moore 2001) learning theories, which posit that the learning process is a social activity, where new knowledge grows from associations with pre-existing knowledge through participatory, as opposed to, passive learning. Hands-on, task-oriented learning, contextualized in real world, relevant examples is followed by critical student reflection (Jose et al. 2017). New knowledge is acquired best when it can be connected to previous knowledge. We provide cooperative and collaborative learning environments that foster student communication offering them ample opportunity to make connections between new information and what they already know. All activities offer moments for critical reflection and challenge the students to apply what they learn within the activity to their own life experiences.

An Interdisciplinary Approach

Many of life's circumstances, work and otherwise, require an amalgamation of different methods and approaches. It naturally follows that an effective educational model emulates what can be expected in life after school. Vars (1991) identified the importance of a curriculum that not only teaches the subject at hand but also addresses students' needs and society's challenges. Interdisciplinarity, therefore, is not solely conceived of as an intermingling of subjects, it includes the teaching of valuable, what Relan and Kimpston refer to as "across-the-domain" (1991, 3), skills such as reasoning, observation, interpretation, strategizing, communication, and discernment.

Science influences and affects change at the social and political level, and social concerns influence and facilitate scientific endeavors. And, these concerns and endeavors are embedded in a historical and archaeological context. It is important that we make these connections explicit (Bybee et al. 1991; Pugh and Girod 2007; National Science Board 1983) to our K–12 students who are also citizens of the communities in which they live. For example, Section 315 of the Post–Katrina

Emergency Management Reform Act (PKEMRA) of 2006, directed the Under Secretary for Science and Technology—the individual responsible for leveraging scientific and technological research to improve national security and increase community resilience in the face of emergencies such as natural disasters—to "establish a comprehensive research and development program" that would improve emergency response efforts during crises. Here is an example of how science and research interact with political and social concerns. This sort of policy implementation, which is based on an event that happened in the past, is designed to address future events and draws on expertise across disciplines.

An education based on discretized subjects does not adequately prepare students to affect change and construct solutions in a world that is not so conveniently compartmentalized (Relan and Kimpston 1991). As students navigate the modules we provide, they learn about the process of inquiry and knowledge production. We provide opportunities to apply these skills to topics (such as the mitigation of natural disasters) that cannot be associated solely with one academic subject. The goal is to help students realize their individual strengths, develop the skills necessary to capitalize on those strengths, determine what they like or do not like, and, in the process, recognize their own value and that of their classmates. We move beyond teaching the prescribed standards pertinent to the learner's grade and subject to a more tangible application of skills that is more relevant and relatable to the world in which the students live.

When students begin to see the process by which an idea becomes imbedded in our worldview, the ordinary can be seen as something extraordinary (Pugh and Girod 2007). Students begin to build a context for concepts and ideas that they may have previously taken for granted. When they understand processes, they can begin to see the germ of an idea, its original implementation, and its transformative power, something so transformative that it becomes imbedded in our world. Then they can begin to appreciate the importance of historical context and the present-day influence of the historical.

Hands-on Learning

In some ways, the old factory-like model of learning still exists in the classroom. This can, in some ways be attributed to the limitations that the physical classroom space imposes. Students need concentrated time and a quiet environment in order to focus and perform certain tasks, such as reading at a desk. However, sitting in a classroom can accomplish only so much. Hands-on learning is a daily necessity for most people and most learning is "on site"—in the garage, in the kitchen, at the store, at a lake, or in the wilderness—away from the classroom.

A conducive learning environment is student-centered and inquiry-based, where teachers facilitate learning by encouraging students to construct their own knowledge. Great teaching has always been about meeting students where they are at and then getting them to take steps forward in their learning. Soluri (2010, 11) supports hands-on learning, stating that "classroom activities should be experiential, involving the students in the activities and processes that help them construct knowledge." Inquiry-based, student-centered learning takes students beyond superficial learning, promotes deep content learning (Ashmore 2005), and verifies the knowledge and ideas studied by students. Active learning removes passivity and increases engagement and motivation. It fosters self-confidence and a desire to learn more. SASSA modules are setup to be exploratory in nature and the value is in the discussion that occurs with peers, college students, and parent volunteers. The true beauty of investigative learning of this nature is that it allows students to learn at their own pace and in a way that is meaningful to them.

Learning that takes place outside the classroom, such as field trips and outdoor learning activities that are guided by experts, is recognized as a valuable, enriching educational tool (Gerber, Cavallo, and Marek 2001; Jose et al. 2017). However, it is not always possible to bring students to the field or there are limitations on the number of students that can be accommodated at a site. By bringing experts, such as archaeologists, into the classroom, we transform the space into something akin to an in-house field trip. A space to which students have grown accustomed is made new and exciting and at a fraction of the cost of facilitating an off-grounds field trip.

Hands-on learning improves concentration, increases student engagement, and makes learning (and teaching) fun. Memory is strongly linked to physical experiences. In his role playing–based courses, Pedelty (2001) found that students more fully grasped the dynamism and complexity of the cultures and themes they were exploring. This approach created a scenario conducive to critical reflection and the foreign became more familiar and appreciable. Not only were students more engaged mentally but so were their senses. For example, in sixth grade social studies at MGMS students learn about Native Americans who crafted stone tools. Most people outside of archaeology are not familiar with flintknapping or see it as a hobby. Students experienced flintknapping by striking hard candy nodules and their success was dependent on their approach, which was guided by lithic specialists (Figures 2.3 and 2.4). Later, students were able to cut celery with different types of stone tools to assess the effectiveness of the stone tool types. Magnetic, 3D puzzles of cores and flakes allowed students to learn about the sequence of flake removal and the level of complexity associated with some stone tool industries (Figure 2.5). Learning

Figure 2.3. SASSA volunteer Sam Porter teaching Maple Grove Middle School students about flintknapping. Photo courtesy of Katrina Yezzi-Woodley.

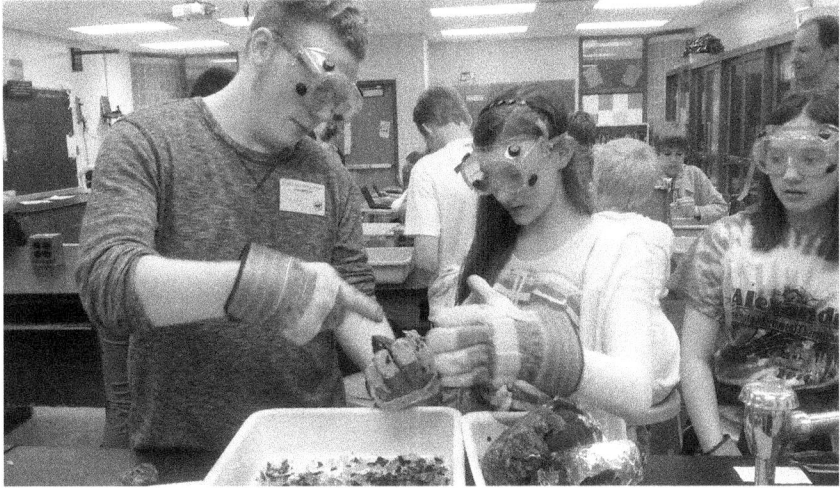

Figure 2.4. SASSA volunteer Thomas Alberg teaching Maple Grove Middle School students about the anatomy of a flake. Photo courtesy of Katrina Yezzi-Woodley.

Figure 2.5. Maple Grove Middle School student learns about stone tool industries by refitting a magnetized, 3D puzzle. Photo courtesy of Katrina Yezzi-Woodley.

about crafting tools helped students appreciate the skills needed to survive in the past. Flintknapping became relevant to the students and they became invested in the outcome of their efforts.

Experiential learning inspires interest in relevant social issues, engendering a concern for community and one's role therein. It offers students opportunities to practice skills that will empower them to be effective, engaged members of their community, both socially and vocationally. Moore sees experiential learning as "contributing to the student's capacity to participate with others in a critical dialog about ongoing processes and problems, to make sense of complex situations by means of alternating intelligently between action and reflection. This strategy is progressive in the sense of democratic discourses that distribute power and social goods more fairly" (2001, 20). As an example, students in Pedelty's (2001) classes were more inclined to collaborate with one another. When they took on roles of iconic, historical figures that have been villainized or heroized in the public eye, they began to understand multiple viewpoints held by variously invested players navigating complex situations.

Experiential learning involves decision-making, which shifts power to students, who become responsible for their learning as they engage with the material. They learn, willingly, to critically reflect on their choices and actions and that of their classmates. Thus, students are trained to critically examine and test the common beliefs and processes in their world and to not necessarily accept the status quo as natural, or right, without careful examination and consideration (Moore 2001). The end result is eloquently described by Moore:

> They search out the historical sources of current practices and relations, understanding that things could be different. And they learn to dig out useful information for answering these questions: they collect artifacts and documents, they interview their colleagues and supervisors, they observe events with a critical eye, they write notes and memos to themselves analyzing and explaining what they see going on. (2001, 21)

What Moore describes here is an individual who is transformed into a knowledge producer, an individual, irrespective of vocation, who cares for and is invested in cultural heritage, not for the purpose of clinging to the past, but for the purpose of eliciting change.

Supporting Core Curricula

The education system has a long history of swinging from left to right and back again with what is seen as "best practices" in staff development and teaching protocol. The current trend is standards-based grading (SBG) where subjects are broken into "learning targets" that allow the teacher to evaluate student's mastery of different components of the subject (Del Schalock 1998; White, Chapter 1). Expectations are set for the scope of material taught which can align schools and districts across a large area to a common set of goals (Hamilton, Stecher, and Yuan 2008).

SBG fosters a growth mindset, teaches self-determination, and encourages self-reflection which promotes student ownership of their education and an intrinsic motivation to learn (Wehmeyer et al. 2004). Teachers are able to provide relevant assignments and differentiated instruction based on the individual needs of students as each learning target is assessed. Students receive feedback throughout the process that allows them to know which learning targets they have mastered and which targets need improvement. The consequences for mistakes made early in the learning process are nominal and students are primarily graded on their mastery of the subject after they have received feedback on learning targets and have had ample opportunity to improve these skills, which ultimately leads to better understanding of the overall topic (Iamarino 2014). This creates an environment that promotes learning without fear.

There are concerns related to SBG. Teachers are often incentivized to focus on standardized test preparation which redirects focus from standards to testing (Ashmore 2005; Hamilton et al. 2008). When K–12 students are prepared primarily for exams, their learning can become "rapid and superficial" (Soluri 2010, 8). The potential superficiality of learning is exacerbated by the fact that SBG is a system in which the teacher is able only to teach or assign grades to outcomes that are tied to standards taught per grade and per subject.

In addition to the concerns surrounding SBG, time and material resources are limited at all levels, including teaching and administrative (Ashmore 2005). The task to develop a continuous teacher training program is daunting as administrators balance the political, financial, and educational trends that surround them. Each teacher has a unique teaching style and teaching performance is variable. SBG does not influence teaching practices and pedagogical methods in a way that is predictable (Hamilton et al. 2008).

SASSA bridges the gap well, allowing for deeper learning that is tied to standards; it supplements what teachers are doing in the classroom without depleting precious time for something that is ancillary. SASSA works with K–12 educators, examining state standards for each grade and finding ways to connect fields of expertise to the curriculum in ways that are fun and engaging.

Making Lessons Relevant to Students

It is not uncommon in the classroom for students to ask when they will ever use what they are learning. We need to make the connections between the classroom and beyond explicit (Coleman and Simpson 1999). Anthropology, by virtue of being the study of people, is relevant to people. Archaeology reveals how skills and topics learned in the core subjects have manifested in the real world through time and it does so with physical artifacts that bring the students close to the topic in a tangible way. When we use "realistic examples and relevant issues" (Soluri 2010, 2) to make these connections between the classroom and the "real world," students become invested in what they are learning and they begin to value the cultural remnants that served as the conduits that made those connections for them in the first place.

By making an effort to understand the diversity of a community and what it means for individuals in that community, we can target our efforts toward helping students unpack issues that are locally and globally meaningful to them (Newman 1990). This has the reciprocal effect of educating SASSA members, volunteers, and collaborators too. Though this may seem like a fortuitous, and possibly negligible, byproduct of community engagement, it is actually a very important component of the SASSA program. We make very little impact by imposing what we deem to be relevant on others. We see it as our job to show how components of science and social studies, which are seen as universally beneficial according to state standards, are inherently part of that which is relevant to the diverse communities within which we work.

Archaeology is a natural amalgamation of science and social studies that uses scientific methods to explore societal issues both past and present. It is by way of this first step that students begin to grasp why archaeology and cultural heritage are meaningful. It might also be a good reminder to archaeologists, who are entrenched in their own immediate research interests, of the broader implications of their archaeological work. Many archaeologists love archaeology for archaeology's sake and many archaeologists come from relative privilege and are pursuing it to satisfy intellectual or scientific curiosity alone. Some archaeologists go into it because it can be a tool of community cultural heritage preservation, and their research and work comes from a place of deep personal connections. This may be especially true for those coming from under-represented populations in archaeology. This will become important for how we ground our work in relevance for students. Again, there is an intrinsic reciprocity that unfolds in which the larger public begins to see meaning in archaeological pursuits and archaeologists remain cognizant of the most grounding purpose in any archaeological inquiry: the meaning of, and the lives impacted by, archaeological endeavors.

Collaboration and Community Involvement

SASSA works at a grassroots level, focusing on the needs of students, volunteers, and teachers to create a transformational program. Graduate students serve as content experts while teachers bring pedagogical knowledge and experience managing thirty-five to forty students to assess the modules for the "doable" aspect of the lessons. Together, we create effective modules.

Students value volunteers and experts in the classroom. A new face brings about novelty and curiosity. When visitors eagerly share knowledge and experience, or validate what is being taught in the classroom, students lean forward and care. When teachers connect with experts, in this case archaeologists, those experts bring a vast knowledge and passion for their career to the classroom. To see that there are people who really work in archaeology, or other related disciplines, is critical to making these fields of study seem accessible.

However, a single classroom visit is not sufficient to meet the needs of the schools and may not justify teachers setting valuable time aside to allow us to come into the classrooms. We are committed to long-term relationships with the schools. We went into this knowing that the first generation of these modules were test runs and that we would improvise and adapt as each group came through the module. It was that flexible thinking that allowed us to analyze the activity and combine efforts from parent volunteers, teachers, and presenters to streamline instruction, supplies, and tasks. Each time the module was presented it was a better product.

We all are members of multiple, connected communities in which social learning is constantly taking place (Wenger 2000). Though we might be experts in some aspects, we are all learners in others. Collaboration invites multiple voices, including the students' voices, to be heard and incorporated into a social learning practice that more effectively connects students to what they are learning and has greater potential to broaden their worldview.

We acknowledge that the level and type of investment of all participants, including that of the students, varies and in so doing we become more effective. Students' level of investment may simply be to earn credit and pass the class. When we offer distractions to that goal, however well-meaning and educational, then we lose our students (Walker and Saitta 2002). When we assume they will be excited about the topic because we are excited about the topic, we risk outcomes opposite to those we wish. Students will not learn to value what they are learning, they will not value cultural heritage and the need for archaeology, and they may actually develop a distaste for it. However, when we welcome our students at any level of commitment, and come to them where they are, then we position ourselves to journey with them through a process that could then increase their level of commitment to the learning experience and to the importance of cultural heritage.

School Partnerships

Each school has diverse student populations and unique challenges which affect how we formulate teaching modules. Here we present our experiences at two local public schools. Maple Grove Middle School is a mainstream, suburban school that provides educational services to sixth through eighth grade. Gordon Parks High School is an urban, alternative learning center that provides educational services for grades nine through twelve. In the following sections we will describe each school and our experience working with each school, including the differences that make each experience unique and the similarities that highlight how we are all connected.

Maple Grove Middle School

MGMS is located in Maple Grove, Minnesota, a northwest suburb of Minneapolis, and is one of four middle schools in the Osseo School District. With over 1,700 students in grades six through eight, its attendance area ranges across parts of Maple Grove, Plymouth, Brooklyn Park, and Brooklyn Center. The Osseo School District is sometimes referred to as a "split district" because of how economic factors and population diversity varies significantly from the eastern and western parts of the district. MGMS has a lower poverty rate and less diversity compared to its sister middle schools. While student achievement is generally on par compared to the state overall, it reflects the wide achievement gap between white students and students of color.

MGMS changed from a junior high to a middle school in the fall of 2015. Ninth graders were moved to the high school and sixth graders were moved in from elementary schools. In the first year as a middle school, 15 out of 16 sixth grade teachers were previous elementary teachers, not junior high teachers. MGMS and its sister middle schools are in a programming transition. The junior high model was basically a high school for young adolescents where students' placement in classes was based on scheduling logistics. With the middle school model, many adjustments were aligned to match the standards set forth by the Association of Middle Level Education (AMLE).

One significant adjustment was arranging students into interdisciplinary teams with "core" teachers. Each grade is subdivided into core teams of about 150 students taught by a specified teaching team comprised of four teachers: English, math, social studies, and science. The purpose is to provide a stronger transition from elementary school. This allows for a greater sense of community with students and for core teachers to collaborate with instruction and communicate with each other and parents about the needs of students more effectively. Students also have choices of "exploratory" classes such as band, orchestra, art, physical education, technology education, and others.

Another significant change was adding an advisory class within each core team. Students on each team are assigned an advisory class from either the math, social studies, English, or science teacher. This class has a number of functions and curriculum designed to build community, foster future career awareness, and build academic accountability and support.

One feature of MGMS's model is each interdisciplinary core team of teachers have common meeting times four days a week. That means a student's math, English, social studies, and science teacher meet to discuss the needs of students, and to plan programming as a team during the school day. This interdisciplinary approach has great potential. For example, curriculum can be planned and reinforced in more than one classroom. The science teacher can support the math teacher's efforts. The social studies teacher can support strategies students experience in English class. The science teacher and social studies teacher can support each other's efforts. The underlying belief is that learning is not always isolated by subject but connected in many ways. This relationship was part of the beginning of SASSA.

Program Development at Maple Grove Middle School

In our first year SASSA designed three learning modules. The "Stratigraphy and Transport" module demonstrates how riverbeds are eroded and bones are transported by flowing water. Students use sand art to make stratigraphic profiles and explore the concept of biostratigraphy and context. In the "Lithics" module, students learn various aspects relating to stone tool technology such as sourcing and choosing raw materials; issues of transport and exchange; aesthetic value and social status; the mechanics of making the tools; the efficacy of using stone tools; and removal sequences as related to complexity. The "Archaeology on the Internet" module explores material culture across time and space. Many archaeologists and cultural heritage programs have created amazing websites that allow visitors to explore different aspects of many important archaeological sites in North America. Students have the opportunity to explore these interactive websites and learn about the artifacts found there. Critical inquiry about artifacts and features at each site unfold and conversations elucidate the meaning of tools across time and geographic space in terms of complexity, socioeconomic importance, identity, and status.

Graduate students volunteered in the classroom to provide expertise. Parents, family, and friends were welcomed to help facilitate activities and generate conversations. No previous knowledge of the

Table 2.1. Maple Grove Middle School program budget for years one and two. Courtesy of the authors.

	Year 1 (2015–2016)	Year 2 (2016–2017)
Total # of Students	~600	~1,330
Grades	6	6, 7, and 9–12
Modules Taught	3	7
Overall Program Cost	$351.00	$325**
Cost per Child	< $0.59*	$0.24
# of Grad Student Volunteers	9	17
# of Undergraduate Volunteers	4	14
# of Local/Parent Volunteers	14	27
UMN Departments	Anthropology	Anthropology; Earth Sciences; Ecology, Evolution, and Behavior

*Each student participated in four modules, so the cost per child per module was $0.15.
**Some expenses were covered directly by the District 279 Innovation Grant and are not reflected here. Also, we were able to reuse materials purchased in the previous year for modules that were repeated in the second year.

material was required. A step-by-step guide accompanied each activity and was distributed to all volunteers. Generalized instruction videos offered visual familiarity with some of the activities. We provided questions in our guides to inspire conversation and example answers to those questions so that community volunteers could be confident when encouraging conversation.

Meeting the Needs of Maple Grove Middle School

As a school in transition, MGMS is establishing a team-based, interdisciplinary program for which SASSA is well-suited. We are able to work closely with the teachers to provide targeted support to the needs of their school and classrooms. SASSA is able to enrich lessons with deeper levels of expertise in real-world applications of the material that is being taught in the classrooms. We are able to bring materials into the classroom that are not readily available in a K–12 setting. Students can better envision possibilities for their own future when they connect with college students in their classrooms.

Outcomes of the Partnership

SASSA reached approximately 600 sixth graders with the Osseo District in the first year. We did so at a cost of less than fifty-nine cents per child, falling under budget and within our funding. Nine graduate students, four undergraduate students, and fourteen parents volunteered in the first year. Sandra Day, Coordinator of Curriculum, Instruction and Educational Standards, visited the classroom, saw the program's potential, and has become an advocate for its future.

In our second year, we separated the "Stratigraphy and Transport Module" into two separate modules, presenting them to approximately 700 sixth graders, and we created an "Ecology" module for the seventh graders. Overall, we presented to approximately 1,300 students at MGMS.

We create a lasting impression with the students we work with and they look forward to our visits each year. We hope to expand into all four middle schools over the next few years so that we can share what we do across the district.

Gordon Parks High School

GPHS is an alternative learning center, renamed and dedicated in 2008, located on the bustling University Avenue in St. Paul near Lexington Ave.

The legacy of the school's namesake guides the intended trajectory of its curriculum. Gordon Parks was an African American photographer, filmmaker, poet, and author who was born in Kansas, but spent his teen and early adult years in St. Paul. Gordon attended an alternative high school in St. Paul, named Mechanic Arts High School, fitting school in between the periods where he was homeless, financially independent, and struggling to follow his dream. Similarly, the students who attend GPHS are considered "at-risk," meaning they wrestle with issues such as homelessness, pregnancy, chemical dependency, or are severely behind in school.

The school's course schedule was designed around students experiencing similar circumstances as Gordon Parks did when he was their age. Classes are organized in three-week blocks, so that if a crisis (housing, family, medical) occurs in a student's life, they do not lose their entire quarter of credits. Correspondingly, one third of a credit is earned in each three-week cycle, so that students (more rapidly than in a traditional nine-week quarter) are rewarded for the fruits of their academic investment. The three-week cycles are also conducive to project-based learning experiences embedded with community engagement efforts.

What is the local community like? GPHS students come from all over St. Paul. The school does not have a specific "draw" area. However, it is useful to consider the local community around the school, as it is the hyper-local context for our multi-year civic engaged digital storytelling work, which will be described later in the chapter. The school is located near the northernmost end of the former Rondo Community, which was the African American business center of St. Paul. Its demolition for the construction of Highway 94 was hugely detrimental for the burgeoning African American middle class of St. Paul.

The school is also part of the Hamline Midway and Frogtown neighborhood, though an aerial view of the school location shows that the south side of University Ave is one of industrial "super blocks," dotted with current and former businesses. Ironically, the block on which Gordon Parks is located has particularly high population density because of the Skyline Tower apartment building. This residence is the largest single subsidized housing complex west of Chicago with five hundred units and approximately 1,500 residents. This affordable housing complex is run by Common Bond properties, and has a mission focus on new immigrants, particularly east African.

The community around GPHS is interwoven with instruction via an approach to curriculum best called Civic Engaged Digital Storytelling (CEDS). This approach to curriculum helps to point educators toward hyper local civic engagement and storytelling opportunities to connect with standards-based instruction. This approach to curriculum shatters the typical scale and scope of school experience, so collaboration has been necessary and in fact SASSA's involvement with the school is highly connected to CEDS.

A quick example of this approach was a project between 2008–14 called "Transitions: University Avenue." A multi-institutional partnership between GPHS, Minnesota Historical Society, and the University of Minnesota supported the production of forty films that told the stories of residents, business owners, and students before, during, and after light rail transit construction on University Avenue. The University of Minnesota portion of project collaboration was through Professor Catherine Squires, and this yielded the introduction of Hayes from the University of Minnesota (and correspondingly Yezzi-Woodley) to the school.

Another example of CEDS was the school's successful effort to promote public awareness and engagement with the prospect of converting three vacant lots behind the school into a park. Students in human geography, science, English and art sustained a multi-year effort between 2011 and the present to promote awareness, build stakeholder support, fundraise, and champion the park effort. After fundraising 2.5 million dollars, the five-acre park was purchased by the city in 2016. Though interest in the park was multi-dimensional, a recurring question was whether there was a potential archaeological project in the space.

So, in the fall of 2016, Hayes started working with GPHS and introduced our science teacher, Mr. Joel Abdella, to Yezzi-Woodley. Hayes continued working with the school's social studies department, and SASSA focused on the science classrooms.

Program Development at Gordon Parks High School

GPHS presented us with an interesting and exciting project in our second year of existence. Between 2011–16, teachers and students at this high school worked with the city to acquire an adjacent property for a park project. Now that the land had changed from private to public ownership, and there was the prospect of an open excavation in 2018, they wanted to conduct an archaeological inquiry and reached out to Hayes.

Hayes began working with Mr. Paul Creager, Curriculum & Media Arts Coordinator at GPHS. Hayes suggested that SASSA might be a helpful collaborator to broaden the collaboration into other subject areas. Yezzi-Woodley met with Creager and teachers Abdella (science), and Mr. Tom Davies and Mr. Ted Johnson (social studies). We decided on a two-pronged approach: the archaeological dig and the in-class training for which we would create modules that provide necessary knowledge and information that would benefit the dig but could also be generalized for use independently in any classroom. Two modules were presented in 2016–17: a "Biology" module and a two-part "GPR" module, the first part of which took place in the classroom, the second part of which took place on the city-acquired land adjacent to the school.

Meeting the Needs of Gordon Parks High School

GPHS as a setting for this work is unique and valuable because it connects this work with students in need of high engagement and relevancy. Most if not all students at this school are significantly behind in credits, and on top of that many students are living independently with part-time work consuming much of their time outside of the school day. Add to this a general distaste among students for traditional education, and you have a list of needs that are quite different than other schools.

During the winter months Yezzi-Woodley, and a number of other graduate students interfaced with Abdella's biology class. Abdella's students were studying evolution at the time, and they developed a laboratory experience to help students grasp some of the difficult concepts found in evolutionary theory via hands-on work with mammal scapulae that they were able to touch, measure, categorize, and build hypotheses from. Questions were posed to the students in such a way as to get at the fundamental understanding that living organisms are connected through similar (homologous) structures. In other words, it was an experience that required high level thinking skills but in a hands-on, tactile rich setting.

Another laboratory station had a number of different primate skulls including *Homo sapiens* (modern humans); *Homo neanderthalensis, Homo erectus,* and *Australopithecus africanus* (human ancestors); *Pan troglodytes* (chimpanzees) and *Gorilla gorilla* (gorillas). Students could touch, feel, and measure the different features of each skull. Questions such as "Which skull is closest in features to the modern human skull?" were asked. Students came up with many plausible hypotheses based on their observations, and at times would defend their answer by describing features that to them represented a closer connection to modern humans. There was also a station showing 500 million-year-old fossils embedded into rock. These fossils ranged from impressions of ferns to sea crustaceans in parts of the world where ancient seas existed at one time. Students were exposed to the idea that the earth did not always look as it does today, and just like life, has evolved over time.

Later in the school year another group of graduate students worked with Abdella's physics students using ground-penetrating radar (GPR) technology to map out the vacant field soon to become a future park space (Figure 2.6). Abdella was already working with physics students on wave theory with sound and light, including concepts such as reflection, refraction, and the speed of light in different mediums, as described by Snell's law. GPR technology was a natural development of those ideas and an excellent way for students to experience the application of physics for the purpose of an archaeological dig. Physics students as well as social studies students by the end of the year went out to the property and started to map out part of the field's underground features with the hope of finding interesting features that might motivate a dig in that area.

Figure 2.6. Dr. Kat Hayes and SASSA volunteers Emily Briggs and Annie Melton teach Gordon Parks High School students how to work the GPR. Photo courtesy of the authors.

During the coming 2017–18 school year Hayes and her students will be working with Abdella's chemistry class doing a study of heavy metal deposits using x-ray fluorescence to measure the concentrations of these metals found in the field and in surrounding areas. Tom Davies and Ted Johnson will be involved in surveying techniques using Light Detection and Ranging (LiDAR) to explore topographical data as well as understanding the history of the area and current industries that are close neighbors to GPHS and the future park space.

Abdella would like SASSA units that help perpetuate the park context in his science classes. He is particularly interested in the soil sample approach. To broaden this topic for relevancy on more instructional days, we will find examples of where soil analysis has saved lives. The most engaging scenario for students would be to put them, as much as possible, in the role that professional chemists would when analyzing soil from the park. We will provide examples where soil analysis triggered awareness of something that impacted human health, especially in an urban setting, to contextualize this work. For example, arsenic testing was done in South Minneapolis because there was an old arsenic plant along what is now Hiawatha Avenue. This led to a massive clean-up by the Environmental Protection Agency (EPA). From 2004–08, the EPA cleaned up properties that put children at immediate risk. The American Revitalization and Recovery Act (ARRA) funded the final phase of the clean-up which ended in 2011. Ultimately, the EPA removed fifty thousand tons of contaminated soil and refilled depleted properties with clean soil.

Outcomes of the Partnership

SASSA brought GPHS resources to deepen lessons. This collaboration brought in resources Gordon Parks did not have—extreme support for a niche component of a unit. State standards are not designed to support such in-depth opportunities. Yet, being able to hold something "cool" engages students with a unit which is why it is important to provide rich projects for kids, especially in schools that serve students who require high engagement.

There is not a lot of innovation in education. The idea of a multi-year project is status quo. But multi-year relationships grow and change. GPHS is able to counterbalance poor attendance through big projects that compel students to engage with community. Curriculum that yields more curriculum provides resources for student action within the community. They are immediately empowered to participate in and influence local initiatives, defying the idea that community engagement is solely the purview of adults.

It takes a special teacher to work at GPHS. Not everyone is qualified. Teachers are really pressured amidst a more rigorous grading schedule and intense focus on experiential learning than those of traditional high schools. Organizations like SASSA provide valuable support with the latter when they are willing to do more than play a bit part and lean in to do the work, remaining flexible in approach to meet the needs of different teachers.

The Valuation of Archaeology

Archaeological approaches to knowledge acquisition and production offer an excellent point of entry for getting people to learn how to produce knowledge critically, which breeds respect and care for archaeological resources and what they can tell us about our shared human history. Therefore, the focus of SASSA is not the valuation of archaeology in and of itself. The practice of archaeology helps individuals develop an innate curiosity and teaches strategies to satisfy that curiosity such that children are transformed from knowledge consumers to knowledge producers.

Archaeology is inherently an interdisciplinary endeavor that calls upon expertise from a variety of fields outside of archaeology and specialties within archaeology. As most archaeologists know, chemists, geologists, geneticists, historians, geographers, and botanists, to name a few, have made incredible contributions to the field. Specialists in lithics, faunal analysis, taphonomy, pottery, metals, and more are called upon to provide in-depth analysis of different aspects within a site. To separate the skills needed in this field, like we do in most schools, would be ludicrous. All of these disciplines work together, which is what we want students to see firsthand.

Life's inherent interdisciplinarity, to which archaeologists are accustomed, carries over when we examine it through a K–12 lens. With this in mind, we opt to provide activities that meld all the core curricula. SASSA is not archaeologically centered; it is social studies and science centered. Archaeology offers approaches that exist at the intersection between science and social studies. So, our approach is largely informed by methods in archaeology and anthropology and grounded in archaeological themes. And, much like what happens in a professional archaeological endeavor, we benefit from the contributions of practitioners in related fields such as geology, paleontology, and ecology.

Archaeology in urban settings like St. Paul also connects our work to more recent histories and diverse communities. Minnesota has a rich immigrant history. Descendants of these immigrant populations live here today as do local establishments. For example, the river flats of Upper Landing in St. Paul were settled by southern Italians in the 1900s. Swede Hollow was home for Swedish, Polish, Italian, and Mexican immigrants and Connemara Patch was home for Irish immigrants. The influence of these past immigrations can be felt today.

Descendant communities of Anishinaabe (Ojibwe) and Dakota (Sioux) have voices which are undeniably necessary for any discussion of historical and sociopolitical importance in Minnesota. Additionally, there is a strong Somali presence in Minneapolis and, according to the popular press, the Cedar-Riverside area has been referred to by its residents as the "Little Mogadishu" (Shah 2017). In fact, Somali-born, Ilhan Omar was elected to the Minnesota House of Representatives in 2016. These are just two examples of the incredible diversity present in Minnesota. The Minnesota State Demographic Center put out a report, "The Economic Status of Minnesotans Chartbook" in 2016 in which they identify the seventeen largest cultural groups in the state: African-American, Mexican, Hmong, Somali, Asian Indian, Ojibwe, Vietnamese, Chinese, Korean, Ethiopian, Filipino, Liberian, Puerto Rican, Lao, Russian, and Dakota. Many of these people were born here, and many represent recent immigrants.

Archaeology occurs in physical places often occupied by these various cultural groups to which archaeologists have an ethical responsibility. All of these cultural groups bring invaluable community expertise. Any archaeological analysis would be remiss, shallow, and largely uninformative if it did not engage with these various experts and resources.

Academics who participate in SASSA benefit from the experience by learning how to communicate their discipline to the larger public. What might be important to non-specialists needs to be at the forefront of the archaeologist's mind. Since most students will not become archaeologists (Newman 1990), it is an important and necessary challenge for us as archaeologists to remember that archaeology is actually not, and is never likely to be, the number one priority for most of the public. We become effective by traveling on a journey with the public, meeting them where they are, and bringing them through a process from which they will develop their own sense of archaeology's importance. We must tap into what is important for non-archaeologists and then demonstrate how archaeology is integral to those concerns.

It is also important to recognize that we are not just talking about differences in students' future vocational interests. When we think of this universal term "student" it conjures up a notion of a youngster with an oversized backpack draped over their shoulder traipsing off to school where they are going to learn their ABCs and it becomes easy to forget they are all individuals with individual stories. Each individual brings their own experience to bear on their education. When we make that connection, recognizing and acknowledging the multiple stories in our students then we open the door for them to do the same. Students begin to realize that they are the most recent participants of a history that continues to unfold and the connection between the present and the past becomes tangible and meaningful.

The purpose of education reaches beyond training students for future careers or vocations. Students need to be prepared to handle change, much of which is unknown or cannot be predicted. It should also ignite the desire in students to become lifelong learners which can be translated into individuals who are resilient. In this way, students are not limited to learning a particular skill, but are taught a way of moving through the world effectively, regardless of the circumstances. Covington states that "the majority of our students understand neither the history of change nor the forces that shape their individual lives; and their loyalties often run to self-indulgence and near-term gratification" (1998, 4). When we are able to situate ourselves within a communal, global, and historical context we can begin to construct purpose.

The Future

One of the challenges in writing this chapter is that our organization is new and we are only beginning to establish what the future of SASSA looks like. Our program has been well-received in its first two years and we are experiencing rapid growth due to the generosity and support of its members and volunteers who can see the benefit of the program and are willing to devote their time and efforts to bring the vision to fruition.

None of us set out with the express intent to create a major outreach program. A shared sense of community brought us together. We care deeply about education and what underpins all of this for us is the desire to bring the community together to benefit our children. What continues to motivate us is knowing that we have an impact. Witnessing the benefits K–12 students experience during presentations, and even a year later when we return, is immediately gratifying and reinforces that what we have begun needs to continue and grow.

We all approach this collaboration with a growth mindset that allows us to experiment, try new things, adjust our methods, and flourish as a result. We recognize that the modules are still a work in progress as we figure out how to best place them in the appropriate grade level as well as tweak the style of delivery and management of supplies.

What is truly amazing about the process is that each participant in SASSA has been integral in making it what it is. Our partnerships are seeded in a true understanding and recognition of what others bring to the table. One of the most incredible parts is knowing that the academic world beyond K–12 is willing to assist in the teaching of their fields, and, reciprocally, the educators at the K–12 level have been willing to take a risk, be flexible, and dedicate time to creating a product that is workable for all.

Concretizing our organization as a nonprofit with a proper business plan, articles, and bylaws is the next step in developing an infrastructure that can support our growth over the long-term. To that end, we are seeking the guidance and support of well-established organizations, such as the Minnesota Council of Nonprofits and Propel for Nonprofits, whose purpose is to help fledgling non-profit organizations establish themselves, and to provide a support network for all local nonprofits.

Creating an effective infrastructure for our program is largely reliant on growing our volunteer base and cultivating valuable collaborations. We continue to collaborate with Maple Grove Middle School, Gordon Parks High School, and have recently begun a collaboration with White Bear Lake Area Learning Center to create a year-long elective course in anthropology. In this academic year, our focus is on formalizing the organization and refining the services we already provide to these schools.

In the coming years, we would like to expand across the Osseo School District to provide programming for all their middle schools, high schools, and eventually elementary schools. We hope to continue the journey with GPHS as the archaeological project unfolds on the city-acquired land. We hope to mainstream the elective we create with White Bear Lake Area Learning Center to the White Bear Lake Area High School.

We also have plans to establish local field schools in the schools' respective communities because outdoor field experiences are effective experiential learning tools that help students to internalize what they are learning in a lasting way. Such experiences offer an additional exploratory atmosphere, which inspires interest in learning (Jose et al. 2017) and builds off of what we bring to the classrooms. Offering the opportunity for students to engage in archaeological digs will deepen the concern for cultural heritage that we have begun to cultivate in the classrooms and will transform students into knowledge producers because they will be doing the work of archaeology.

A more impactful approach also involves making efforts to understand ethnic and cultural experiences of students (Newman 1990). To fully realize our vision, we must look for opportunities to work with diverse groups and individuals. We want to reach out to the various and diverse cultural groups, such as the Somali and the Dakota among others, within our community. We know that our educational materials will be strengthened by incorporating different perspectives. We serve diverse students who will benefit from seeing diverse volunteers in their classrooms with whom they can connect on various levels.

We are interested in expanding our source of volunteers to other departments within the University of Minnesota and expanding our efforts to include other local colleges and universities. We hope to collaborate with the University of Minnesota and the Minnesota Historical Society's Heritage Studies and Public History Program to provide internship opportunities for their Master's students (P. Messenger, Chapter 5). Continuing to work with those who focus on cultural heritage will ensure that as we grow and diversify, that we will reify our grounding in the community values that we hold dear. Collaborations with education programs will also be beneficial. Individuals who have committed to training in education will strengthen the pedagogical value of our modules and we hope that our program will offer them the opportunity to hone their teaching skills and gain exposure to various local schools.

Conclusion

SASSA's mission is to bring community experts and volunteers together to educate and inspire K–12 students with an interdisciplinary, hands-on approach to learning to foster curiosity, confidence, and a connected community of engaged individuals. Individuals that are engaged in their community care about its history and its heritage. We accomplish our mission by: connecting and collaborating with our local community; engaging students with volunteer and graduate student role models; preparing relevant, innovative, and creative interdisciplinary modules from state standards using investigative, exploratory, and hands-on strategies; using a flexible and individualized approach to accommodate the needs of students and schools; and, seeking the viewpoints and influence of diverse individuals, groups, and perspectives. We are a new program and as such we are learning and growing. We look forward to continuing our partnerships and seeing the vision unfold—a vision that nurtures a future that values archaeology and heritage stewardship.

Acknowledgments

Thank you to the Anthropological, Environmental, and Geological Interdisciplinary Sciences (AEGIS) group, who funded our first year and part of our second year, and the University of Minnesota Anthropology Department, the Office for Public Engagement, and District 279 Innovation Grant who funded our second year. Dr. Gil Tostevin offered guidance for the Lithics Module and allowed us to use his 3D magnetic puzzles. Dr. Ellery Frahm provided the idea for flintknapping rock candy. The Anthropology Labs and the Bell Museum loaned materials for the modules. Matt Edling helped facilitate the loans from the Anthropology labs. Carrie Miller, Evan Whiting, Emily Briggs, Annie Melton, Katharine Baldwin, and Caithryn Garcia designed and created modules that were presented in the classrooms. Several more graduate students, undergraduate students, and parents volunteered in the classrooms. We have a feeling of incredible gratitude to all who have contributed time, effort, expertise, and creativity to **SASSA**. We are also grateful to the teachers, administrators and students at Maple Grove Middle School and Gordon Parks High School, who have embraced the program and who, through continued participation and feedback, are helping build the program's identity. We look forward to many more years to come.

Katrina Yezzi-Woodley, PhD Candidate, Department of Anthropology, University of Minnesota.

Chris Kestly, Social Studies Teacher, Maple Grove Middle School, ISD 279.

Beth Albrecht, Science Teacher, Maple Grove Middle School, ISD 279.

Paul Creager, Curriculum & Media Arts Coordinator, Gordon Parks High School, St. Paul Public Schools.

Joel Abdella, Science Teacher, Gordon Parks High School, St. Paul Public Schools.

Katherine Hayes, Associate Professor of Anthropology and affiliate faculty in American Indian Studies, University of Minnesota.

References

Ashmore, Pamela C. 2005. "Role of physical anthropology in intermediate and secondary education." *American journal of physical anthropology* 128(S41): 154–62.
Blake, Barbara, and Tambra Pope. 2008. "Developmental Psychology: Incorporating Piaget's and Vygotsky's Theories in Classrooms." *Journal of Cross-Disciplinary Perspectives in Education* 1(1): 59–67.
Bybee, Rodger W., Janet C. Powell, James D. Ellis, James R. Giese, Lynn Parisi, and Laurel Singleton. 1991. "Integrating the History and Nature of Science and Technology in Science and Social Studies Curriculum." *Science Education* 75(1): 143–55.
Coleman, Simon, and Bob Simpson. 1999. "Unintended Consequences? Anthropology, Pedagogy, and Personhood." *Anthropology Today* 15: 3–6.
Covington, Martin. 1998. *The will to learn: A guide for motivating young people.* Cambridge: Cambridge University Press.
Del Schalock, H. 1998. "Student progress in learning: Teacher responsibility, accountability, and reality." *Journal of Personnel Evaluation in Education* 12(3): 237–46.
Gerber, Brian L., Anne M. Cavallo, and Edmund A. Marek. 2001. "Relationships among informal learning environments, teaching procedures and scientific reasoning ability." *International Journal of Science Education* 23(5): 535–549.
Hamilton, Laura, Brian Stecher, and Kun Yuan. 2008. "Standards-based reform in the United States: History, research, and future directions." Santa Monica, CA: Rand Education. Commissioned by the Center on Education Policy in Washington, DC.
Iamarino, Danielle L. 2014. "The benefits of standards-based grading: A critical evaluation of modern grading practices." *Current Issues in Education* 17(2): 1–12.
Jose, Sara, Patricia G. Patrick, and Christine Moseley. 2017. "Experiential learning theory: the importance of outdoor classrooms in environmental education." *International Journal of Science Education* Part B: 1–16.
Moore, David T. 2001. "Experiential Learning in Anthropology: Another Perspective." *Anthropology of Work Review* 22: 19–23.
National Science Board. 1983. *Educating American for the 21st century.* Washington, DC: US Government Printing Office.
Newman, Stanley M. 1990. "Teaching Anthropology to 'Nonelite' Students: A Beginning Discussion." *Anthropology & Education Quarterly* 21(2): 141–45.
Pedelty, Mark 2001. "Teaching Anthropology through Performance." *Anthropology and Education Quarterly* 32: 244–53.
Piaget, J. 1970. "Piaget's theory." In *Manual of Child Psychology*, vol.1, 3rd ed, edited by P. H. Mussen. London: John Wiley.
Pugh, Kevin, and Mark Girod. 2007. "Science, Art, and Experience: Constructing a Science Pedagogy from Dewey's Aesthetics." *Journal of Science Teacher Education* 18(1): 9–27. doi:10.1007/s10972-006-9029-0.

Relan, Anju, and Richard Kimpston. 1991. "Curriculum Integration: A Critical Analysis of Practical and Conceptual Issues." Paper presented at the Annual Meeting of the American Educational Research Association, Chicago, IL, 3–7 April 1991.

Shah, Allie. 2017. "Go inside 'Little Mogadishu,' the Somali capital of America: The Cedar-Riverside area has long been a magnet for new arrivals; Today, it's mainly East Africans breathing new life into it." *Star Tribune.* 2 March. Accessed 12 September 2017. http://www.startribune.com/inside-little-mogadishu-no-one-is-an-outcast/414876214/

Soluri, Kathaeryne E. 2010. "Engaging bioanthropology college students: The role of active and cooperative pedagogies." PhD diss., University of California, Berkeley.

Vars, Gordon F. 1991. "Integrated curriculum in historical perspective." *Abstracts International* 20: 1830–31.

Walker, Mark, and Dean J. Saitta. 2002. "Teaching the Craft of Archaeology: Theory, Practice, and the Field School." *International Journal of Historical Archaeology* 6: 199–207.

Wehmeyer, Mark, Sharon Field, Bonnie Doren, Bonnie Jones, and Christine Mason. 2004. "Self-Determination and Student Involvement in Standards-Based Reform." *Council for Exceptional Children* 70(4): 413–25.

Wenger, Etienne. 2000. "Communities of practice and social learning systems." *Organization* 7(2): 225–46.

CHAPTER 3

Strengthening a Place-Based Curriculum through the Integration of Archaeology and Environmental Education

Elizabeth C. Reetz, Chérie Haury-Artz, and Jay A. Gorsh

Environmental education (EE) is a well-established educational field that teaches children and adults how to learn about and investigate their environment and to make intelligent, informed decisions about how they can take care of it (North American Association for Environmental Education [NAAEE] 2017). Archaeology education has strong parallels and intersections with the field of EE, especially regarding common goals and objectives to create an informed citizenry that acts in positive ways to care for our natural and cultural resources. However, it is widely acknowledged that cultural history is one of the weaker components of EE, and many archaeology educators are likewise unfamiliar with EE.

Understanding the fundamentals of EE, including the history of the field and a selection of pedagogical approaches, can help archaeologists to recognize connections with using archaeology education to inspire heritage stewardship and provide a theoretical grounding for future archaeological projects and collaborations of all kinds. Archaeologists can strengthen and expand their outreach efforts by integrating with EE programs and initiatives that align the goals and objectives of the two fields. In this chapter, we present a case study that details the pilot year of a place-based archaeology curriculum as part of a larger, well-established EE program called School of the Wild (SoW). The pilot year yielded promising results for using EE as a tool to promote archaeological and environmental stewardship, and also provided insights into how integrating archaeology and cultural history content can enhance a traditionally natural resources–based EE program.

Following this case study, we then take a deeper look at decades' worth of EE research on attitudes toward conservation and pro-environmental behavior and generalize that research against the results of the SoW partnership. A common thread to this research involves the importance of significant life experiences (SLEs) during childhood and their impact on pro-environmental behaviors and attitudes in adulthood. Similar research is lacking in archaeology education, but we can take a critical look at EE research and its potential applications to guide future research and program development in archaeology and historic preservation.

What Is Environmental Education?

EE is closely related to outdoor education, adventure education, experiential education, and interpretation, yet it is a separate field of study. The modern EE movement began in the late 1960s, although it has deep roots in the nature study movement of the late nineteenth to early twentieth century and the conservation education movement inspired by the Great Depression and Dust Bowl. The rise of environmentalism in response to rampant pollution, waste, and pesticides, among other environmental problems in the 1960s and 70s, fueled the beginnings of the modern EE movement. Another influence was a concern that the shift of US communities from predominantly rural to urban would negatively affect the amount of time citizens intimately associated and interacted with the basic natural resources in their immediate environment, while at the same time citizens were increasingly being asked to make decisions that both directly and indirectly affected their environment (Stapp 1969). An early definition of EE, as defined by a committee led by William B. Stapp from the Department of Resource Planning and Conservation, School of Natural Resources at the University of Michigan states that, "EE is aimed at producing a citizenry that is knowledgeable concerning the biophysical environment and its associated problems, aware of how to help solve these problems, and motivated to work toward their solution" (Stapp 1969, 34).

In 1975, representatives from the United Nations met in the former Yugoslavia to draft a document that further defined EE and established its basic objectives. This became known as the Belgrade Charter.

Two years later, the world's first intergovernmental conference on EE in Tbilisi (in the former Soviet Republic of Georgia) built on the Belgrade Charter and released an official statement on EE known as the Tbilisi Declaration (UNESCO 1978). Part of this declaration outlined five objectives of EE (Table 3.1). As the field evolved, these goals have been tested and refined by individuals and organizations working in the field to create a strong foundation for an internationally shared view of the core concepts and skills that environmentally literate citizens need.

As more people became aware of modern environmental concerns and the benefits of EE, the discipline established a small foothold in the educational policies of most US states. EE in schools is supported by the No Child Left Inside Act of 2013, which amended the Elementary and Secondary Education Act of 1965 to increase environmental literacy among elementary and secondary students by encouraging and providing assistance to states for the development and implementation of environmental literacy plans and promoting professional development for teachers on how to integrate environmental literacy and field experiences into their instruction (No Child Left Inside Coalition 2015). The most recent development in institutionalizing EE occurred during the Obama administration, where the Every Student Succeeds Act recognized environmental literacy programs as a part of a child's well-rounded education and created federal grant opportunities for EE programs and schools (Espinoza 2016).

EE has a strong focus on inquiry-based and experiential learning. Experiential education, in the most basic sense, is defined as learn-

Table 3.1. The categories of environmental education objectives, as outlined in the Tbilisi Declaration. Source: UNESCO 1978; author-generated table.

Foundational Objectives of Environmental Education
AWARENESS – to acquire an awareness and sensitivity to the total environment and its allied problems;
KNOWLEDGE – to gain a variety of experiences in and acquire a basic understanding of, the environment and its associated problems;
ATTITUDES – to acquire a set of values and feelings of concern for the environment and motivation for actively participating in environmental improvement and protection;
SKILLS – to acquire the skills for identifying and solving environmental problems; and
PARTICIPATION – to encourage citizens to be actively involved at all levels in working toward resolution of environmental problems.

ing by doing (Adkins and Simmons 2002). Pedagogical research indicates that these learning strategies improve students' understanding and retention of information (California State University 2017). When students pose questions and undertake their own investigations, they think more deeply about the problem. Gathering information through their own efforts gives them ownership of the knowledge and demonstrates to them that they can take on large problems and solve them. Active, experiential learning that involves the whole human sensory system (sight, hearing, touch, taste, and smell) is a more appealing way to acquire knowledge compared to passive listening in a classroom or lecture setting. The experiential learning model, as defined by Kolb (1984), outlines learning as a process whereby knowledge is created through the transformation of experience.

Place-Based Education

Place-based education is a cornerstone of EE, community-based learning, and service learning. Place-based teaching and learning are by design situated in places, which are spatial or physical localities that are given meaning by human experience in them or relating to them (Semken 2012). It is cross-disciplinary and intercultural, and it seeks to connect learning to the unique history, culture, environment, and economy of a particular place (Greenwood 2010). Place-based curriculum and instruction is primarily intended to motivate students through humanistic and scientific engagement with surroundings and to promote sustainability of local environments and communities (Gruenewald and Smith 2008), and secondarily intended to meet specific disciplinary standards or achievement tests (Ault 2008; Smith and Sobel 2010). It is not simply a way to integrate the curriculum around the study of a place, but a means of inspiring stewardship and an authentic renewal and revitalization of civic life (Sobel 2004).

Place-based education often involves a strong field-based component and/or service-learning component where the learner is immersed in place with active, hands-on learning. Benefits of such instruction are that it fosters comprehension and retention of course content and an increased motivation to learn; it promotes self-confidence, critical thinking, self-motivation, and socialization skills; and it improves environmental stewardship (Sheppard, Donaldson, and Huckleberry 2010; Sobel 2004; van der Hoeven Kraft et al. 2011). It also fosters a sense of place, which is the set of all meanings and attachments affixed to a place by an individual or group that encapsulate cognitive and affective connections between people and places (Gruenewald 2003; Sobel 2004).

Place-based education links well with using cultural landscapes as learning tools. Studies with a stronger focus on history, heritage, and multidisciplinary studies conclude that linking history with place-based education is not simply an interesting way to introduce teachers and students to the central themes of American history, but it inspires them to engage as social and political actors in their own communities (Gruenewald, Koppelman, and Elam 2007; MacDowell and Kozma 2007). As students are immersed in local places rather than familiarizing themselves with exotic far-away landscapes through books, they become part of an informed citizenry that is developing their knowledge and awareness of their environment and the processes by which it is shaped.

Archaeology as a Form of Environmental Education

Efforts at archaeology education began with regional programs as early as the 1950s. After the passage of the Archaeological Resources Protection Act (ARPA) in 1988, which required federal action to protect archaeological resources, efforts expanded to a national level (Ellick 2016; King 2016). Archaeology education takes place in many forms in both formal and informal settings. It has found its way into the classroom via archaeology-based books, teacher manuals, resource guides, electronic media, and classroom activities for precollegiate audiences. The quality of the programs often varies widely depending on training of the educators in both archaeology and pedagogy, funding, and institutional support.

Several organizations and universities have developed standards-based print and online archaeology curricula and resources for classroom teachers including Project Archaeology (2017), the Florida Public Archaeology Network (2017), and the Haffenreffer Museum of Anthropology (Hoffman, Boyd, and Urbanus 2010). Additional resources have been compiled by the Society for American Archaeology (SAA), the Archaeological Institute of America (AIA), and numerous other state and federal agencies, museums, and universities with the expressed interest in fostering stewardship of archaeological and historical resources.

These groups recognize that the first line of defense in the preservation of cultural resources exists in the minds and comprehension of the next generation of decision-makers (Smith 1998, 112). Teachers embrace these resources because archaeological topics are multidisciplinary, interactive, and cooperative. As Smith summarizes, archaeology is a humanistic pursuit, yet it uses rigorous scientific methods and theories, and draws on: history, geography, natural and physical sciences, art, mathematics, and engineering, to name a few—to assemble a complete picture of the past (1998, 113). Archaeology also emphasizes social and critical thinking skills and offers an interesting alternative to text book learning. However, while these classroom resources have all of the aforementioned benefits, the curricula largely focus on indoor or simulated activities rather than authentic outdoor experiences.

In the field of EE, archaeology can be an educational tool used to inspire children to spend more time in the outdoors, participate in experiential outdoor activities, and interpret their own archaeological heritage. Studying human activity from the past through the recovery and analysis of material culture involves looking at both cultural and physical landscapes in and through the environment. To practice archaeology is to study human adaptation to the natural world by using the environment as a vehicle for the development of knowledge. In short, we can learn the story of the land through archaeology. Although archaeologists may not have realized it before, this is actually a form of EE.

Because archaeology is a field-based profession, it has the potential to serve as an educational avenue toward experiential learning opportunities, which are so critical in EE. These benefits are summarized, as explored by multiple researchers:

> Hands-on, active learning, which typifies field-based education (Orion 1989; Tucth and Wikle 2000), fosters comprehension and retention of course content (McKenzie, Utgard, and Lisowski 1986). Additionally, other benefits accrue from field-based instruction, including self-confidence (McConnell 1979), critical thinking (McNamara and Fowler 1975), self-motivation (Giardino and Fish 1986), and socialization skills (Falk, Martin, and Balling 1978), all of which are desired outcomes of education generally. (as cited in Sheppard et al. 2010, 296)

Archaeology that focuses on cultural landscapes as tools for learning can immerse a learner in place, and field-based activities that focus on a learner's local community can foster a sense of place.

School of the Wild: A Case Study

In 2016, staff from the University of Iowa Office of the State Archaeologist (OSA) and University of Iowa Recreational Services Outdoors Program (Outdoors Program) integrated archaeology and EE into a place-based, outdoor curricular unit to complement other natural resources-focused units in a week-long EE program called School of the Wild (SoW). The authors of this chapter participated in the project as program developers and directors, curriculum developers, teacher orientation leaders, instructors, and evaluators. In addition to evaluating the results of exploratory research on the pilot program in this case study, the authors reflect and provide observations regarding this educational approach from their perspectives as archaeologists and as a science educator with no prior experience in archaeology or archaeology education.

The OSA, which formally organized in 1959, has been a leader in archaeological education in Iowa since the office's foundation. Education initiatives occurred with in-kind staff efforts and project-based funding until 1999 when internal University of Iowa funds supported a part-time position for a Public Archaeology Coordinator. In 2002, OSA professionalized this position as a Director of Education and Outreach, with sixty percent funding from the University and forty percent supplemented from grants and contract support. The Director of Education and Outreach became a full-time, University-supported position in 2013 due to an integration with cross-campus partnerships, but University support for OSA education and outreach program activities was eliminated in 2016. Nonetheless OSA continues to make educating the public a priority, utilizing collaborative efforts with the Iowa Archeological Society, the Association of Iowa Archaeologists, grants, and donor-funding as available. Additional staff assist with education initiatives as grants and contracts allow. Since establishing a full-time position, the Director and OSA colleagues have conducted a wide variety of community engagement and archaeology education programming in over eighty percent of Iowa counties and beyond, reaching more than seventy thousand people, including over seven thousand K–12 school children.

EE programs at the University of Iowa are managed by the Outdoors Program and include SoW, Wildlife Camps, and Iowa Raptor Project. These programs take place in the Macbride Nature Recreation Area (MNRA), a 485-acre peninsula that the US Army Corps of Engineers leases to the University of Iowa, under the management of the University of Iowa Recreational Services. MNRA is situated north of the communities that make up the Iowa City Community School District, and ranges from four to twenty miles from the schools that participated in SoW.

In the spring of 1999, the Outdoors Program launched Wild 2000, a week-long nature experience that served as a school-year expansion of the Wildlife Camps program that started in 1991. Six schools participated in the pilot year, which led to the development of SoW. In 2000, SoW became the first North Central Association (NCA) accredited special purpose school, and the first accredited environmental school in Iowa. Prior to the 2016–17 school year, Iowa City Community School District (ICCSD) classes, typically in grades 3–5, attended SoW when funding and opportunity allowed. In 2016, ICCSD, with assistance from community businesses, grants, private donations, and the ICCSD Foundation, began to fully cover the cost of this program for all ICCSD sixth grade students. Each year over 1100 students from up to twenty-two elementary schools participate in SoW. As the success of the program continues to grow, so does the expanse of its programming.

The partnership between archaeology educators and environmental educators at the University of Iowa developed organically based on shared goals and interests. The director of education activities at the OSA has a graduate-level background in EE and approached Outdoors Program staff regarding potential partnerships. Regular campus gatherings among faculty and staff in STEM fields provided an opportunity for the partners to continue to get to know one another and become familiar with each other's interests, skills, and departmental activities. The partners had a strong mutual interest in integrating EE and cultural history, in part due to their shared acknowledgement that cultural history and the humanities are lacking or poorly represented in EE.

In spring 2016, SoW staff wanted to restructure their program to integrate a stronger cultural history unit into the week and eliminate a weaker activity-based unit they loosely identified as Survival Skills. In particular, they wanted to better align with recently developed state and national standards and benchmarks for learning. They also wanted to better utilize elements of MNRA well-suited to study cultural history, including the ruins of a large historical farmstead and the Iowa River, which is culturally significant to Iowa's Meskwaki Nation. They partnered with OSA archaeology education staff to pursue a grant from the Iowa Department of Natural Resources (Iowa DNR) Resource Enhancement and Protection Conservation Education Program (REAP–CEP). REAP–CEP awarded a grant to OSA in May, and we drafted a curriculum over the summer, in preparation for the 2016–17 school year. This unit was called People and the Land, and it was implemented in fall 2016.

Because the education area was already steeped in cultural history and evidence of human impact, adding an archaeology unit was a natural fit. The nature area provided an ideal setting to explore archaeological concepts using noninvasive techniques. This was especially important to the archaeologists who often work to dispel the public misconception that archaeology equates to excavation. People and the Land was designed to emphasize human impact on the environment through three activities: building simple, expedient shelters; exploring a Meskwaki wickiup; and investigating the ruins of a historical turn-of-the-century farmstead. These activities totaled approximately five hours of instruction time. The expedient shelter building reframed a favorite activity from the Survival Skills unit as a necessary part of the life of small bands of people moving across the landscape, leaving a small footprint in an ongoing search for seasonal resources. Developing activities centered on the Meskwaki wickiup involved consultation and collaboration with staff from the Meskwaki Tribal Museum. Archaeologists conducted background research on the historic ruins and documented it as an archaeological site.

To understand how People and the Land was integrated, we provide a brief overview of the structure of SoW. Area elementary schools are assigned a week, typically five consecutive days of programming, to attend SoW. SoW provides transportation and staff are licensed to bus the students to and from their elementary schools. Students arrive by 9 a.m. and depart by 2 p.m. Each day of programming is based around a particular curricular theme; historically the units were: Woodlands, Wetlands, Ornithology, Prairies, and Survival Skills. At the beginning of the program, students are divided into five groups, and groups rotate to a new unit each day. SoW employs three full-time instructors who teach three of the units, and teachers from the elementary school attending for the week are trained to provide instruction for the other two units. Each day begins with an introduction before students are sent off with their instructor to explore for the day. A short debrief is conducted at the end of each day to highlight experiences from the day of exploring.

People and the Land was assigned to visiting elementary school teachers. Since fall 2016 marked the first year of SoW as a required program for all ISCCD sixth graders, not only was this unit new, but teaching at MNRA in an outdoor setting was new to many teachers. SoW and OSA staff held an in-service training workshop prior to the school year to introduce the new curriculum with the ICCSD teachers responsible for teaching the lessons to their students (Figure 3.1). The training was about two hours long compared to the five hours of instructional time it takes to teach the curriculum, so the archaeology educators only modeled portions of the lessons. Fourteen out of the twenty-two teachers who would be teaching the unit attended the workshop. Although some of the teachers had participated in the SoW

Figure 3.1. Teacher orientation. Archaeologist Chérie Haury-Artz works with sixth-grade teachers at the historic archaeological site. Photo courtesy of the University of Iowa Office of the State Archaeologist.

program in the past, the People and the Land curriculum was new to everyone, including the SoW staff. Along with modeling the lessons, it was necessary to familiarize teachers and staff with some basic tenets of archaeological investigation such as leaving artifacts in place so that the integrity of the site context is not disturbed.

The People and the Land Experience

During the unit, students are guided on a journey back through time to explore three different types of shelters. Students learn that all people need shelter and that people use elements from their environment to create different kinds of shelters. The curriculum emphasizes that archaeology is not about finding cool or beautiful artifacts, but that archaeologists want to know what those artifacts can tell us about the lives of the people who made and used them. As an introduction, students learn how an archaeologist uses material evidence such as artifacts, buildings, foundations, animal bones, and plants to learn how people lived in the past. The archaeologists analyze this evidence and give it meaning. The students are told that they are about to embark on a journey in which they will investigate how people may have lived on this land during different times in the past.

People and the Land starts with a journey into a wooded section of MNRA that was once a fully functioning farm (Figure 3.2). Historical records indicate that this site was originally homesteaded in 1824. The property changed hands numerous times during the nineteenth century as the local farm economy developed and changed. The 1900 county atlas shows that it was owned by S. M. and W. L. Mahaffie, which is probably an alternative spelling of Mehaffey, a name familiar to all in the area as it is used for the nearby road and the bridge across the reservoir that is visible from the site. The students learn that all the land surrounding them was once a part of this farm. Many are surprised when they are reminded that the lake adjacent to the site, which is an artificial reservoir, did not exist at that time. Aerial photographs taken at intervals throughout the twentieth century clearly show dramatic changes in land-use and vegetation. As the farm economy changes, structures come and go, gardens and orchards disappear, and fields become larger as the woodlands shrink. The farm ceased to function after it was purchased, prior to the creation of the dam and reservoir on the Iowa River. Students are told that the buildings were destroyed, but that the foundations ("ruins") and scattered artifacts remain. The students are asked to work in small groups as they engage in a process of scientific inquiry in which they are challenged to explore each of the foundations to gather clues to try to determine the functions of

Figure 3.2. Historical archaeological site 13JH1479 and adjacent Iowa River. Photo courtesy of the University of Iowa Office of the State Archaeologist.

the buildings that once stood there. This method aligns with science standards that recommend students engage in a scientific process of developing questions, formulating theories, and gathering evidence to support those theories. The activity concludes with a discussion of their claims and the evidence they gathered to support their reasoning.

During the second activity of the day, students are taken further back in time to the days just prior to and concurrent with European settlement. Students learn that the area would have been the winter home of the Meskwaki tribe. In their oral history, the Meskwaki originally came from eastern North America, near present-day Quebec. Over many centuries they gradually moved westward and arrived in the early 1600s in what is now Wisconsin. The Meskwaki left Wisconsin in the 1730s and moved to the Iowa–Illinois region. Throughout their history, the Meskwaki lived in areas covered by hardwood forests and drained by many rivers and streams. Students are led down a trail to a wickiup frame, which students constructed during the first week of SoW in 2016 with guests Johnathan Buffalo and Suzanne Wanatee Buffalo of the Meskwaki Nation near Tama, Iowa (Figure 3.3). Students learn how wickiups were traditionally constructed and discuss

Figure 3.3. Chérie Haury-Artz works with Johnathan Buffalo and Suzanne Wanatee Buffalo to build the wickiup frame in the fall of 2016. Photo courtesy of the University of Iowa Office of the State Archaeologist.

why the site would have been an appealing location for the tribe to build their winter homes. Students are then challenged with the task of covering the wickiup frame with canvas to provide protection from the elements. Students learn how, and why, the methods for constructing a wickiup have changed over time (Figure 3.4). Students also learn the cultural significance of the wickiup and how they are used today, using an oral history from Johnathan Buffalo included in the Project Archaeology curriculum, "Investigating a Midwestern Wickiup." To conclude this portion of the day, students are taught ancient methods for fire building and discuss a selection of material culture items that are associated with wickiups such as a scapula hoe, gourd bowl, and gourd spoon (Figure 3.5).

The final portion of the day takes students back to the time of ancient hunter-gatherer societies. Students are challenged to build their own shelter using materials in the environment, and to construct a temporary shelter that is as effective as possible for providing protection from the elements (Figure 3.6). It is stressed that although these

Figure 3.4. Elizabeth Reetz and students listen as Suzanne Wanatee Buffalo and Johnathan Buffalo explain Meskwaki traditions associated with wickiups. Photo courtesy of the University of Iowa Office of the State Archaeologist.

Figure 3.5. Students stand around the hearth in the completed wickiup frame. Photo courtesy of the University of Iowa Office of the State Archaeologist.

Figure 3.6. Expedient, temporary shelters built by School of the Wild students. Photo courtesy of the University of Iowa Office of the State Archaeologist.

shelters are simple and temporary, ancient hunters and gatherers in Iowa were innovative and had an intimate knowledge of the land and its resources. Ancient cultures all over the world were adapting to their specific environments and the particular needs of their community, whether they were hunter-gatherers, pastoralists, or farmers, and these environmental and cultural adaptations influenced how they built their shelters.

Evaluation

The REAP–CEP grant that funded the development of the People and the Land curricula required the archaeologists to assess the efficacy of their project. The proposed evaluation at the time of the grant application was to modify an existing SoW questionnaire by adding quantitative questions related to the archaeology unit and survey all students at the commencement and completion of their SoW experience. Further into the project, we realized that although there was a SoW questionnaire, the content was outdated and it had not been used for several years. We proceeded with administering a questionnaire of eight questions that related to archaeology and attitudes toward nature. This questionnaire did not evaluate the other four SoW content units.

The results from this evaluation are best described as exploratory research. We did not create a study design or statistical design for this evaluation, as data was collected for internal program improvement. Prior to this evaluation, no previous structured or in-depth evaluation of SoW programming had been performed. Therefore, we had to determine, through trial and error during the pilot program, what type of evaluation could be administered and how it could best be done. The results of this pilot helped us to gain an understanding of the advantages and disadvantages of our chosen survey instrument, research questions, and data collection methods. What we learned will help us to lay the groundwork for future assessment, with more rigor and control to provide validity and reliability. Because this is exploratory research, our results are not generalizable.

Data Collection

The classroom teachers indicated it was not possible for the archaeologists to visit each classroom to administer pre- and post-tests due to pressure to maximize instruction time, so SoW staff administered the questionnaires on a day-by-day basis as time allowed. The administration of this questionnaire was not a prioritized component of the commencement and completion of each school's SoW experience. Instead, students were surveyed, as time allowed before and/or after instruction on the actual day of their People and the Land experience. This impacted the evaluation in several ways. First, the survey sample was relatively small and amounted to approximately fifteen percent of the total number of students who participated in SoW, with 166 students taking the pre-test and 168 taking the post-test. These students came from classes in eight out of twenty-two schools that attended, but we could only compare pre- and post-test results confidently from seven of the schools. Second, because it was not possible to survey every school, it was not possible to measure whether each teacher was meeting or missing the main goals and objectives outlined in the curricula. Lastly, students could not be surveyed in the classroom before and after their SoW experience as proposed, but instead were tested the day of their People and the Land experience. Given the brevity of this program, this could result in what is called a "test effect," where students may have remembered their answers from the morning (Ernst, Monroe, and Simmons 2009). Finally, pre- and post-tests were not consistently administered. At times, a late start or rushed afternoon impacted the staff's ability to administer both the pre-test and post-test to the same group. Therefore, we cannot quantify measures of individual changes in knowledge and attitude, nor can we measure the change among particular groups pre- and post-instruction. Several factors influenced this inconsistency, which is typical among this type of data collection in an outdoor setting, such as late or early buses, time management, and unexpected teachable moments with a greater priority.

Results were organized by school, with no information collected on student identity or classroom group. Because each school was divided into five groups throughout the week, and only a random sample of groups were surveyed, it is not possible to identify the student tested. In short, the data analysis presents a general overview of the attitudes and knowledge of students from each school tested in the span of one day during the 2016–17 SoW sessions.

The Survey Instrument

The questionnaire designed for the students totaled eight questions, including three questions on a Likert scale, two true or false questions, two multiple-choice questions, and one open-answer question (see chapter appendix). These were modeled after questions on the original, outdated SoW survey, with the intent that they could be incorporated into that questionnaire when updated. Because one of the objectives of REAP–CEP funded projects is to foster healthy attitudes about the environment, we included three questions from the original

SoW questionnaire that assessed environmental attitudes on a five-point scale (1 = strongly disagree and 5 = strongly agree). The new true/false and multiple-choice questions assessed knowledge or awareness of archaeology and Native Americans in Iowa. The final question was an open-ended qualitative question that asked students to list at least three environmental factors that influence how people create shelter.

Results of the Questionnaire

Three questions addressed students' attitudes toward nature or learning outside. As Cheng and Monroe (2010) noted in their research on children's affective attitude toward nature, attitudes change slowly, therefore it was not reasonable to expect significant differences between the pre- and post-test measures of attitudes toward learning outside. Because of the difficulties with assessing changes in attitude, combined with the problematic data collection, we will not discuss an in-depth analysis of the Likert scale questions in this chapter, but our data is available upon request. This data overall hints toward a slight improvement in attitudes toward conservation behavior, and we now have a baseline assessment for future studies. On both the pre- and post-tests, about 90 percent of students either strongly agreed or agreed with the statement in the first question, and more than 75 percent disagreed or strongly disagreed with the second statement. The results of the third statement showed an improvement from 66 percent of students who either agreed or strongly agreed on the pre-test to 72 percent on the post-test. These results indicate that the students already overwhelmingly enjoyed exploring and learning outside in nature, and future surveys conducted with more structure and rigor should focus on more nuanced attitude and behavior questions.

Four questions measured students' knowledge about Native Americans, human interaction with the environment, and archaeology. We totaled the frequencies of each response, and present the percentage of students who chose each response (Table 3.2). We did not tabulate a breakdown of data from the seven schools we could confidently compare but can provide this data upon request.

We included a true/false question on the statement, "Native Americans only lived in the past" because of our own anecdotal experiences as archaeology educators. It is an all too frequent misconception with adults who visit us at events and make remarks that indicate they do not realize that Native Americans have living communities and thriving cultures that blend past traditions with contemporary adaptations. On occasions, adults have exclaimed surprise when they learned Iowa has its own resident tribal community, and many are unaware that

Table 3.2. Students' responses to People and the Land questions, showing the percentage of students who chose each response and the percentage of increase or decrease between the pre- and post-tests. Courtesy of the authors.

Question	Response	Pre-test Response (% of students)	Post-test Response (% of students)	% Increase (+) or Decrease (-)
Native Americans only lived in the past	True	8.4	9.5	+13.1
	False	91.6	90.5	–1.2
People change their environment when they build shelters	True	78.3	79.8	+1.8
	False	21.7	20.2	–6.9
An archaeologist is a scientist who studies _____ from the past	a) fossils and dinosaurs	33.7	16.7	–50.5
	b) climates	1.8	0.6	–66.7
	c) people and the objects they leave behind	59.0	81.0	+37.1
	d) water and wetlands	4.8	1.2	–75.0
Which Native American tribe lives in Iowa today?	a) Cherokee	25.9	4.8	–81.5
	b) Navajo	15.1	7.1	–53.0
	c) Meskwaki	28.3	85.1	+200.6
	d) Sioux/Dakota	27.7	3.0	–89.2

Iowa was named after a living Native American tribe. Additionally, popular representations of Native Americans often create an image of them as living in the past, and people are fixated on these representations. Similar occurrences happen in other states, where people are not aware that federal- and state-recognized tribes exist (Istre 2017). The results of the responses indicate that over ninety percent of students answered this question correctly on both the pre-test and post-test. The same number of students answered correctly each time; however, more students took the post-test and answered incorrectly, resulting in a technical decrease in knowledge. Overall, these results indicate that students already have a good grasp of this concept, and we can potentially choose another research question to focus on in the future. However, when looking at a breakdown of results from seven of the schools, four of the schools had a negative decrease in correct responses, ranging from 0.5 to 9.2 percent. One school had no change and two schools had an increase in correct responses of 4.0 and 22.2 percent. Perhaps the teachers are not properly emphasizing contemporary Meskwaki culture, or they are not reading Johnathan Buffalo's ethnographic piece. Alternatively, the students may be fixated on the elements from the past and remember those more strongly. We need to investigate why more than half of the schools had a decrease in correct responses.

The second true/false knowledge question asked, "People change their environment when they build shelters." We asked this question to get at the link between humans and the environment. The frequency of correct responses was very similar on both the pre-test (78.3 percent) and post-test (79.8 percent), with more than three-quarters of the students already knowledgeable about this concept. We would like to see a stronger gain with the students who did not know this to be true. However, now that we know the students, at a baseline, know this to be true, we could rephrase this as a more detailed question that assesses what they know or do not know about the extent of human impact on the environment.

The first multiple-choice knowledge question asked was, "An archaeologist is a scientist who studies [fill in the blank] from the past." On the pre-test, 59.0 percent of students answered correctly, while 33.7 percent answered, "dinosaurs and fossils." On the post-test, 81.0 percent of students answered correctly, which shows a 37.1 percent overall increase in the frequency of correct answers. The response rate of "dinosaurs and fossils" decreased by 50 percent. Initially, the archaeologists had doubts regarding how strongly archaeological concepts would be communicated by teachers without discussing the typical excavations or artifacts that people usually associate with archaeology. Although more than half of the students who were tested could already successfully answer this question, a 37.1 percent increase in knowledge is notable. These responses help us to know that overall, many of the teachers were successfully communicating an essential understanding of what archaeology is without relying on the typical field methods and objects traditionally associated with archaeology. When we look at a breakdown of data for each school, we do see that the degree to which teachers successfully communicated this essential understanding varied greatly. Two schools only had a gain of one additional correct response, with less than two-thirds of students knowing the correct definition of archaeology, and another school had less than half of the students answering correctly on the post-test. Other schools had less than 25 percent of students answering correctly on the pre-test and increasing to over 90 percent on the post-test. Clearly some teachers are not focusing on archaeology as we intended, while others are excelling at it.

The next multiple-choice question asked was, "Which Native American tribe lives in Iowa today?" Our partnerships with tribal communities across the Midwest are incredibly important to the OSA, and consultation with these communities is an integral part of our education and outreach. Part of our intent with the People and the Land unit was to raise awareness about both past and present tribal communities in eastern Iowa, because we often find with guest teaching in classrooms that many students are not familiar with the Meskwaki Tribe (federally known as the Sac and Fox of the Mississippi in Iowa) who reside in central Iowa. Students were given choices that reflect (with the exception of "Meskwaki") many of the common responses we get when we ask this same question in elementary classrooms. On the pre-test, only 28.3 percent of students answered correctly with "Meskwaki." However, this was the most frequent response. This question saw the most significant increase in the frequency of correct responses, with 143 out of 168 students (85.1 percent) answering correctly on the post-test. A breakdown of the data by school also shows significant gains in each classroom. One school had zero out of twenty-six correct answers on the pre-test and 80 percent correct answers afterwards, while the smallest increase was seen in a school that answered 89 percent correctly on the pre-test and 100 percent correctly on the post-test.

The final question was qualitative and asked, "List at least three environmental factors that affect how people build shelter." Our objective behind this question was to find out if students made connections between identifiable elements in the physical environment (e.g., topography such as high ground versus low-lying marshes, the proximity of the Iowa River and its potential resources, the Midwest climate) that influenced the construction of the various types of shelter. It was apparent from the responses that the sixth grade students did not understand what an "environmental factor" was, and their answers primarily included types of natural building materials such as, "wood," "leaves," or "rock." Some responses hinted at environmental factors such as topography, climate, or resources like, "surroundings," "weather," and "animals," but we cannot confirm this is what they meant without further investigation. Many answers were clearly copied from one student to the next, affirming our suspicion that the students did not understand what we were asking for. In the end, we did not conduct a qualitative analysis of this question. Instead, we need to reassess whether or not we will use this question in the future. If so, we must determine how we might rephrase this question in a way the students can understand. In reflection, this is a higher order question that we did not execute correctly. In their own worlds, this is a very adult concept, with their parents or guardians deciding where they live or camp and why. Therefore, we need to brainstorm a question that both addresses our research question and is analogous to something in the students' own lives.

Additional Observations on People and the Land

In addition to the survey data used to evaluate this program and the literature reviewed as a contextual framework, we offer some naturalistic observations on aspects of the development and implementation of People and the Land as part of this case study. Our intent is that this program inspires others to create comparable programs or similar partnerships among archaeologists and environmental or science educators. We offer these anecdotes and observations as archaeologists and a science educator, and overall as program developers.

Observations from Jay Gorsh, Science and Outdoor Educator

Before this partnership and new curricular unit, I had no prior experience teaching archaeology. In my opinion, the archaeology unit plays a critical role in the SoW experience. During SoW, students explore different habitats to learn about the flora, fauna, and microorganisms that make up that ecosystem. Each of those experiences is grounded in the present as students discover what flora and fauna happen to be around on that particular day. What makes the archaeology unit critical is that it gives the students a link to the past, a historical perspective. During this unit, students gain a better understanding of how the land has been used over time. They learn how the land usage impacts the flora and fauna living in the area and how decisions made by the people living on the land impact the greater ecosystem. They also gain an understanding of how different people have designed and built shelters to allow them to live on the land.

In speaking with the ICSSD teachers, I have learned that this unit is much better aligned with their overall school curriculum, which is particularly important to us as an accredited institution. They can make connections between the archaeology unit and their curriculum that they were not able to make with the Survival Skills unit. In the past, some instructors occasionally explored the ruins with their students, but did not have any background knowledge or context for the ruins. It was just an activity. Likewise, the shelter building, originally part of Survival Skills, was just an activity without context. Other unrelated activities that took place included archery, animal tracking, and fire building. People and the Land took the shelter building activity and connected it to one of our big objectives—people change their environment when they build shelters.

Observations from the Archaeologists

Whenever the topic of archaeology is introduced, there are many common misconceptions that must be addressed along with the new concepts being taught. This was true for both the public school teachers and the SoW educators. SoW educators, working closely with the archaeologists over several weeks, caught on quickly and adapted their program concepts. The very brief training that was provided to the teachers who attended the orientation session was not enough to address misconceptions along with communicating many of the scientific concepts of archaeology, the background of the historic site, and the history of the Meskwaki Nation. It was a great deal of new material. Some were uncertain about using the curriculum and requested assistance from the archaeologists for their first day, and we were happy to provide this assistance. That said, many of those who participated were enthusiastic about using inquiry and exploration to stimulate their students' curiosity about the materials that they were finding. We observed students who seemed quite liberated in the outdoor setting, coming up with many theories and explanations for the materials they were finding as they explored the historic archaeological site. They freely changed their ideas as they found more evidence and included the discoveries and theories of their comrades as they chatted about the area. They did not seem to worry about having a "right" answer the way they often do in a classroom discussion.

These observations are more challenging to document or quantify, but we do know that the People and the Land experience at SoW succeeded in inspiring at least one student to learn more about archaeology and raised awareness among others about Iowa archaeology in general. In particular, one student signed up for a class on Iowa Archaeology at College for Kids, a summer enrichment program for talented and gifted students, following her SoW experience. The Iowa Archaeology class is taught by co-author and archaeologist Chérie Haury-Artz, who also helped develop People and the Land. She notes that many of the students who take her class tell her they were inspired to learn more, even after just a brief exposure to archaeology. Examples that piqued their curiosity and inspired them to learn more about Iowa's cultural heritage at College for Kids also include field trips to a local conservation center where they threw darts with an atlatl, and visits to burial mound sites. Additionally, docents who staffed the University of Iowa Mobile Museum, which included an exhibit on archaeology and the Oneota culture, noted that students who viewed the exhibit expressed recognitions at some of the concepts and items like the reproduction scapula hoe. When asked where they learned about these items, they answered, "School of the Wild!" These are brief and immeasurable connections, but it is fulfilling to witness youth express this awareness and familiarity several months after their SoW experience.

Reflections as Educators

As educators, we acknowledge the challenges in creating any EE curriculum to be a "one size fits all" for every classroom teacher and their diverse instructional styles, level of comfort teaching in an outdoor setting, and classroom management skills. There will always be inconsistencies when multiple different teachers teach any one lesson. We observed that some classroom teachers struggled with the new curriculum and that the fidelity of implementation—the degree to which teachers understood the concepts and followed the prescribed procedures—was highly variable. The breakdowns of data by school shows us this variability, and we observed it first-hand. Some veteran SoW teachers taught the day as they did in previous years, with more of a focus on shelter building and unstructured exploration of the ruins. One teacher chose to ignore the new curriculum and do other activities, like archery, instead. Even with an orientation training and curriculum guide, it was apparent that the content was so new to teachers that it was challenging for them to meet the proposed goals and objectives. Like other new units, it would likely take teachers a few years or rounds of teaching to get comfortable and find their stride with the unit instruction.

Without talking to the teachers in depth, we can only speculate reasons for some of this dissonance. If they do not have a lot of prior experience, their insecurities may step in, and they may adopt an "I don't know how to help them" attitude. Not only is the unit new, but it is a new requirement for many of these teachers to teach unfamiliar concepts in an outdoor setting. As archaeologists who work with teachers, we often hear teachers express perceptions of archaeology as something that does not relate to what they teach. When teachers are unfamiliar with archaeology, we often hear, "That is social studies, I teach science" or "That's science, I teach social studies." It is our job to do better at demonstrating—and understanding how to communicate to teachers—the interdisciplinary nature of our field. Moe observed something similar when initially evaluating the *Project Archaeology: Investigating Shelter* curriculum (2016, 445). She noted that fidelity of implementation among the fifteen classrooms studied was highly variable, with only five of the fifteen teachers completing the entire unit before administering the assessment instrument. The best implementation of the curriculum took place in schools that had the strongest relationship with archaeology educators.

The archaeologists recognized that after working closely with the Outdoors Program staff, those instructors gained a solid understanding of the archaeological concepts being communicated. The SoW instructors not only have a stronger grasp on the archaeological concepts but see clearly the role that the unit plays in the SoW overall experience. They can use this understanding to guide the students to developing a historical perspective. Therefore, we propose to pivot and designate an Outdoors Program staff member to teach the People and the Land unit and have the classroom teachers teach a less abstract unit, such as Prairies.

Significant Life Behavior and Research on Attitudes Leading to Environmental Stewardship

For the past few decades, environmental educators and other researchers have attempted to understand what variables or experiences impact pro-environmental attitudes and behavior. Significant life experiences (SLE) research focuses on connections between childhood and environmentalism or pro-environmental behavior in adulthood, and a wealth of additional research investigates factors that impact children's attitudes toward nature. Heritage preservation professionals lack a body of research that examines variables that inspire pro-stewardship behavior among both adults and children. A deeper look at select research in EE helps to provide additional insight into the efficacy of the People and the Land unit at SoW. Additionally, we connect this research to archaeology education and potential approaches to designing programming that inspires heritage stewardship.

The foundational study on SLE in EE took place in the 1980s. Tanner wanted to know what motivated professional conservationists to dedicate their lives to environmental issues (1980). The results of this landmark study concluded the following as the most frequently mentioned variables that influenced the respondents: interaction with natural, rural, or other relatively pristine habitats; growing up with easy access to rural or natural habitats; and parents who foster, reinforce, or tolerate a child's interest in nature. To a lesser extent, in order of frequency, respondents also mentioned: teachers who foster, reinforce, or tolerate a child's interest in nature; nature-oriented books; other adult mentors; the loss of beloved habitats; and time spent in nature in solitude. Several of these variables have shown up in the results of research over the next three decades that were influenced by Tanner's work. These studies (not an exhaustive list) focused on: connections between childhood and adult environmentalism (Chawla 1999; Wells and Lekies 2006); teachers' attitudes toward the environment and the impact of their teaching (Torkar 2014); children's attitudes, knowledge, and behavior concerning the environment (Cheng and Monroe 2010; Stevenson et al. 2014); and a meta-analysis of literature that explores people's accounts of the sources of their environmental interest, concern, and action (Chawla 1998). We present common recurring variables that influence various aspects of environmental stewardship, which could have potential applications toward inspiring heritage stewardship.

Time Spent in Nature

The single most important influence on individuals that emerged from these studies was many hours spent outdoors in natural habitats like forests, parks, farms, or cabins during childhood or adolescence—alone or with others (Wells and Lekies 2006). Some researchers distinguish between time spent in groups and time spent in solitude (Tanner 1980; Palmer, Corcoran, and Suggate 1993; Chawla 1998). Wells and Lekies differentiated between "wild nature" (e.g., hunting, camping, or hiking) and "domesticated nature" (tending a garden), with participation in wild nature before the age of eleven as a particularly potent pathway toward shaping both environmental attitudes and behaviors in adulthood (2006, 13). Researchers also differentiate at times between the frequency of time spent in nature or access to nearby areas (Chawla 1998), but in short, all forms of spending time in natural areas as children are hugely significant predictors of adult pro-environmental behavior, whether it is becoming an environmental/conservation professional (Tanner 1980), an environmental educator (Chawla 1999), or a teacher who expresses care for the environment in their teaching

(Torkar 2014). Many of these studies were conducted in the 1980s or 90s, and there is some evidence that this is changing. A recent study of middle school students found that there was a statistically significant relationship between spending time outdoors and environmental knowledge and behavior, but this relationship was weak (Stevenson et al. 2014). Although children are still spending time outdoors, organized activities and activities involving electronics are increasing in popularity while there is a shift away from activities such as the nature-based use of national parks (Pergams and Zaradic 2008).

Could time spent at archaeological sites and heritage areas as children be equivalent to time spent in nature with regard to inspiring heritage stewardship? The findings suggest that archaeologists should find more ways to engage the public through experiential activities at sites related to cultural heritage, in addition to the services offered by archaeological parks across the country. In order to apply the significance of these findings in SLE to heritage stewardship, we have to acknowledge some differences between archaeological sites and natural spaces. Natural spaces, including backyards, parks, and nature areas, are typically more accessible than archaeological sites, and spending time in nature is a common way to recreate. The locations of many local archaeological sites are often protected; there are far fewer archaeological parks than nature areas. With SoW, we were fortunate to have an accessible archaeological site already located in an experiential learning area with a strong place-based connection. The presence of this site was one of the driving factors behind the creation of new curriculum. Outdoors Program staff knew they did not have the content knowledge expertise to create a curriculum that incorporated archaeology and cultural history with their knowledge of EE, but the partnership with archaeologists filled this gap. Archaeologists who connect more with EE professionals such as naturalists, interpreters, and teachers in their communities could help them develop programs with stronger connections to archaeology. EE professionals know how to create experiential learning opportunities, but they may not have the content knowledge to address archaeology and cultural heritage. Seek these professionals out, find nature areas rich in archaeology and cultural history, and create opportunities for children to spend time experiencing archaeology at these sites.

Adult Role Models

Adult role models who facilitate outdoor experiences such as parents, teachers, or other adult mentors such as scout leaders, repeatedly show up as an influential factor in SLE studies (Tanner 1980; Chawla 1999; Stevenson et al. 2014). Family members are most commonly mentioned in the retrospections of environmentalists and educators, mainly as fostering or reinforcing a child's interest in nature. Family values toward nature, or perceived family values as interpreted by children, are also a strong predictor of children's connection to nature and their interest in environmentally friendly practices (Cheng and Monroe 2010). To a lesser but still important extent, educators and other adult mentors are mentioned. Quality teachers matter. Stevenson et al. found a statistically positive, although limited relationship, between the presence of role models and pro-environmental behavior among middle school students (2014). The researchers acknowledge that their findings would be explained by the effect of role models not being well-expressed until children reach adolescence and adulthood (Stevenson et al. 2014, 169). In a survey of teachers who teach environmental topics, they recognize the importance and influence of being role models, as well as providing their students with direct experiences in nature, active and experiential participation in environmental activities, and discussions about environmental problems (Torkar 2014).

Programs like SoW are on the right track in providing role models to both teach about human interaction with the land and the importance of conservation and stewardship. Knowing the importance of role models in SLE research, we propose to focus on strengthening the efficacy of the People and the Land instructors. In a perfect world, we would work more closely with the classroom teachers to improve their efficacy in teaching People and the Land and create a cohort of twenty additional area teachers knowledgeable in teaching archaeological concepts. However, the ability to be a mentor to classroom teachers and other community members certainly has barriers. If we had the ability to continue to work closely with SoW classroom teachers so they could teach the curriculum with a high degree of fidelity, we would certainly do so. With the staff time our budget allowed, we were more effective working with fewer of the Outdoors Program staff to communicate a strong understanding of archaeological concepts. In turn, these staff members could take over the People and the Land curriculum while they use their resources to train the teachers in another unit. As a result, there are fewer but stronger mentors teaching this cultural history unit.

This research makes it clear that it is important for archaeologists to work more closely with teachers and find ways that allow families to experience and foster pro-stewardship attitudes. Family-friendly opportunities to experience archaeology are common. Families can freely explore archaeological sites at state, national, and other parks; they can participate in archaeology fairs and events found across the country; and they can learn about archaeology in museums. Future research could assess the impact of more events geared toward families and explore their knowledge, attitudes, and behaviors related to stewardship after these events. Many archaeologists have training in educational theory and pedagogy that allow them to be effective role models in the classroom. Project Archaeology has a strong national network of archaeologists and educators in nearly every state who create effective workshops and professional development for teachers. Archaeologists who realize they may not have the skills to effectively deliver experiential education opportunities to youth should foster relationships with people in their communities who can complement their archaeological content knowledge with pedagogical skills.

Indirect Experiences

To a far lesser extent than the above variables, consuming media during childhood such as books, magazines, television, and movies are often mentioned as influential factors toward pro-environmental behavior as adults. Chawla's (1998) meta-analysis of SLE research found that books only sometimes inspired new understandings and decisions regarding the environment, with the total percentage of respondents mentioning books as: 29 percent (Tanner 1980), 18 percent (Peterson 1982), 15 percent (Palmer et al. 1993), 22 percent (James 1993), and 20 percent (Chawla 1999). Television was mentioned once as an influential variable in 23 percent of respondents (Palmer et al. 1993). In the research reviewed, indirect media does not show up as a variable measured until 2014. Stevenson et al. found that time watching nature-related television was a negative predictor of environmental knowledge (2014).

Archaeology is an engaging topic in pop culture, as it sparks wonder and imagination about the lives of past peoples. As archaeologists, we often encounter members of the public who have misconceptions about archaeology because of the influence of pop culture and popular media—particularly television. When archaeology is portrayed incorrectly or negatively through popular media, archaeologists serve on the front line to correct those misconceptions, with varying degrees of success. We also produce much of our own informational media such as pamphlets, booklets, websites, and video, often as an add-on to grants and projects that stipulate an outreach product. We typically create these products without an assessment or critical examination of their impact. Informational media most certainly provides a much needed way for archaeologists to share information with the public, but consumers of this information are likely adults who are already interested in these topics. Are we doing ourselves and the public a disservice by not producing more media at an accessible learning level for children? The intent of much of our own media is to share knowledge and increase awareness, not to influence behavior and attitudes. If attitudes and behavior toward conservation are largely influenced during childhood, it would benefit archaeologists to create more media products at appropriate learning levels for children. To take it further, if our intent is to ultimately inspire preservation and stewardship behavior, we need to focus on alternative forms of outreach that provide experiences and active participation, and we need to both serve as and mentor effective role models.

A Connection to Nature

Other studies touch on SLE research but focus more on attitudes in children. Torkar (2014) and Tanner (1980) wrote that children must first come to know and love the natural world before they can become concerned with its care. Cheng and Monroe developed and tested a connection to nature index to measure children's affective attitude toward the environment (2010). A connection to nature is a strong predictor of environmentally friendly practices. Things that increase a child's connection to nature include an enjoyment of nature, an empathy for creatures, a sense of oneness, and a sense of responsibility; and factors that positively influence attitudes include previous experiences in nature, perceived family value toward nature, and a perceived control regarding making an impact (Cheng and Monroe 2010). Building knowledge and skills through EE is important, but a child's belief in their own competence to solve problems affects the extent to which they participate in environmentally friendly practices. This boils down to experiential learning in the outdoors, which teachers view as the most important educational approach for the development of young people's care for the environment and nature (Torkar 2014).

Researchers also acknowledge that fostering attitudes alone may not be a sufficient strategy for building environmental stewardship (Stevenson et al. 2014). You have to pair attitude with knowledge. Archaeologists do a great job at sharing knowledge, but we understand less about fostering attitudes and inspiring action. If archaeologists can understand what variables impact a child's attitude toward archaeology, cultural sites, or various aspects of heritage and community, they can more effectively nurture these variables in archaeology education and outreach. But what exactly impacts a stewardship ethic and what do we measure? Is it a connection to archaeology and the past? Or living cultures and community? Environmental issues, although complex, are broader and more concrete than heritage issues. Pro-environmental behavior can be reflected in daily habits such as recycling, making wise consumption choices, or monitoring energy usages, but pro-stewardship behavior takes places on a larger and broader scale. What we do know from the research is that experiential learning and a sense of responsibility matter, as well as a child's perceived ability to make an impact. This is where place-based education and civic engagement initiatives can assist archaeologists. Fostering a stewardship attitude needs to start with a project where children can see that they are making a difference or see that they have made a positive impact, but to do so may take a long-term investment on the part of the archaeologist.

Conclusion

Environmental education and archaeology education have parallel and overlapping goals and pedagogy. The ultimate goal of EE is to produce an informed citizenry that is knowledgeable concerning the biophysical environment and its associated problems, aware of how to help solve these problems, and motivated to work toward their solution (Stapp 1969). Similarly, our goal as archaeology educators is to create informed and engaged citizens who act in positive ways to care for cultural resources. In the field of EE, archaeology can be an educational tool used to inspire children to spend more time in the outdoors, participate in experiential outdoor activities, and interpret their own archaeological heritage, particularly through experiential learning opportunities. When these experiential opportunities take place in the learner's community, they foster a sense of place and in turn, promote sustainability of local environments and communities.

The development and implementation of the People and the Land curriculum and pilot evaluation serves as a case study for the integration of archaeology and EE at a nature area familiar to the local community. The curriculum emphasized the interconnectedness of humans and Iowa's landscapes, from its first inhabitants, to the Meskwaki Nation, to Euroamerican immigrants. It actively engaged participants in learning about past environments and how native people in Iowa incorporated natural resources into their everyday lives. Students experienced activities designed to inspire them to make informed decisions about natural and cultural resources, with the understanding that stewardship is everyone's responsibility. Results of the pilot evaluation show that students had an overall remarkable increase in knowledge regarding the definition of archaeology and the Meskwaki Nation in Iowa, and restructuring the rigor and control of future evaluations will strengthen this assessment. It is also evident in the evaluation that the classroom teachers individually had varying degrees of success communicating some of the curriculum's main objectives. Because of this, we will pivot and assign the teachers a less abstract, nature-based unit, while an Outdoors Program staff member takes over the teaching of People and the Land. We are confident that this instructor has a robust grasp of archaeological concepts and will serve as a strong role model while teaching this unit.

The Outdoors Program acknowledged that cultural history was one of the weaker components of their EE initiatives. A partnership with experienced archaeologists, who were also trained educators, strengthened this weak link and rounded out the SoW five-day experience. Additionally, this unit helped their program better align to teacher's curricular standards. By partnering with SoW, the OSA increased the number of students they reached exposing 1,100 additional school children to archaeology through high-quality, inquiry-based activities.

EE offers tried and tested teaching methods that can be adopted by archaeologists to make a stronger impact through their outreach. Environmental educators have long tried to understand the variables that impact pro-environmental behavior, to better design and implement programs that foster these variables. Tanner reasoned that if educators understood the type of experiences that motivate responsible environmental behavior, they would be better able to foster the development of an informed and active citizenry (Chawla 1999, 15). As archaeologists, we need to do better at understanding the experiences that motivate responsible stewardship behavior and develop education and outreach initiatives with intentional objectives that connect to these experiences. Although not every variable that impacts environmental stewardship applies to archaeology, we can learn from those that do. Several decade's worth of research on SLE and attitudes toward the environment show that the most important variables that impact pro-environmental behavior include time spent in nature, strong role models including parents and teachers, and a strong connection between a child and nature. When we create more experiential learning opportunities that allow children to spend time at archaeological sites with informed teachers, mentors, and parents, we may see a marked increase in heritage stewardship down the road. When we reach out to children and adolescents, they could grow up to be cultural heritage professionals, the teachers who incorporate stewardship topics into their curricula, or adults who value cultural heritage sites and act to protect them.

Elizabeth C. Reetz, MA, ME, Director of Strategic Initiatives, University of Iowa Office of the State Archaeologist.

Chérie Haury-Artz, MA, Archaeologist and Educator, University of Iowa Office of the State Archaeologist.

Jay A. Gorsh, PhD, Assistant Director, University of Iowa Recreational Services and Coordinator of School of the Wild.

Appendix: Questionnaire Designed to Assess Student Understanding of the People and the Land Unit at School of the Wild

My school is: _____

Circle the best answer

1. I enjoy exploring and learning outside in nature.
   Disagree   Agree   Not sure   Agree   Strongly agree
2. Being outside in nature is scary or dangerous.
   Disagree   Agree   Not sure   Agree   Strongly agree
3. I am committed to living in a way that leaves little negative impact on the land.
   Disagree   Agree   Not sure   Agree   Strongly agree

Circle the best answer

4. Native Americans only lived in the past.
   a. True
   b. False
5. People change their environment when they build shelters.
   a. True
   b. False

6. An archaeologist is a scientist who studies _____ from the past:
   a. Fossils and dinosaurs
   b. Climates
   c. People and objects they leave behind
   d. Water and wetlands
7. Which Native American tribe lives in Iowa today?
   a. Cherokee
   b. Navajo
   c. Meskwaki
   d. Sioux/Dakota

Short Answer
8. List at least 3 environmental factors that affect how people build shelters.

Source: Courtesy of the authors.

References

Adkins, Carol, and Bora Simmons. 2002. *Outdoor, Experiential, and Environmental Education: Converging or Diverging Approaches?* Charleston, WV: ERIC Clearinghouse on Rural Education and Small Schools, AEL.

Ault, Charles R. 2008. "Achieving Querencia: Integrating a Sense of Place with Disciplined Thinking." *Curriculum Inquiry* 38(5): 605–37.

California State University. 2017. "Merlot Pedagogy." *California State University.* Accessed 25 August 2017. http://pedagogy.merlot.org/TeachingStrategies.html.

Chawla, Louise. 1998. "Significant Life Experiences Revisited: A Review of Research on Sources of Environmental Sensitivity." *Environmental Education Research* 4(4): 369–82.

———. 1999. "Life Paths into Effective Environmental Action." *Journal of Environmental Education* 31(1): 15–26.

Cheng, Judith Chen-Hsuan, and Martha C. Monroe. 2010. "Connection to Nature: Children's Affective Attitude Toward Nature." *Environment and Behavior* 44(1): 31–49.

Ellick, Carol J. 2016. "A Cultural History of Archaeological Education." *Advances in Archaeological Practice* 4(4): 425–40.

Ernst, Julie A., Martha C. Monroe, and Bora Simmons. 2009. *Evaluating Your Environmental Programs: A Workbook for Practitioners.* Washington, DC: North American Association for Environmental Education.

Espinoza, Ambar. 2016. "New Federal Education Law Promotes Environmental Education." *Rhode Island Public Radio.* Accessed 14 September 2017. http://ripr.org/post/new-federal-education-law-promotes-environmental-education#stream/0.

Florida Public Archaeology Network. 2017. "Resources, Lesson Plans." *Florida Public Archaeology Network.* Accessed 17 August 2017. http://www.flpublicarchaeology.org/resources.

Greenwood, David A. 2010. "Why Place Matters: Environment, Culture, and Education." In *Handbook of Research in Social Foundations of Education*, edited by S. Tozer, B. Gallegos, A. Henry, M. B. Greiner, and P. Graves-Price, 1–14. New York: Routledge.

Gruenewald, David A. 2003. "Foundations of Place: A Multidisciplinary Framework for Place-Conscious Education." *American Educational Research Journal* 40(3): 619–94.

Gruenewald, David A., Nancy Koppelman, and Anna Elam. 2007. "Our Place in History: Inspiring Place-Based Social History in Schools and Communities." *The Journal of Museum Education* 32(3): 233–42.

Gruenewald, David A., and Gregory A. Smith, eds. 2008. *Place-Based Education in the Global Age: Local Diversity.* New York: Lawrence Erlbaum Associates.

Hoffman, Geralyn, Cara Boyd, and Jason Urbanus. 2010. "Dig It!: Discovering Archaeology, a Standards-Linked Resource Packet for Teachers." *The Haffenreffer Museum of Anthropology.* Accessed 15 August 2017. https://www.scribd.com/document/80002019/Dig-It-Enabling-teachers-to-broaden-their-tools-for-teaching-about-archaeology.

Istre, Elista. 2017. "Interpreting Living Cultures: Indians, Cajuns, and Creoles." *Legacy* 28(2): 15–17.

James, Katherine. 1993. "A Qualitative Study of Factors Influencing Racial Diversity in Environmental Education." PhD diss., University of Minnesota, Minneapolis.

King, Eleanor M. 2016. "Systematizing Public Education in Archaeology." *Advances in Archaeological Practice* 4(4): 415–24.

Kolb, David A. 1984. *Experiential Learning: Experience as the Source of Learning and Development.* Englewood Cliffs, NJ: Prentice Hall.

MacDowell, Marsha, and LuAnne G. Kozma. 2007. "Folkpatterns: A Place-Based Youth Cultural Heritage Education Program." *The Journal of Museum Studies* 32(3): 263–73.

Moe, Jeanne M. 2016. "Archaeology Education for Children: Assessing Effective Learning." *Advances in Archaeological Practice* 4(4): 441–53.

No Child Left Inside Coalition. 2015. "No Child Left Inside." *No Child Left Inside.* Accessed 2 February 2017. http://www.legacy-cbf.org/ncli/landing.

North American Association for Environmental Education (NAAEE). 2009. *Guidelines for Excellence: Nonformal EE Programs.* Washington, DC: The North American Association for Environmental Education.

———. 2017. "About EE and Why It Matters." *NAAEE.* Accessed 5 August 2017. http://www.naaee.org/about-us/about-ee-and-why-it-matters.

Palmer, Joy A., Peter Blaze Corcoran, and Jennifer Suggate. 1993. "Formative Experiences of Environmental Educators." *Environmental Education* 52: 5–8.

Pergams, Oliver R. W., and Patricia A. Zaradic. 2008. "Evidence for a Fundamental and Pervasive Shift Away from Nature-Based Recreation." *Proceedings of the National Academy of Sciences of the United States of America* 105: 2295–3000.

Peterson, N. 1982. "Developmental Variable Affecting Environmental Sensitivity in Professional Environmental Educators." Master's thesis, Southern Illinois University, Carbondale.

Project Archaeology. 2017. "Project Archaeology." Accessed 10 September 2017. http://projectarchaeology.org.

Semken, Steven. 2012. "Place-Based Teaching and Learning." In *Encyclopedia of the Sciences of Learning*, edited by N. M. Seel, 2641–42. New York: Springer.

Sheppard, Paul R., Brad A. Donaldson, and Gary Huckleberry. 2010. "Quantitative Assessment of a Field-Based Course on Integrative Geology, Ecology, and Cultural History." *International Research in Geographical and Environmental Education* 19(4): 295–313.

Smith, K. C. 1998. "Pathway to the Past: Archaeology Education in Precollegiate Classrooms." *The Social Studies* 89(3): 112–17.

Smith, Gregory A., and David Sobel. 2010. *Place- and Community-Based Education in Schools*. New York: Routledge.

Sobel, David. 2004. *Place-Based Education: Connecting Classrooms and Communities*. Great Barrington, MA: The Orion Society.

Stapp, William B. 1969. "The Concept of Environmental Education." *Journal of Environmental Education* 1(1): 33–36.

Stevenson, Kathryn T., M. Nils Peterson, Sarah J. Carrier, Renee L. Strnad, Howard D. Bondell, Terri Kirby-Hathaway, and Susan E. Moore. 2014. "Role of Significant Life Experiences in Building Environmental Knowledge and Behavior Among Middle School Students." *Journal of Environmental Education* 45(3): 163–77.

Tanner, T. 1980. "Significant Life Experiences: A New Research Area in Environmental Education." *Journal of Environmental Education* 11(4): 20–24.

Torkar, Gregor. 2014. "Learning Experiences that Produce Environmentally Active and Informed Minds." *NJAS -Wageningen Journal of Life Sciences* 69: 49–55.

UNESCO. 1978. "Final Report of Intergovernmental Conference on Environmental Education." UNESCO UNEP Conference on Environmental Education, Tbilisi, USSR, 14–26 October 1977, Paris: UNESCO ED/MD/49.

van der Hoeven Kraft, Katrien J., LeeAnn Srogi, Jenefer Husman, Steven Semken, and Miriam Fuhrman. 2011. "Engaging Students to Learn Through the Affective Domain: A New Framework for Teaching in the Geosciences." *Journal of Geoscience Education* 59: 71–84.

Wells, Nancy M., and Kristi S. Lekies. 2006. "Nature and the Life Course: Pathways from Childhood Nature Experiences to Adult Environmentalism." *Children, Youth and Environments* 16(1): 1–26.

CHAPTER 4

Engaging with the Past through Writing Accountable First-Person Creative Fiction
BACAB CAAS

Lewis C. Messenger, Jr.

In 1992, I began to experiment with an archaeological teaching methodology using archaeologically grounded fiction writing. It has developed into a structured writing assignment that I believe is quite useful and effective on a number of levels and can be used in a wide range of topical courses. This chapter describes the ongoing development of this method, its current structure, and suggestions for future applications in a variety of courses.

I teach in a relatively small anthropology department at Hamline University, a liberal arts university in St. Paul, Minnesota. Our student body demographic generally reflects the Upper Midwest, however the Twin Cities has increasingly become more diverse, including large numbers of people from the Horn of Africa (Somalia, Ethiopia), Southeast Asia (Hmong, but also Lao and Karen), as well as an increasing Latino presence (predominantly Mexican, but representative of all of Latin America). The Twin Cities is also home to the largest urban concentration of American Indian peoples in the nation. Hamline has been working hard to attract students of diverse origins. As an anthropological archaeologist, I have found it an exciting challenge to use the knowledge I have gained working with people from many cultures around the world to help students come to recognize for themselves the richness of their own and others' heritage.

My personal background is in Maya studies and my archaeological fieldwork has focused on the Mexican Southeast, Belize, Honduras, and Minnesota. My PhD program at the University of Minnesota under Professor Dennis Puleston introduced me to an incredible holistic spectrum of research methodologies available to archaeology through studies of paleogeography, geology, palynology, and archaeobotany, as well as understanding the contemporary life sciences of botany and its various subdisciplines, and zoology. He was the first to introduce me to trying to replicate technological experience, both through what later became known as "experimental archaeology," as well as going out into "natural" areas to learn how to identify, gather, process, and consume wild foods. Little did I know that this was all part of helping me develop a strong sense of cross-cultural empathy.

My anthropology is rooted in cross-cultural empathy, meticulous scientific analysis, and epistemology. These concepts underlie virtually everything that I teach.

When students take an archaeology course from me, I am mindful that they may have little or no background in anthropology and their experience with other cultures may be limited. So, I want to know what knowledge and skills they bring into the classroom with them, and what they expect from the class. I hand out a standard questionnaire on the first day of every class, before introducing anything about the course or me. I ask if they have had personal experience with, say, descendant communities or relevant archaeological sites. What countries or locations have they visited? Have they ever kept a journal? And finally, what do they hope to get out of the course? This questionnaire gives me baseline information about students in the class and helps me understand their initial levels of interest in and enthusiasm for the class. For this class, I also administer several other questionnaires, which I discuss below.

My own background in history, anthropology, and archaeology has made me sensitive to epistemology—how we know what we know. I think that a lot of students just coming into archaeology classes often do not even ask themselves that question because they assume that what is written, online, on television, and supposedly, coming out of the professor's mouth is correct and based upon fact. What we say about archaeology—as having proven a useful technique to gain the knowledge we now have about ancient cultures—in class is true. Beginning students often assume they know what they know archaeologically because of the abovementioned factors. In a sense, such students have taken on the position of a sort of unquestioning audience for stories about the ancient past, a grand form of historical fiction. (I found myself critical of sloppy historical fiction, especially when some of its central tenets seem to masquerade as facts.)

Reading fiction of any kind truly is an immersive experience. The reader enters a different reality, where suspension of disbelief depends upon the details and accuracy of how that world is presented. Many contemporary readers of science fiction demand literature grounded in science and reality, calling this hard science fiction.

In this genre, Robert Silverberg does well with his planet Majipoor. It has geology, present and past environments, its own "First Nations" (the "Piurivar"), its archaeology, and its history (Silverberg 1995). Even though Majipoor is purely fictional, knowing these kinds of "facts" about the planet's characteristics provides a logical consistency—a sense of reality about the place—and we can suspend our disbelief because this author has really done his homework. He has created a place, one that the reader can recognize as a candidate for a biologist to visit: one that would be a really interesting place to explore and learn the ancient history of!

Perhaps a better example of hard science fiction might be what Silverberg edited with several other authors to create *Murasaki. A Novel in Six Parts* (Silverberg 1992), a "shared universe" novel taking place in a bi-planetary system (hypothetical) that rotates around Gleise 205 (HD 36396, which is an actual red dwarf star). Poul Anderson, one of the authors of the six chapters and a holder of a degree in physics from the University of Minnesota himself (Barrett 2001), was also responsible for the hard science behind the hypothetical dwarf star and its larger-than-earth bi-planetary system. Establishing these kinds of baselines (atmospheric pressure and composition, sunlight, etc., necessary for these environments) that could be available on these planets provided opportunities within which the remaining authors could generate their own stories. They could also do so knowing that their readers would recognize a high degree of scientific logical consistency.

I consider it bad science fiction when writers of such fiction rely too much on overly speculative technology—gadgetry—without enough background research to develop the context that could convince us that such devices would, or even should, logically exist. For me, this is just another example of too much emphasis upon plot and not enough planning and research, or, in academic jargon, "homework."

A different genre of fiction exists that could be called "archaeological fiction," as it addresses ancient times only accessible through the archaeological record. A number of authors have written about such ancient times and created archaeological scenarios that seem exceptionally realistic and thus, we find little reason to question their veracity. This is the case with books like Jean Auel's *Clan of the Cave Bear,* made so, in particular, because of her endnotes and bibliographic references (1980). The mere presence of such references can lend a sense of legitimacy. Examples like that made me think that people who wrote fictional accounts about ancient human times, and gave the impression that they were historically accurate, should be held to extremely high standards.

This has been done successfully by people like Janet Spector in *What This Awl Means,* in which she, as a highly qualified archaeologist and specialist, was able to illustrate how the doing of archaeology can focus upon understanding the lifeways of ancient individuals (1993). She used what was learned and interpreted through archaeology to tell the story of one person and placed it at the beginning of her book. She placed the various categories of data, graphs, and tables, which often comprise the body of many archaeology articles and reports, in the appendices. She demonstrated what I, and probably most of us, ultimately believe archaeology to be about.

I kicked around the idea of having a fiction writing assignment in one of my regional survey classes, North American Archaeology. I would have students account for the details of life that they presented in their story—what food they ate, what structures or artifacts they might have used, and so on. Students would have to use endnotes to indicate both their sources and their own commentary. References would have to be from legitimate scholarly sources, such as journals or book chapters.

My original North American Archaeology syllabus had a standard hypothetico-deductive term paper assignment. Then, during 1992, I decided to consider that assignment as Plan A, adding the optional archaeological fictional writing assignment as Plan B. Over half the class opted for Plan B, no doubt attracted by the words *creative writing*. Students had leeway in choosing the site and time period they wanted to focus on, with the restriction that their scenarios had to take place prior to European contact and somewhere in North America. The "vehicle" they chose, how they got into the time and place, was open. It could be through dreams, time travel, whatever they came up with, but ultimately, they would have to document the details of life back then, preferably from archaeological reports.

This assignment was part of Hamline University's Writing-Intensive curricular program. The syllabus contained a clear set of nine steps leading toward the final product, described below, and students always had access to the final evaluation form, kept on Blackboard.

Students began by identifying the time and place they wanted to learn more about. For many, this was hard, because the average college student is pretty clueless of the options at the beginning of an archaeology class such as this. Given that these creative writing assignments have varied depending upon my class focus (ancient North America, Mesoamerica, and Southeast Asia), the textbooks for the class have been a resource I have promoted as a primary place to begin to browse. For those new to the topic, perusing the visual inventory of their texts might inspire or pique their interest for each of the classes indicated. These texts have always provided extensive visual opportunities for searching. Furthermore, I keep asking them to try to think about where and when they would like to go—often making reference to the services of a time-traveler like Dr. Who. I ask them to do some active daydreaming. This part is important, as it is where they try to find somewhere/when to focus on and anchor themselves. Sometimes, when they begin the next series of steps, they might find that there is insufficient data to proceed, and thus have to change their focus to a different place and time.

The next few steps involved coming up with potential references that would be useful to them in developing their paper. This usually involved individual consultation with me, but I also directed them to other tools students might not think about, such as indices and the bibliography of their textbook.

After they gathered at least four scholarly references, students began to write a fictional account. I would stress to them that I was less interested in plot and more interested in accuracy and detail. I told them I would be overjoyed if I could receive an incredibly boring, but accurate and detailed description of the day in the life of an unnamed person from Chaco Canyon, for example. As students gave me first drafts of their writing, I usually found that most students still preferred plot and claimed that they just could not find details of ancient life. I reminded them that, yes, this might be true, in part, and we, as archaeologists, will never be able to get at all of the details of ancient life. However, we have tools and data that other archaeologists have developed to enlighten our understanding of the past.

I guess it was during one of those moments of trying to reinforce why I was doing this that I came up with the acronym, BACAB CAAS, standing for "Bringing Ancient Cultures Alive by Creating Archaeologically Accountable Stories." I was trying to develop a pedagogical approach that combined concepts of cross-cultural empathy and archaeological epistemology in a meaningful way for undergraduate students. This led to a number of potential questions. For example, what would it be like to be excavating a site of your ancestors, or the ancestors of your classmates? What difference might these relationships make in how students think about the archaeological record? My hope was that this research and writing experience might lead toward greater sensitivity toward the lives of persons in the past, while understanding how we know what we know.

In later years of teaching with this assignment, I began to require that the writer speak in the first person as a way to compel students to experience cross-cultural empathy. In other words, the writer "becomes" the storyteller of the time and place, a sort of "avatar" having responsibilities and direct experience within the community under study. At the same time, they are developing an awareness of issues of representation and place and the importance of traditional Indigenous knowledge. The other part, the archaeological epistemology, relates to how the average student comes to know what the greater "we" (that is, scholars and other specialists) know about the ancient world. What do we actually know, and how do we know it? This makes them stop and think about what is often taken for granted.

Students need to have a sense of the knowledge and processes that underlie statements of fact or conjecture about the past. They need to understand what is involved in determining the age of that cameloid bone with a projectile point in it, or what those folks in Ipiutak ate, or who those people in Etowah may have been concerned about, or when the crops might be getting back to normal in Chaco Canyon. They might also be glad to know that ancient human beings actually were capable of spitting rocks, developing calendars, and creating straight lines in the desert *without* the aid of extraterrestrials. There are multiple epistemologies that we as archaeologists employ, including an incredible array of scientific techniques. We can also learn from Indigenous ways of knowing, and that these are fundamental to this entire process, and that these should be exploited as best as possible, through consultation, and collaboration, and recognition of Indigenous-initiated research as well.

The "How-To" of Implementing BACAB CAAS in Classes

BACAB CAAS projects must reflect the regional and temporal focus of the class for which they are assigned. For instance, in the BACAB CAAS for Ancient Mesoamerica, students develop their avatars for that region, while for North America, the focus is on that area, and so on. BACAB CAAS assignments and the class sequence of other activities run in tandem throughout the term. Scheduling major assignment due dates so that they do not overlap with examinations is clearly recommended.

In many respects, the professor becomes the "coach." There is a sequence of assignments, spaced over a semester. These start by sensitizing students to their own material culture, then asking them to make a decision about where and when they want their avatar to have lived. Then there are four weekly literature searches (here, the word "coaching" may have more meaning). This is followed by assembling materials into a draft narrative and ultimately crafting their paper. This should take the form of a well-formatted, information- and detail-rich engaging first-person narrative that captures what life was like for an individual in a particular location during a specific time period in the past. It should be something the student is proud of and would be willing to show to someone of a descendant community.

The Steps

There are nine assignments throughout the semester, including four literature searches and several reviews of drafts, with students receiving instructor feedback and coaching throughout.

Step 1: Focusing on "Things"

Assignment 1: Autoethnoarchaeological Student Questionnaire. This is an eight-page detailed questionnaire beginning with Question 1, "When you first open your eyes, what do you see within about 6 inches of your face?" and ending on page 8 with, "Would the answers to these questions be different for different times of the year? If so, why? and how?" Its goal is to get students to begin to think about the specific details of their daily lives; things that are meaningful to them and relevant to their material culture; and eventually, how having these background questions might inform their wanting to learn about ancient people. This is passed out on the first day of class; the completed questionnaire is due the following class day.

Step 2: Focused Archaeological Daydreaming

Assignment 2: Proposed Culture—Free Write. Since each student will be responsible for writing a first-person narrative, taking place in a location of their choice (determined by the topic of the course, such as ancient North America, Mesoamerica, or Southeast Asia), and in a time period of their choice, they have to think about where and when they would like to travel back to and learn about, and then do some free writing about it. For the lucky few who already have an idea of what they want to know about a particular part of the world at a particular point in time, and perhaps even a named culture that was there then, this should prove quite easy. For others, this may involve more delving into one of their textbooks to do some searching and browsing for something that could pique their interest.

For all three courses, their main texts have been chosen for their breadth of coverage—something to provide an "anchor" for students to have throughout the semester, and in this case, for them to delve into for images, photographs, and bolded topics to pique their interest and help them decide upon a time and place for their **BACAB CAAS** research.

Their textbooks are: Brian Fagan's *Ancient North America: The Archaeology of a Continent* (2005) for North American Archaeology (ANTH 3040-01); Susan Toby Evans' *Ancient Mexico and Central America* (2013) and Mary Ellen Miller's *The Art of Mesoamerica* (2012) for Ancient Civilizations of Middle America (ANTH 3310-01); and Michael Coe's *Angkor and the Khmer Civilization* (2003), or Charles Higham's *The Civilization of Angkor* (2004), and later Dougald O'Reilly's *Early Civilizations of Southeast Asia* (2007) for Ancient Civilizations of Southeast Asia (ANTH 1980-01).

All of these texts and readings, plus my coaching, allow students to find and settle into the culture that they will be focusing on throughout the semester—the one within which they ultimately will be functioning as an avatar. This assignment will be due one week later.

Step 3: Literature Search

Students find out what kinds of research may have been done about the place and time that they are beginning to get interested in. They can search in scholarly journals and various other sources. They are encouraged to come to talk to me about their ideas.

Assignments 3–6: Literature Search (References 1–4). This involves students doing four separate literature searches related to their proposed archaeological time period, culture, and site, with one handed in approximately every week. They must find minimally one legitimate scholarly source per assignment, so that their final bibliography will have four individual references that they can expect to use in their final paper.

Step 4: Organizing and Putting It Together

Bits of knowledge about landscape, shelter, food, activities, maybe art and ritual, are starting to allow the student to begin to put together fleeting scenarios of what it would have been like in the time and place they have selected. This is when students start to bring it together in drafts for feedback.

Assignment 7: First Draft of Your BACAB CAAS. In this assignment, students formally organize and sort the information they have gathered from their four literature searches. Formatting and specific order are introduced here. Their papers must follow a prescribed format, using the following as a final checklist:

I. **Title.** This includes terms relevant to the cultural scenario.

II. **Brief Summary Statement.** This is similar to an abstract, an approximately 500-word introduction, informing the reader of the location and time period of the narrative, plus any additional rationales the writer wants to add indicating why they chose what they did.

III. **Narrative.** This is the finished product—the final draft. It must be minimally ten pages, written in first person, with only endnote numbers indicating references, or the author's comments.

IV. **Endnotes.** These are critically important. This is where the details of ancient life must be accounted for and referenced to a legitimate source. Annotations on references inform the reader and the reader should feel confident about the legitimacy of what they are reading. This is not a bibliography, but can refer to references as one might find in the text, or to comments made about details not to be presented in the text.

V. **References Cited.** This is where the sources consulted and referenced in the narrative and the endnotes are presented alphabetically in either *American Anthropologist* or *American Antiquity* format.

VI. **Evaluation and Suggestions for Further Research.** In this required section, students must confront what this project has meant to them. How did their research go? Would they have liked to do more work? Do they have any suggestions for others doing **BACAB CAAS** projects in the future, in general, or specifically related to the topic that they wrote about? They are informed clearly that this part must be taken seriously, and if it is not included in their final paper, points will be lost, and/or the paper will be returned until it is added.

Step 5: Optional Narrative Feedback

Assignment 8: Second Draft. This step is optional, but I make myself available during extended office hours for the week that this assignment is scheduled.

Step 6: Final Narrative

Assignment 9: Third—Final Draft. This is where a student's final product, following the sequence indicated in Step 4, Assignment 7, is submitted. It should be a seamless project reflecting the outline as seen in the evaluation sheet (see chapter appendix). It is graded separately from the grades done for students' previous assignments, and then both tallies are compared for the final grade. If students have completed all of the assignments and taken heed, and advantage of, the feedback given, their final project grade should be high.

BACAB CAAS's Developments: Stopping and Taking Account

Currently at Hamline, we are trying to establish online archives of course "artifacts" for assessment purposes, therefore student BACAB CAAS papers will be uploaded to Blackboard, both for other students in the class, and for outside reviewers.

As I used this teaching methodology over the years, I began to notice patterns. At the beginning of the semester, when students hear about the creative-writing side of the assignment, they tend toward euphoria. About halfway through the semester, when it becomes apparent that I am requiring them to produce evidence of legitimate sources of details mentioned in their narratives, there is a sense of panic. Then, students begin to find that they really want to know more about the specifics of the environment, the material culture, and the social and cultural milieu within which the characters of their scenario lived. They want to know for themselves more than for me. Thus, they begin to take ownership of the assignment.

The definition of a successful BACAB CAAS project has evolved over the years to focus on one day in the life of a person, thus challenging students to document it to the best of their ability. A truly excellent paper could be an account of an incredibly boring, but detail-filled day in the life of someone in the past. This is where the detailed autoethnographic introspective assignment students had to complete by the end of the first week of class keeps popping up—where they had to focus on the observable material culture around them for a day. That had been a kind of metaphor for the details archaeologists would love to be able to work with in reconstructing past lifeways. Students will discover that that level of detail does not exist in the archaeological record, and they will have to grapple with the epistemological implications.

BACAB CAAS Examples

Of the more than four hundred BACAB CAAS papers that I have received, there are many that deserve mention. Here are just a handful of my favorite examples of student narratives.

"The Day of the Death of a Crooked Aztalan Princess," by Kristina Orlikowski (1998), tells the story of a young disabled girl visiting an archaeological exhibit of Mississippian materials in the Milwaukee Museum with her parents. She faints, only to awaken, still with disabilities, but in a different place and time, where she describes activities using things she read about or saw in the museum.

A beautifully hand-crafted book, "Names From the Fire, The Story of a Native American Family," by Joelle Pocklington (1998), is a fictional account of a pre-white contact western Great Lakes Potawatomi family. It was illustrated by an artist friend of the author, including charcoal portraits of the individuals mentioned in her text.

In "The Maya Stone-Carver of K'umarcaaj," by Ellen Schousboe (2008), we learn about a jade carver in the late Post-Classic period of the Guatemala highlands, in the Quiché Maya city of Utatlán. Based on this assignment, Ellen was a recipient of the annual Alfred D. and Hazel Stedman Endowed Writing Award. This prestigious award was established in 1983 to encourage excellence in writing by students in any discipline at Hamline University. Three of my students have won this award for their **BACAB CAAS** papers.

One year I decided to offer the option for students to create their **BACAB CAAS** as a children's book. I pointed out that this was not license to write a few simple sentences and do some nice drawings. There would have to be consideration of the parents who would want to be educated about the archaeological resources available on the topic. At the end of each book, there had to be explanatory text, with equivalent reference entries, geared toward adults.

One of my students, Emma Swank, produced a well-written and thoroughly illustrated **BACAB CAAS** children's book, "A Rainforest Adventure Involving Silvery Gibbons and Jambu Fruit Doves," written in fall 2006 for *Ancient Civilizations of Southeast Asia* (Figure 4.1). It gave readers a sense of the environmental context of one of the world's great ancient monuments—Borobudur on Java (Figure 4.2). Her art is simple and inviting, as is her prose. Her explanations and resources listed at the end of the book would have been very useful to any parent. There, parents can find information on the construction of the structure, the layout of the terraces and the galleries and narrative reliefs, with finally the statues of the Buddha at the summit, all within the context of Mahayana Buddhism. In her final paragraphs, she gives the reader a sense of what it was like to have visited the monument during its heyday (Figure 4.3). Emma Swank was another winner of the Stedman Award as a result of this project.

Figure 4.1. Title page of "Rainforest Adventure ... involving Silvery Gibbons and Jambu Fruit Doves" by Emma Swank (2006). Courtesy of Emma Swank.

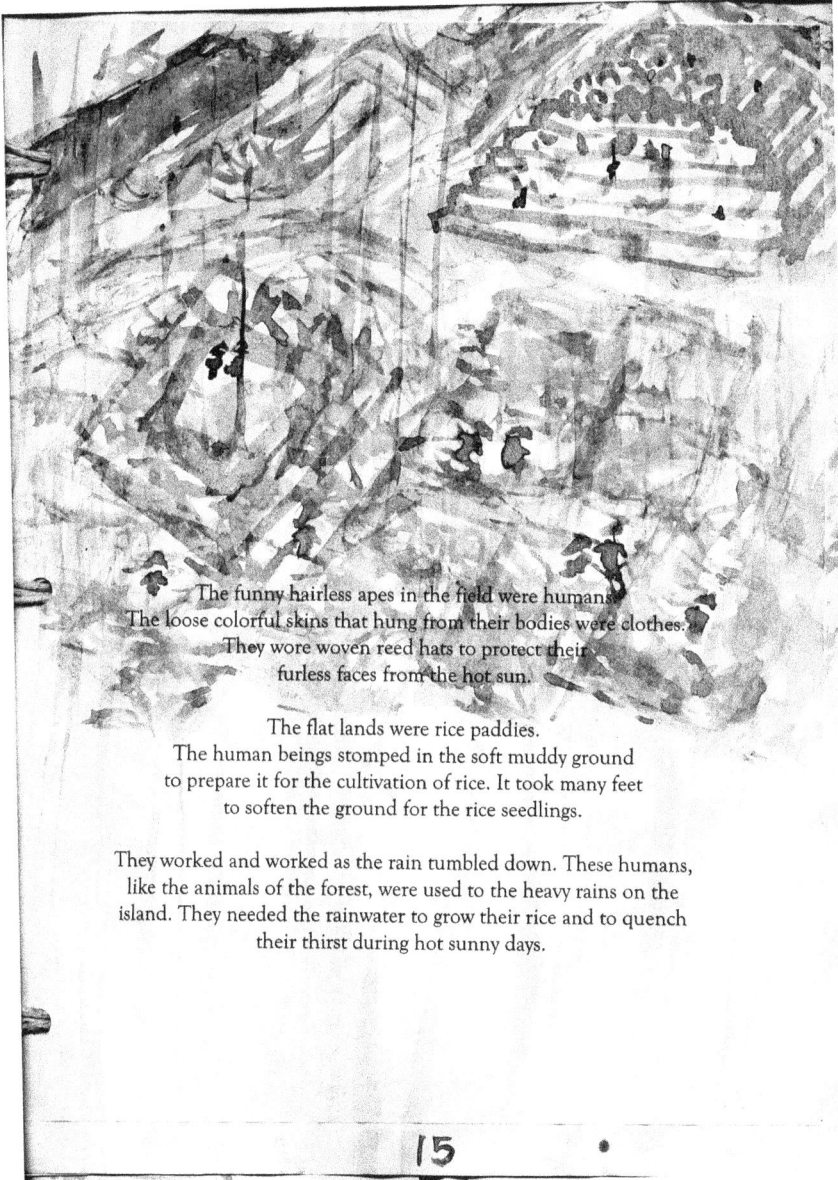

Figure 4.2. Colorful apes and the Stone Mountain—Borobudur. From "Rainforest Adventure ... involving Silvery Gibbons and Jambu Fruit Doves" by Emma Swank (2006, 15). Courtesy of Emma Swank.

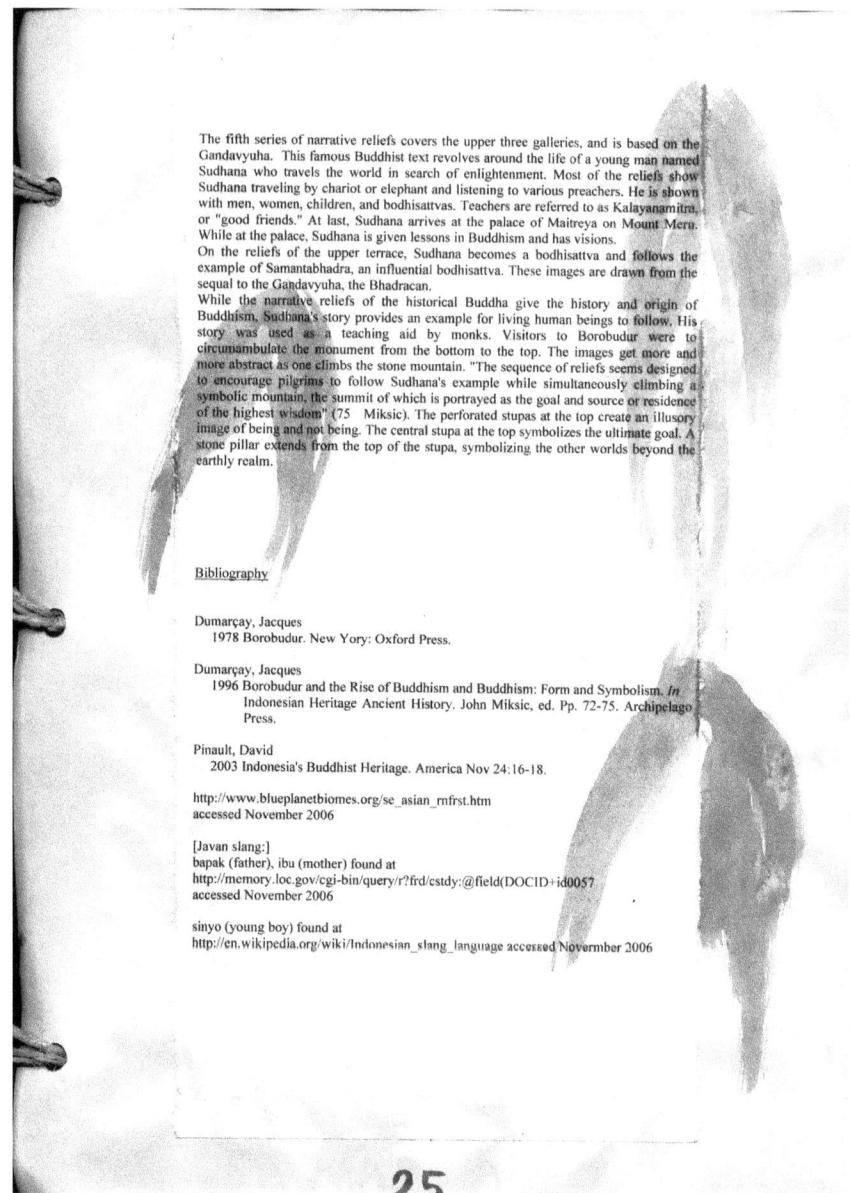

Figure 4.3. Final page of explanation section for parents from "Rainforest Adventure ... involving Silvery Gibbons and Jambu Fruit Doves" by Emma Swank (2006, 25). Courtesy of Emma Swank.

Another student, Bonnie Wetherby, produced an illustrated children's book called "Suchin and the Prince of Angkor" (Figure 4.4). Written in fall 2006, the story is a vehicle for a quick trip through the center of Angkor, most likely during its peak. We learn about details of what life was like there through narrative in word and picture following the chase of a naughty dog by his master, a young prince (Figure 4.5). They run past temples, markets, elephants, and other buildings in a circle, back to the palace where both Suchin, the dog, and her master, the Prince, live (Figure 4.6). Bonnie provides the reader (parents) with

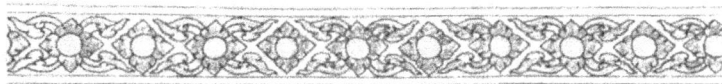

Suchin and the Prince In Angkor Thom

By Bonnie Wetherby

Figure 4.4. Title page of "Suchin and the Prince in Angkor Thom" by Bonnie Wetherby (2006). Courtesy of Bonnie Wetherby.

"Long ago, there was a king that built many things. In his grandest city, near one of the grandest Wats," lived a boy. He was about your age Sunan, but this boy was a prince. He was a younger prince among many princes, and his favorite thing in the entire city was his little dog. This little dog's name was Suchin, and she was a good dog...most of the time."

Figure 4.5. Text and images introducing Angkor Thom, the Prince, and Suchin. From "Suchin and the Prince in Angkor Thom" by Bonnie Wetherby (2006, 5–6). Courtesy of Bonnie Wetherby.

Figure 4.6. Suchin runs through Angkor Thom's market. From "Suchin and the Prince in Angkor Thom" by Bonnie Wetherby (2006, 12–13). Courtesy of Bonnie Wetherby.

her own explanatory endnotes and references, plus background information and sources for the inspiration for her drawings.

BACAB CAAS Assessment

How do we know what students are learning? Can BACAB CAAS, as an approach or technique, be assessed, and if so, do my assumptions about its value in increasing students' empathy and cross-cultural awareness hold up? In recent years, I developed three approaches to try to find out: a questionnaire sent to graduates, surveys administered to students working on BACAB CAAS assignments, and an open-ended question included with final exams.

My first assessment strategy used a questionnaire sent out to students who had graduated. I was interested in seeing if this creative-writing project had affected them. Did it have an impact on their studies, work, and life experiences in any way? Did they think differently about archaeological sites, materials, or descendant communities as a result of the writing project?

A student responding to my inquiry about how the BACAB CAAS experience affected understanding of archaeological epistemology put it succinctly: "It is eye-opening to realize all of the details that you do not think about not knowing until you try to imagine in depth the lives of people in the past."

Another student wrote, "The creative writing assignment I did at Hamline allowed me to look at the archeological sites and artifacts I have seen as not just 'cold faceless objects,' but instead, as products of living cultures and peoples."

One student, writing about my class on ancient Mesoamerica, responded: "When I was writing the story, I frequently had to use creative license which to an extent disturbed me. I did not necessarily want to make things up or to come off as ethnocentric; however, since we do not have extensive knowledge of the Olmec I had no other alternative at times. Therefore it helped me appreciate careful meticulous archaeology and the importance of provenience."

Regarding the question about whether or not the experience of writing creative archaeological fiction has influenced their choice of vocation, one student wrote, "Working on these various projects was the most useful exercise I encountered at Hamline. I do not think that I would have pursued archaeology as a vocation without them."

My second assessment strategy involved administering pre- and post-surveys at the beginning and end of Spring and Fall semester classes in 2015. Here are some examples:

Question 1. *How have your ideas about the role of storytelling in archaeology changed over the course of this semester?* A student responded: "I originally thought it was very dumb. I figured that all the information could be written in a scholarly article and everything would be fine. Well, as I started researching the culture, I realized how difficult it was to read and comprehend those scholarly articles. I found myself appreciating the stories a lot more because it could help teach people other than professors." Another wrote: "I had never really considered storytelling to be a part, and such a significant one in archaeology. It puts a new perspective on the field as I thought about archaeologists as looking for the who/where, but this brings in the question of the why!" And yet another: "I have come to realize that w/o the role of storytelling in anthropology, specifically Archaeology has been a part of a large disconnect between the representation of a people and the artifacts information that we already have."

Question 2. *What surprised you about the process of writing archaeological fiction?* Most students said it was "harder" to "much harder" than they expected. One student wrote: "It was WAY harder than I thought it would be. In fact it was probably the most challenging paper I've ever written. It was a lot of work and required me to think in a different way that I am not used to." Another wrote: "I was surprised by the amount of research that had to be done in order to produce 10 pages of narrative." The exceptions generally involved the assignment being "easier than I thought once I read all I could about my topic. Once I had that base of information, it came very easily." Yet another student agreed with the others about it being hard to write and added: "I didn't feel comfortable with dialog and fear of misrepresentation of the people I was researching."

Question 3. *What new insights did you gain about what it takes to write about the past? Are you seeing movies, pictures from the past, in a different light?* One student wrote: "It gave me a lot of new insight into how cultures are portrayed. It was interesting watching documentaries and movies about ancient North America and other cultures and think about how they are giving information. They guess and make a lot of conjectures similar to what I had to do for this project." Another wrote: "I am! It makes me appreciate films and books set in the past, but it also makes me more angry when a high-budget film is historically inaccurate because now that I know what goes into these and the level of research it takes to make sure you are accurately portraying a culture, it makes me upset to know that some films just simply are not doing the research necessary." Another student responded: "I mainly gained insight about the sheer difficulty of writing about the past. I felt almost a 'responsibility' to this culture I was writing about to make my journal as accurate as possible. Now I appreciate stories, movies, and pictures from the past even more."

One of the most profound responses to this question was short and to the point: "Stories shape how we see the world as they shape us." Another wrote: "I gained a lot of new insight regarding a culture I knew nothing about til [sic] doing all this research on it. I cannot say I am seeing things differently, but instead [have] more appreciation for different cultures."

Question 4. *What does it take to write about the past? What grabs you about stories, movies, videos, pictures from the past?* Said one student, "The best advice I can give is to research, research, research, and then digest what has been read." Another recommended, "K.I.S.S. Keep It Simple Stupid. Forget the plot, and just write as accurately as you can. Day in the life is simple, so stick with it. If you want to make life interesting, write from a tool's perspective or some otherwise inanimate object." A third student suggested, "Don't write with the language of only your discipline. Try to incorporate everyday language."

My third assessment strategy is based on a question I always include in my take-home final exams: *What have you learned that will be of direct relevance to your expected career choice and/or discipline?* Students are told that this is not to be viewed as a course evaluation, rather they are to talk about what was of value to them that they take away from their semester. Here are two responses from non-anthropology students in BACAB CAAS classes. One student reported, "Rather than just writing or learning for the sake of doing it—this style of output really requires you to think about the human implications of your research." Another wrote, "I was also greatly impacted by the difficulty of drawing conclusions from objects left behind by ancient peoples. After writing the BACAB CAAS paper, I learned first-hand the difficulty archaeologists have deciding whether they are justified in drawing conclusions about a past civilization."

BACAB CAAS's Potential Long-Term Impacts on Students' Future Cultural Awareness

Development of cross-cultural empathy as a goal has not been explicit in anthropology for much of its history. At the same time, I feel that every one of us—be we ethnographers, linguists, biological anthropologists, archaeologists, or generalists—wish we could become culturally comfortable and conversant within the culture of "the other."

Comments made by students who have previously done BACAB CAAS projects suggest that they indeed have come to realize the importance of trying to understand the perspective of one of those "others," in this case, someone from the distant past. The sampling of responses suggests that a heightened awareness of the importance of the part they, as anthropologist archaeologists, have to play in representation of people/cultures. They have confronted the epistemological quandary in archaeology. How do we know what we know about the lifeways of peoples in the past? How much do we know, and how much are we as yet unable to know, about what it was like then? Students also become aware that archaeologists have a responsibility to the descendants of those whose ancient belongings–usually referred to professionally as artifacts–they have been excavating. Archaeological data alone cannot provide a complete picture of the past. Students show a concern for engagement with descendant communities. Misrepresentation of lifeways of particular groups of the past becomes a real concern, just as is the case with those working with living societies today. Such lessons have clear implications for the ethics, attitudes, and future behavior of our student citizens[1].

BACAB CAAS—Impacts, Implications, Suggestions for the Future

As I have continued teaching classes using the BACAB CAAS writing assignment, I find that student responses to questionnaires and assessment tools confirm my own personal observations and anecdotes. The BACAB CAAS methodology does increase students' ability to empathize with people from other times and cultures. Evidence I have collected to date convinces me that, along with keeping up with the growing variety of technical skills that are constantly emerging, archaeology is well served by having students develop skills of empathy and cross-cultural awareness. This in no way diminishes the scientific quality of our discipline. If anything, developing such skills continually challenges ours, and our students', epistemological assumptions in ways beyond what traditional analysis of form, function, and process alone ever can. I feel confident that students of mine who have gone through the BACAB CAAS writing experience will approach archaeological sites and Indigenous descendant communities with respect, and a wish to learn more from them. In informal conversations with other archaeologists about this approach, I have come to the conclusion that both students and specialists alike could profit from this kind of pedagogical experience.

I would like to offer several suggestions for future BACAB CAAS directions and applications:

—Interdisciplinary Collaboratives in Children's BACAB CAAS Projects,
—BACAB CAAS in the Precollegiate Classroom,
—BACAB CAAS in Professional Archaeological Writing.

Interdisciplinary Collaboratives in Children's BACAB CAAS Projects

I would like to see the BACAB CAAS methodology used more intentionally in writing children's books, involving direct interdisciplinary collaborations between students in anthropology, creative writing, and visual arts. As indicated earlier in this paper, a successful BACAB CAAS project requires considerable research and cultural interpretation such that one can attempt to situate oneself within an ancient society. Doing a successful children's book adds layers upon this that the student often does not anticipate, mostly in the form of visual presentation and attention to a different type of audience that demands focus. Producing an entertaining children's story might be done through engaging prose and/or striking visual imagery, yet still leave them with an inaccurate picture that sticks with them through adulthood.

For example, years ago, when my wife and I were in the market for children's books for our own children, we saw and quickly bought *The Cucumber Princess* by Jane Wahl (1981). As Mesoamericanists, we were attracted to Caren Caraway's beautiful illustrations, done in a stunningly Mixtec/Aztec codex-style. Each page took the reader along a story reminiscent of the *Popol Vuh*, 8-Deer, and others. The princess was quite a heroine, and the story and illustrations seemed just right for our daughter. Still, something bothered me. Years later, I realized that the central figure could not have existed in ancient Mesoamerica because the Spaniards introduced cucumbers to the region. Had the author looked for an indigenous crop for her princess, perhaps this children's book could have held up under scholarly scrutiny. This was one example of how even minimal academic research by someone writing a children's book could have produced something of long-term value.

As it turned out, few of my students created children's stories. Instead, many students who began writing a children's book became bogged down, unable to deal with the visual part, or they focused too much on that part at the expense of the research component, leading them to give up for the more standard BACAB CAAS project.

I suspect that an interdisciplinary three-pronged collaboration bringing the skills of a studio artist, someone who had experience working with creative writing, and finally the anthropology and archaeology student, would be a win, win, win situation for all. We saw a hint of this with Joelle Pocklington's "Names from the Fire" (1998), for which she worked with an artist friend. She herself had some experience in book design, which also strengthened her project.

BACAB CAAS in the Precollegiate Classroom

The BACAB CAAS concept should be adaptable to the precollegiate curricula. The driving goal of BACAB CAAS has been development of skills and cross-cultural empathy, in this case, focusing on people of the past. Archaeology fascinates little kids (too), and children who want to know about people of the past have lots of opportunities to learn, such as the Discovery Channel, too many computer games to imagine, television shows with archaeological themes and characters, going-back-in-time-to, and so forth.

The very idea of time travel is intriguing to all of us. We know that the movie *Avatar* was a success. The idea of time travel exists in popular culture (*Back to the Future, Terminator, Dr. Who*). One can imagine that a class based upon learning how to become an avatar in some ancient time might sound fascinating to children. Keeping them on track to acquire the knowledge they would need to live in a particular time and place in the past so they could become that avatar could be difficult. I can imagine a whole lot more interest in things like chariots and pyramids rather than morning gruel, personal cleanliness, and what kinds of tasks non-elite children might be expected to be doing outside the city walls. Beyond just survival during their chosen time, how to appropriately act once they were wherever or whenever their avatar lived would provide additional cultural layers for them to think about. All these would result in children gaining respect for the knowledge they would have to acquire to become their ancient avatar.

Clearly, "precollegiate" is an expansive term and what I have just described most likely focuses on upper level students. However, the fundamental idea of BACAB CAAS is flexible and adaptive to various levels. Even developing a series of curricular units of Q&A's for students focusing on "What would it take to be able to have lived in . . . ?" could be tailored to different age groups.[2]

BACAB CAAS in Professional Archaeological Writing

As professional anthropologists and archaeologists, we do not, as a general rule, write fiction. We fill out forms, write reports, write papers for submission to journals or conferences—all quite legitimate and appropriate professional activities directed toward traditionally appropriate audiences. Many of us teach as well and spend time developing curricula, assignments, exams, and reading and grading them. The concept of "free time" for many in academia is often viewed more than ever as "catchup time." There are a lot of things that contribute toward minimal fiction writing among archaeologists. I present that our discipline would be greatly served if more of us did in fact do it.

Having written much of this paper and reflecting upon it, I once again looked online, under searches like "hard historical fiction." It strikes me that much of what is important in our own historical, prehistorical, or archaeological fiction writing, ultimately revolves around quality control—just trying to get it right.

"Hard archaeological fiction" is something that I have tried to make my students think about as a pedagogical learning stratagem. They learn about various kinds of paths that can be taken to reveal as much as we can learn about the past and ancient human lifeways. Student searches lead them to often question the knowledge potentials of those pathways and techniques, and how the knowledge is perceived, and how it has often been parsed historically and academically. In the BACAB CAAS scenarios, students are participants in the past. As part of quality control, getting it right, students should be kept mindful that, whenever possible, collaboration with Indigenous peoples involved in curricular affairs should be a goal. While not easy, making the effort, and thereby showing your students that the effort IS worthwhile, ultimately helps create legitimate, well-grounded, "hard" archaeological fiction. This clearly has been the case for my BACAB CAAS projects as a pedagogical approach for university students. I also believe this should be considered by professionals who want to reach a greater public.

Acknowledgments

I want to extend special gratitude to the following students for their willingness to share the content of their papers and their authorship of them: Hannah C. Klumb, Kristina Orlikowski, Joelle Pocklington, Ellen Schousboe, Emma J. Swank, and Bonnie Wetherby. Producing these final BACAB CAAS narratives has involved a lot of work and sometimes frustration, but in retrospect, I am so proud of these students, and many more who are not mentioned here. As a professor often spending long hours grading works like these, I must confess to sometimes actually feeling a small tear form as I would read on and realize that this particular student really did take ownership of this assignment. She or he went on and really *did* get it. Those are the kinds of moments I am especially grateful for.

Lewis C. Messenger, Jr., PhD, Professor Emeritus, Department of Anthropology, Hamline University.

Appendix: BACAB CAAS Final Draft Evaluation Form Used in North American Archaeology Class

Student name: _____

☐ A. Title (5 points): _____
_____

☐ B. Summary statement (5 points for an Abstract): _____
_____

☐ C. Fictional account/"Novel" (10 points): _____
_____

☐ D. Endnotes (5 points):_____
_____

☐ E. Bibliography (or References cited) (5 points):_____

_____
_____

(Formatting must follow format for the *American Anthropologist* or *American Antiquity*)

☐ Evaluation and suggestions for further research (5 points): _____

_____

General comments on paper: _____

_____
_____
_____
_____

☐ Total points for final version

☐ Total points as percentage of 35

☐ Letter grade for final version

(Note that this Assignment 9 grade [worth a total of 35 points] is added to the other grades for your earlier paper assignments with the final total of all of them—Assignments 1 through 9—being 100 points.)

Source: Courtesy of the author.

Notes

1. One student in my most recent BACAB CAAS became so interested in the region and ancient cultures of Oceania that she plans to try to do graduate work there and try to further understand the ancient Lapita culture she studied for the first time in this class (Klumb 2017).
2. Examples of questions that students might come up with are: Gee, how do I figure out that? What kinds of clothes will I need? Will I have to make them? Whoa, you mean I can't take anything with me? What? You mean just because I have red hair I can't . . . ? No toilet paper back then!

References

Auel, Jean. 1980. *Clan of the Cave Bear.* New York: Crown.
Barrett, David V. 2001. Obituary: "Poul Anderson, Prolific writer of science fiction's golden age." *The Guardian,* 4 August. Accessed 23 June 2017. https://www.theguardian.com/news/2001/aug/04/guardianobituaries.books.
Coe, Michael D. 2003. *Angkor and the Khmer Civilization.* New York: Thames and Hudson.
Evans, Susan Toby. 2013. *Ancient Mexico and Central America: Archaeology and Culture History,* 3rd rev. ed. New York: Thames and Hudson.
Fagan, Brian M. 2005. *Ancient North America: The Archaeology of a Continent,* 4th ed. New York: Thames and Hudson.
Higham, Charles. 2004. *The Civilization of Angkor.* Berkeley, CA: University of California Press.
Klumb, Hannah C. 2017. "The Daily Life of a Lapita Woman." Student paper submitted for Prehistory of the Non-Mediterranean World, St. Paul, MN, Hamline University.
Miller, Mary Ellen. 2012. *The Art of Mesoamerica: From Olmec to Aztec,* 5th ed. New York: Thames and Hudson.
O'Reilly, Dougald J. W. 2007. *Early Civilizations of Southeast Asia.* Lanham, MD: Altamira Press.
Orlikowski, Kristina. 1998. "The Day of the Death of a Crooked Aztalan Princess." Student paper submitted for North American Archaeology, St. Paul, MN, Hamline University.
Pocklington, Joelle. 1998. "Names from the Fire, The Story of a Native American Family." Student Paper submitted for North American Archaeology, St. Paul, MN, Hamline University.
Schousboe, Ellen. 2008. "The Maya Stone-Carver of K'umarcaaj." Student paper submitted for Ancient Civilizations of Middle America, St. Paul, MN, Hamline University.
Silverberg, Robert. 1995. *Lord Valentine's Castle.* New York: Harper.
———, ed. 1992. *Murasaki. A Novel in Six Parts.* New York: Bantam Books.
Spector, Janet. 1993. *What This Awl Means: Feminist Archaeology at a Wahpeton Dakota Village.* St. Paul, MN: Minnesota Historical Society Press.
Swank, Emma J. 2006. "Rainforest Adventure Involving Silvery Gibbons and Janu Fruit Doves." Student paper submitted for Ancient Civilizations of Southeast Asia, St. Paul, MN, Hamline University.
Wahl, Jane. 1981. *The Cucumber Princess.* Illustrated by Caren Caraway. Owings Mills, MD: Stemmer House Publishers.
Wetherby, Bonnie. 2006. "Suchin and the Prince in Angkor Thom." Student paper submitted for Ancient Civilizations of Southeast Asia, St. Paul, MN, Hamline University.

PART II

FOSTERING A DEEPER RESPECT FOR ARCHAEOLOGICAL HERITAGE

CHAPTER 5

Archaeologists and the Pedagogy of Heritage
Preparing Graduate Students for Tomorrow's Interdisciplinary, Engaged Work in Heritage

Phyllis Mauch Messenger

Heritage studies and public history are the publicly engaged and community-accountable practices of historical scholarship, whether that scholarship is based in archival research, archaeology, architecture and preservation, landscape studies, or other related areas. Archaeologists share a commitment to public interpretation, education, and preservation with these other disciplines, and graduate education has a commitment to reflect this reality. Today's scholar-practitioners need to understand the connections and common issues shared by all these perspectives in a heritage field increasingly characterized by interdisciplinary integration and innovation, a diversity of voices and authorities, and responsibilities shared broadly among agencies and with various publics.

In 2017, the University of Minnesota, Twin Cities (UMN) launched an interdisciplinary graduate program in Heritage Studies and Public History (HSPH), in partnership with the Minnesota Historical Society (MNHS). The HSPH graduate program gives students a solid scholarly/professional grounding, offers practical training for working with public audiences, and contributes to the diversity of scholar-practitioners entering the heritage field. The program's designers, coming together from humanities, social sciences, and professional fields, recognized that heritage professionals need to understand the connections and issues common throughout heritage as it is understood and practiced today. Incoming students, including professionals returning to school for advanced degrees, increasingly are seeking interdisciplinary perspectives in their academic studies, diversity and inclusion in their learning communities, and opportunities for meaningful, sustained, hands-on learning experiences in professional settings as part of their curriculum.

The HSPH program addresses the needs of archaeologists and other heritage professionals who wish to manage federally funded projects. In heritage work today and in the future, they also must be ready to work in and with diverse, community-engaged, technology-savvy organizations, ranging from museums and educational institutions to public agencies and consulting firms (cf. Sabloff 2008; Schofield 2014). This chapter delves into the intersection of archaeology with other areas of heritage studies while examining the philosophical perspectives of the faculty and professional staff, including the author (an archaeologist/anthropologist on the university's professional/administrative staff), who led the multi-year effort to establish the program.[1]

The practice of archaeology in the United States has changed dramatically since the late twentieth century with the passage of such federal legislation as the Archaeological Resources Protection Act (ARPA) and the Native American Graves Protection and Repatriation Act (NAGPRA), as well as numerous international conventions protecting cultural property and heritage. Archaeology has become more broadly interdisciplinary and more deeply connected with practitioners in other disciplines (see Carman 2015; Carman and Sørenson 2009; Little 2009; Smith, Messenger, and Soderland 2010; among many others). Archaeologists find themselves, by choice or by necessity, more connected with and more dependent upon institutions and constituencies beyond their own university or agency. Practicing archaeologists working in this context of public engagement continue to hone the skills and perspectives necessary to be effective and productive partners in the heritage field (Derry and Malloy 2003; Little and Shackel 2014; Rubertone 2008). Archaeologists think about how they can make the preparation and training of the next generation of archaeology and heritage practitioners more relevant to the realities of their work today (Harrison 2013; Messenger and Smith 2010). Archaeologists and colleagues believe that archaeology, historic preservation, public history, and related academic fields of study cannot address the needs of today's students, their future employers, and their communities if we stay in our traditional academic and organizational siloes.

Archaeologist Kat Hayes, one of the lead faculty in HSPH, argues that heritage studies is a way to acknowledge the intersection of these fields, and in the case of archaeology, the various subfields (e.g., Native

American, African American, feminist), as well. "This is what I love about collaboration," she says. "We don't come together because of methodological concerns, but because of the communities that value [their heritage]. They don't care about which discipline it is. They want to be involved in whatever way they can" (Messenger 2016, 20).[2]

Chris Taylor, MNHS's chief diversity officer, agrees. For him, heritage studies is "about culture, understanding people and how people live. [Heritage] has an implied sense of value" (Messenger 2016, 58). As a co-instructor for the HSPH core courses (described below), he expects students to come out of the program prepared to look for what is missing in museum exhibits and other heritage projects "related to perspective, voice, and power dynamics." He wants this new generation of heritage professionals to ask different questions than their professors and mentors have been asking.

In a similar way, many archaeologists today are focusing attention on how our work intersects with issues of diversity, social justice, ethics, access to educational and work opportunities, and creating public spaces for untold narratives (Ashmore, Lippert, and Mills 2010; Stottman 2010), in addition to the basic tenets and principles of our fields. As Barbara Little discusses in the concluding essay of *Archaeologists as Activists*, "The changing of archaeology as a scholarly field aside, this book is about changing the world in a different sense: the need for scholars to take seriously both citizenship and the privilege of their positions in order to contribute in a positive way to our society" (2010, 155). One of the most salient themes in the book, she argues, "concerns how archaeology can unsilence people, places, and stories that have disappeared through willful destruction or neglect" (2010, 155–56).

Developing a Master's in Heritage Studies and Public History (HSPH)

The general outline of the Heritage Studies and Public History graduate program took shape during several years of research, consultation, and relationship-building among university faculty and MNHS colleagues (discussed below in "Building a University-based Heritage Collaborative"). We knew we wanted a program that built on (and more than likely would subsume) existing master's-level programs in archaeological heritage management and historic preservation, and that supported a growing interest in developing a public history program. As the groundwork for the new program was laid, we identified these core questions: How can we prepare and train professionals who hold the interdisciplinary concept of *heritage* as central to their approach? How do we (and our future professionals) understand the role of *engagement* in our practice, with community partners, multiple public audiences, other institutions, even other disciplines? How do we shift our fields to be more representative of a shifting demographic to represent multiple narratives and attract more diverse practitioners? (Heritage Collaborative 2016).

The proposed program drew the interest of administrators and faculty in several colleges within the university, especially the College of Design (CDES) and the College of Liberal Arts (CLA). Program goals are aligned with college and university strategic plans, including the University of Minnesota Twin Cities Strategic Plan (2014) and the CLA Roadmap (2016), which emphasizes readiness, research, diversity, and engagement. Because of this strong interest by these two colleges, the program is administered jointly by them, in collaboration with the Graduate School. Core courses are listed under a unique course designator, HSPH. Faculty structures for curricular oversight, student recruiting and advising, and procedures for course approvals had to meet the standards of both colleges, and be approved by all the relevant committees and dean's offices of each, before the program could be reviewed by the provost and submitted to the Board of Regents, the governing body of the university.

The Master's in Heritage Studies and Public History and a concurrent PhD minor were approved by the Regents in December 2016. Program administration was to reside in CDES for the first three years, per a Memorandum of Understanding (MOU) with CLA, to be reviewed periodically. The program's web page was launched in early 2017 (http://hsph.design.umn.edu/), and the first cohort of eleven students began their studies in fall 2017. Anticipated maximum annual enrollment is fifteen, with a total enrolled population by year three of thirty (fifteen first-year and fifteen second-year master's students). Enrollment numbers for students completing PhD minors is more flexible.

In the HSPH program, each cohort of students takes five required courses over a two-year period, plus several electives in their chosen area of focus, for a total of thirty-seven credits (see Table 5.1). The required courses are co-taught by faculty from the university and the historical society.

During the first year, students take three foundational courses (three credits each). In HSPH 8001, "Who Owns the Past?" students discuss the history and social contexts of heritage studies and public history, the potential conflicts, and positive interventions that can be made through the work of affiliated professions. HSPH 8002, "Core Practices in Heritage Studies and Public History," is a survey of methodologies,

Table 5.1. University of Minnesota Heritage Studies and Public History Graduate Program two-year curriculum and sample archaeology track. Courtesy of the author.

Year 1, fall		Year 2, fall
HSPH 8001, Who Owns the Past? 3cr HSPH 8002, Core Practices Survey 3cr **ELECTIVE, 3cr** HSPH 8005, Leadership/Hist. Orgs., 1cr (10 cr total)	Summer paid position at MNHS dept. or site	**ELECTIVE, 3cr** **ELECTIVE, 3cr** Internship OR **ELECTIVE**, 3cr HSPH 8005, Leadership/Hist. Orgs., 1cr (10 cr total)
Year 1, spring		**Year 2, spring**
HSPH 8003, Race and Indigeneity/Heritage, 3cr **ELECTIVE, 3cr** Internship OR **ELECTIVE**, 3cr HSPH 8005, Future/Hist. Orgs., 1cr (10 cr total)		HSPH 8004, Capstone, 3cr Internship OR **ELECTIVE**, 3cr HSPH 8005, Future/Hist. Orgs., 1cr (7 cr total)

Total enrolled credits=37.
All students are required to enroll in HSPH 8001, 8002, 8003, 8004 once, and in 8005 each semester.
All students complete 2 internships in-semester, one within MNHS and one with another organization.
Students have 5 elective options, though one will likely be a track requirement (see track sample curriculum).
Note that in Year 2 students may opt for a fall *or* spring internship, to allow coordination with course scheduling.
For more information on course descriptions and program tracks, see http://hsph.design.umn.edu/curriculum.html.

Sample Archaeological Heritage Track Course Schedule

Year 1, fall		Year 2, fall
HSPH 8001, Who Owns the Past? 3cr HSPH 8002, Core Practices Survey 3cr **Anth 5990, Historical Archaeology, 3cr** HSPH 8005, Leadership/Hist. Orgs., 1cr (10 cr total)	Summer paid position at MNHS dept. or site	**Collections Management, 3cr** **GEOG 5561, Principles of GIS, 3cr** **Anth 5601, Archaeology & Native Americans 3cr** HSPH 8005, Leadership/Hist. Orgs., 1cr (10 cr total)
Year 1, spring		**Year 2, spring**
HSPH 8003, Race and Indigeneity/Heritage, 3cr **Anth 5448, Applied Heritage Management 3cr** Internship, 3cr HSPH 8005, Future/Hist. Orgs., 1cr (10cr total)		HSPH 8004, Capstone, 3cr Internship, 3cr HSPH 8005, Future/Hist. Orgs., 1cr (7 cr total)

See also Historic Preservation track sample and Public History track sample: http://hsph.design.umn.edu/curriculum.html.

in which students learn about professional practice, alignment to institutional mission, customization of programs for diverse audiences, professional evaluation, and management of financial resources. In a seminar on "Race and Indigeneity in Heritage Representation," HSPH 8003, students explore the changes in how diversity has been represented in historical interpretations in the past, and how practice is changing in response to the contemporary social context of the United States. In addition to these courses, all students participate in a one-credit course each semester (HSPH 8005), "Leadership and Future of Historical Organizations." This course operates as a series of lectures and discussions in which leaders from a broad range of historical organizations (both in Minnesota and nationally) explain how they are navigating major changes and challenges associated with their professional practice.

Students also complete two in-semester internships, one with MNHS and one with a partnering institution, as well as a paid summer professional fellowship after their second semester in the program. Depending on a student's interests and intended area of specialization, these opportunities may include work with collections, development of exhibit and interpretive programs, research in archives, or other community-focused work. These experiences, in addition to HSPH coursework, will help build each student's set of skills for work in diverse institutions, their professional networks, and mentoring relationships.

In the final semester of the program, students complete a three-credit capstone course (HSPH 8004). This course is taught as a workshop, drawing together a cohort of students, working with a faculty supervisor, to craft research projects that have multidisciplinary perspectives and aspects of diversity, and that are accountable to stakeholder(s) identified by the students.

We anticipate that these culminating projects will reflect the unique cross-institutional experiences that are the foundation of HSPH. But such a program built on multiple disciplines and institutions did not emerge fully formed out of a few meetings. It required relationship building, experimentation, and persistence. This history is explored in the following section.

Building a University-Based Heritage Collaborative

Relationship building can be a long, slow process. The work to develop a durable partnership capable of supporting an interdisciplinary and inter-institutional graduate program began in 2009–10 with the establishment of a Research and Creative Collaborative called "Locating Heritage," which was funded by a small start-up grant from the University of Minnesota's Institute for Advanced Study (IAS). This collaboration among university faculty and students and community partners provided a space to meet other interested scholars and practitioners, discuss existing interests in heritage work, and consider opportunities for shared teaching, research, and public programming.

One of the earliest findings of participants in this group was that they understood and employed the word *heritage* in many different ways. There are numerous definitions of heritage, often revolving around attitudes and relationships with the past, rather than around definitions of things or movements. Harrison (2013) and Sørenson and Carman (2009), for example, devote whole chapters to definitions of heritage and the development of heritage studies. Harrison says that most of us would recognize a "contemporary 'operational' definition of heritage as the series of mechanisms by which objects, buildings, and landscapes are set apart from the 'everyday' and conserved for their aesthetic, historic, scientific, social or recreational values" (2013, 14). Sørenson and Carman argue that heritage has come to constitute "an influential force in society . . . expressed, for instance, in the strong links between identity formation and heritage," among many other qualities (2009, 3).

In discussions among participants in the heritage collaborative since its inception, there has been a growing understanding that *heritage* is about how people make sense of the past and use it in the present. It has qualities of engagement with multiple stories and cultures, understanding people and how they live. It involves both tangible and intangible aspects of history and cultural heritage. According to Hayes, "Heritage has become a useful way to talk about historical research that is engaged. [It helps us] account for the value that it has for particular communities or individuals" (Messenger 2016, 2). MNHS archaeologist Patricia Emerson notes that, while her orientation is toward tangible elements of heritage, we must also think more broadly about oral traditions and traditional (especially Indigenous) knowledge (Messenger 2016, 16). Historian Kevin Murphy cautions that heritage can be tied to more traditional, conservative, and nationalist roots. Now, he argues, "both heritage studies and public history are trying to think critically about what the past means, how sites of historical memory and monuments are interpreted" (Messenger 2016, 2).

Supporting documents for Minnesota's Arts and Cultural Heritage Fund also offered language for the understanding of heritage. This fund has supported projects throughout the state since 2008, when Minnesota voters agreed to a self-imposed tax in support of arts and the environment. According to a twenty-five-year visioning document, "When we say cultural heritage, we mean the values and traditions that serve to identify us collectively as Minnesotans, and the distinctive values and traditions of the many groups and institutions that make up Minnesota" (Minnesota Historical Society 2010, 5).

In 2011–12, the IAS-funded collaborative sharpened its focus with a new name, the Teaching Heritage Collaborative, and a new goal: to assess the feasibility of establishing a more formalized program of heritage research and education. An overarching question throughout the year was, "How can we train heritage professionals who hold the interdisciplinary concept of heritage as central to their approach?" (Teaching Heritage Collaborative 2012). Each year the collaborative hosted visiting scholars who gave public presentations and provided consultation on our proposed initiative; together we read and discussed current scholarly works (e.g., Chilton and Mason 2010). These discussions were of special importance to the early career faculty who were responsible for master's programs in archaeology and in historic preservation; these faculty were especially interested in exploring how their programs might become more interdisciplinary in response to changes they were seeing in their fields.

By the end of 2012–13, the collaborative, which until then had been largely internally focused, was exploring the feasibility of establishing a more formalized partnership between the university and the historical society, in order to regularize and strengthen opportunities that would benefit both institutions and their constituents, but especially students. These opportunities were initially seen as focusing on carrying out projects in a museum setting or with museum collections. The process of study and consultation, however, was also leading to the conclusion that a new graduate-level curricular offering was needed (Heritage Studies Collaborative 2014). The specifics of what such a program should include remained to be fleshed out, but the possibility of a curricular collaboration with the Minnesota Historical Society seemed to be an opportunity that could set a new program apart from other heritage initiatives. This new initiative would be developed through parallel efforts shaped and funded by the collaborative (renamed the Heritage Collaborative in 2014–15) and a new MNHS/UMN Heritage Partnership, as described below.

Establishing a Museum–University Heritage Partnership

In spring 2013, the University of Minnesota received a $49,000 grant from the Historical and Cultural Heritage Partnerships grant program (which is managed by MNHS on behalf of the Minnesota Arts and Cultural Heritage Fund) to establish a heritage partnership between the historical society and the university. Key players were leaders in the Heritage Studies Collaborative and their MNHS counterparts in sites management, Fort Snelling archaeology, and Minnesota History Day, a statewide program to involve middle and high school students in public history projects. The stated purpose of the partnership was to nurture future generations of professionals who recognize the interdisciplinary and collaborative nature of work across heritage fields. Objectives included engaging students and communities in collaborative work that explores the contemporary significance of heritage issues, to promote an ethic of heritage stewardship in students of all ages, and to place an emphasis on work with communities whose heritage may be overlooked or undervalued (Heritage Education Partnership 2013).

One of the partnership's first projects was to carry out a survey of interested MNHS staff and UMN staff and students to identify key themes and areas of intersection for the partnership. The survey identified areas of mutual concern and provided momentum to establish and build the partnership. Survey respondents agreed on key goals: 1) creating a better coordinated partnership across programs and departments to improve heritage education opportunities in Minnesota, 2) engaging diverse student communities in heritage projects, 3) developing collaborative public outreach opportunities at the History Center and MNHS historic sites, and 4) creating more internship and practical learning opportunities for UMN students (Heritage Partnership 2014).

The general agreement on these goals provided a foundation for further development of partnership initiatives, beginning with collaborative research projects. In fall 2013, the first two partnership projects were selected, one focusing on nineteenth-century immigrant settlements along the Mississippi River near campus, to be carried out by university faculty and students, and the other focusing on Historic Fort Snelling, to be led by MNHS staff in collaboration with UMN faculty and staff. Participants agreed that the nature and extent of collaboration on these projects would unfold as the partnership developed. Additional sites of study, especially MNHS properties, also would be identified as areas of focus for graduate student research as additional funding became available. These initiatives are described more fully below.

The idea of developing a heritage studies graduate program that would draw on the strengths of two of Minnesota's oldest and most prestigious institutions was gaining momentum from other directions, as well. It received strong endorsement in early stages of discussions from the historical society's director, Stephen Elliott, and the university's provost, Karen Hanson, and deans of participating colleges. They were familiar with the successes of two existing collaborations involving undergraduates: the statewide History Day program (in which undergraduates served as mentors to middle and high school students) and a Museum Fellows program (a semester-long mentorship program with a summer trip to Smithsonian Museums). If these short-term programs and mentorships provided so much benefit to the undergraduate participants, institutional leaders agreed, then the long-term impact and benefits would be even greater if the university and the historical society worked together to offer a graduate program. Students admitted to the program, especially those from communities currently underrepresented in museum work, would benefit from the opportunity to study heritage and public history at the graduate level in a collaboratively run program. But the program needed proof of concept, which was provided, in part, by projects that brought students together with museum staff, sites, and collections, as well as their university faculty over several years as the curricular framework of the graduate program was under development.

Interdisciplinary Student and Community-Centered Projects

The process of developing a sustainable partnership relationship has benefitted throughout from projects that engage students and faculty with community partners in collaborations to study and tell heritage stories from diverse perspectives. Projects have included a study of early immigrant neighborhoods on the Mississippi River flats, a series of projects focusing on Historic Fort Snelling, archival research pertaining to several other MNHS properties, and student research on sites of conscience.

Bohemian Flats

One of the first projects undertaken focused on a low-lying area along the Mississippi River, which came to be known as the Bohemian Flats. The river bisects the university's Minneapolis campus, which is within the boundary of the National Park Service's Mississippi National River and Recreation Area. It is just downstream from MNHS's Mill City Museum, created within the ruins of the Washburn Crosby A Mill, once part of the largest flour mill operation in the world. Between the 1870s and the 1930s, Bohemian Flats was home to newly arriving immigrants from Europe who were drawn to work in the St. Anthony

Falls/Mill City industrial waterfront area. Now the space, a grassy park managed by the Minneapolis Parks Board, sits below the Cedar-Riverside neighborhood, which is currently home to some of the Twin Cities' most recent immigrant communities, including East Africans (cf. Immigration History Research Center 2009, 2011).

The Bohemian Flats project began as an undergraduate honors project by anthropology student Rachel Hines in spring 2013 (see Messenger 2016, 24–27). Her interests in preservation, archaeology, public history, and the river landscape led to an honors committee comprised of key players in the ongoing development of the heritage initiative: Donofrio, Hayes, Murphy, and Nunnally. This intersection of faculty interests, as well as Rachel's ongoing work on the project as a researcher and blogger (Hines 2015), has provided valuable insights into the potential for the interdisciplinary heritage program being developed at the university. In addition, Hayes modified a spring 2014 archival re-

Figure 5.1. The *Remembering the Bohemian Flats: One Place, Many Voices* exhibit was visited by descendants of families who had lived there. The exhibit was held in the central lobby of the Mill City Museum on the Mississippi River in Minneapolis. Exhibit developers used QR codes for each panel to provide access to additional research done by students in a spring 2014 archival research class. Photo by David Stevens, courtesy of the Minnesota Historical Society.

search methods course in archaeology so that teams of students could continue to delve into MNHS archives and other sources. Teams of students identified themes (e.g., living on the Mississippi, health and sanitation, crime and vice) and gathered supporting documents (ranging from census data and court documents to photographs and transcripts of WPA interviews) to develop stories. With the help of museum staff, they created exhibit panels that became part of a public exhibit at the Mill City Museum (see Hines 2015; Kowalczyk 2015; Moberg 2015).

This project, and several subsequent collaborations, provided opportunities to test how the MNHS/UMN partnership might support an interdisciplinary graduate program in heritage studies, which would also span both institutions.

Historic Fort Snelling

Another set of projects developed out of an MNHS initiative to rethink how a significant historic site in its care should be reimagined and reinterpreted as a site of conscience. Built in the 1820s, Historic Fort Snelling is a National Historic Landmark at the confluence of the Minnesota and Mississippi Rivers. Excavations in the 1970s were carried out so that a new interpretive center could open in time for the US Bicentennial in 1976. Since that time, Fort Snelling's interpretation focused largely on 1820s military history. A long-anticipated redesign of interpretive programming at Fort Snelling, under way as part of a twenty-year initiative, has begun to tell stories of different communities and different time periods (Minnesota Historical Society 2015). The MNHS–UMN Heritage Partnership focused its initial efforts on a long-overdue collections inventory project at Fort Snelling and on planning for use of archaeological materials and data in the rewriting of site programming. Cohorts of undergraduate interns and anthropology graduate research assistants worked on the project for several years (Figure 5.2) and in 2016 the university carried out a three-week summer archaeology field school to corroborate the location of building foundations covered over during 1970s excavations.

Archaeologists Hayes and Emerson, with a team of student researchers and Fort Snelling staff, explored new research areas, using scanned historic maps and georeferencing, as well as the newly digitized collections catalog to match Fort Snelling structures, both extant and destroyed, with artifacts excavated forty years ago. They envision being able to create 3D renderings of buildings with their associated materials, making new interpretive tools available to the site managers and staff (Messenger 2016).

Figure 5.2. University of Minnesota students participated in collaborative research on Historic Fort Snelling as part of the MNHS–UMN Heritage Partnership. Graduate research assistant Kelly Wolf (*top center*) and undergraduate Meron Tebeje (*lower right*) inventory artifacts from the Fort Snelling Collection. Photo by Nancy Buck Hoffman, courtesy of the Minnesota Historical Society.

Oliver H. Kelley Farm

Research projects carried out at other historic sites owned or managed by the Minnesota Historical Society benefitted multiple constituencies. University students could undertake research projects during a semester-long research assistantship, site managers and staff would have new materials and insights to work with, and school children and other visitors to sites would be the beneficiaries of new interpretive programming. Such initiatives also strengthened collaborations that could be drawn upon as the graduate program was launched.

One of the test sites for such research and programming was the Oliver H. Kelley Farm, which is both a National Historic Landmark and a functioning farm, focusing on nineteenth-century practices. The Historic Landmark designation is the result of its association with Oliver H. Kelley, one of the founders and central figures in the late nineteenth-century agrarian movement, The Patrons of Husbandry, more widely known as the Grange. MNHS had begun a substantial overhaul of the site, including development of a new visitor center and new interpretive programming to address development of agriculture in Minnesota into the twentieth century, an area of knowledge that the public was asking for, but which was outside the expertise of MNHS staff. Background research on agriculture and rural development in Minnesota, carried out by graduate students funded through one of the partnership grants, was given to site managers and interpreters, as well as members of the partnership, as a series of reports, bibliographic entries, and modules that can be used to orient further investigations (see Heritage Partnership 2015; Heritage Collaborative 2016).

Guantánamo Public Memory Project and Humanities Action Lab

The Heritage Collaborative helped support development of an exhibit at the Minnesota History Center curated by UMN students involved in Guantánamo Public Memory Project (GPMP) courses taught by historians Kevin Murphy and Brenda Child (Guantánamo Public Memory Project 2013). According to Murphy, "The most interesting thing about the GPMP project was that it helped to put a pressing contemporary issue into a more complex and interdisciplinary context" (Messenger 2016, 39). "And it was done with collaboration from many layers: undergrads, archivists, historians, archaeologists and anthropologists, graduate students, artists. . . . We were involved with MNHS, the U's Human Rights Program, the Center for Constitutional Rights," Murphy added (2016, 39). He and the students were understandably proud to be invited to Washington, DC by Minnesota US Congressman Keith Ellison for a recognition ceremony. The skills gained in a project like this are applicable to the Heritage Partnership, as well, Murphy says. Putting collaboration at the core is a good principle for organizing the development of a program. Then it is important to allow students to explore difficult topics, including sites of conscience, to think critically about the past, and to develop critical analytical skills.

The Humanities Action Lab (HAL), a multi-year international project inspired by GPMP, provided similar opportunities for students, including courses, conferences, and work on a traveling exhibit. The 2015–16 HAL theme, Global Dialogues, incorporated UMN student projects developed during a fall 2015 class taught by Murphy on "Public Memory and Mass Incarceration" (Humanities Action Lab 2015).

Focusing on incarceration of American Indians, students met with individuals from Native communities and organizations in the Twin Cities. "There is very little scholarship on it, regionally and nationally. Students are doing new research and interpretation," Murphy observed (Messenger 2016, 40). The class also met with MNHS staff to learn about the ongoing re-interpretation of Fort Snelling as a place of contested history, as Bdote or Dakota homeland, and as a site of conscience. "There is never consensus on a site of atrocity. You cannot reach agreement," Murphy explained. "You have to create space for multiple stories" (Messenger 2016, 41).

Benefits of Student Involvement

As described above, the Heritage Partnership, in tandem with the IAS-funded Heritage Collaborative, provided funding for research projects and courses involving dozens of university students working at MNHS sites. The benefits to all stakeholders were articulated by participants in the interviews carried out as part of program evaluation (Messenger 2016). According to John Crippen, who oversaw MNHS historic sites, the background research carried out by graduate students was extremely important for the historical society as they redesigned public programming at their historic sites. "Site managers and interpretive staff, many of whom have MAs and PhDs, are eager to build on the graduate student work" as they develop new interpretive programs at such sites as the Oliver H. Kelley Farm and Historic Fort Snelling, says Crippen, because the long-term investment of research-based interpretation gives their public programs a sound underpinning (Messenger 2016, 7–8).

Chris Taylor emphasizes the importance of mentoring students as they consider heritage work. With support from Legacy funds, the Museum Fellows program (another collaboration between the university and the historical society, as mentioned above) is doing this for undergraduates, especially those from underrepresented communities, through a semester-long course and summer internship. "The purpose is to encourage more diversity in cultural institutions," he says (Messenger 2016, 47). "If you don't like how others tell your story, you should have a stake in telling it." The Museum Fellows program, which draws participants with a commitment to diversity, inclusion, social justice, history, and work in museums, has a consistent placement rate of 75 percent for its students. Several graduates of the Museum Fellows program were among the first cohort of HSPH students. What museum staff and program participants have learned through their seminar work together, their field trips to visit museums in Washington, DC (see Figure 5.3), and their commitment to long-term mentoring relationships is helping to inform development of the museum-based components of the graduate program.

The opportunities that brought university students and faculty together with historical society staff have provided tangible, ongoing collaborative projects through which we have identified the multiple ways in which we carry out our work. They have helped us identify the different vocabularies and ways of knowing that we employ. They have exposed our different scopes of work and timeframes for decision-making and completion of tasks, and helped us develop new skills to work out inter-institutional differences. These collaborations have provided real-world examples, objects, and projects for classrooms and internships that help build heritage literacy as an "enduring value" for the participants. The experience gained through each of these initiatives continues to inform development of the graduate program in heritage studies and public history.

Figure 5.3. The Museum Fellows group from the University of Minnesota toured museums in Washington, DC, and met with Lonnie Bunch, Founding Director of the National Museum of African American History and Culture. Photo by Chris Taylor, courtesy of the Minnesota Historical Society.

Conclusion

We remain committed to core values of diversity, inclusion, and equity.[3] We agree that our program must be interdisciplinary with no one perspective privileged above others. Students will have the opportunity to specialize within a broad interdisciplinary framework. Currently, there are three track options (archaeological heritage, historic preservation, and public history), and additional tracks may be added as the program continues to develop. Students will carry out their required coursework in cohorts, with strong mentorship from faculty and museum staff. Internships and paid summer fellowships will provide multiple and varied opportunities for experiential learning. Students will have the opportunity to meet Secretary of the Interior standards to direct federally funded projects.

Themes that are woven throughout the program include diversity and inclusion, public engagement, applied learning, interdisciplinarity, networking, and professional museum-based experiences. Students will gain a wide range of skills needed for work in diverse heritage-related institutions.

We expect that students completing the HSPH Master's program and PhD minor will become leaders in the heritage field as curators, interpreters, managers, and researchers in a range of institutions. We believe they will help diversify and transform existing positions and organizations and create new ones that we cannot yet imagine. Yet with these high expectations, we also are mindful of words of wisdom and cautions from our colleagues. As archaeologists (along with our colleagues in other heritage fields) engaged in heritage work, Little reminds us, we need to engage in "our own self-defined activism . . . to bring about social or political change, but we must be vigilant and continually self-critical and questioning about the types of changes we advocate" (2010, 158). As the Heritage Studies and Public History graduate program evolves and grows, we will maintain vigilance, and continually seek to measure successes and make improvements, following the lead of our graduates as they lead us into the future of heritage.

Phyllis Mauch Messenger, EdD, RPA, Grants Coordinator and Journal Editor, Institute for Advanced Study, University of Minnesota.

Notes

1. A forthcoming book chapter, authored by an interdisciplinary team that contributed to development of the HSPH program, will discuss more fully the several disciplines represented in the program (Hayes et al. 2019).
2. During January–February 2016, the author carried out a series of interviews with ten faculty, staff, and students who participated in the MNHS/UMN Heritage Partnership and research projects funded by it. The goal of the interview project was to document participants' experiences with the partnership and its projects and gather perspectives on heritage studies and public history in relation to development of the new graduate program. A transcript of the interviews is on file at the University of Minnesota (Messenger 2016).
3. In March 2018 the Andrew W. Mellon Foundation awarded a two-year $350,000 grant to the University of Minnesota for the HSPH program in support of "Diversifying the Heritage Profession through Immersive Interdisciplinary Graduate Training."

References

Ashmore, Wendy, Dorothy Lippert, and Barbara Mills, eds. 2010. *Voices in American Archaeology*. Washington, DC: Society for American Archaeology.

Carman, John. 2015. *Archaeological Resource Management: An International Perspective*. New York: Cambridge University Press.

Carman, John, and Marie Louise Stig Sørenson. 2009. "Heritage Studies: An Outline." In *Heritage Studies: Methods and Approaches*, ed. Mary Louise Stig Sørenson and John Carman, 11–28. New York: Routledge.

Chilton, Elizabeth S., and Randall Mason. 2010. "NSF White Paper: A Call for a Social Science of the Past. SBE 2020: Future Research in the Social, Behavioral, and Economic Sciences." Accessed 26 January 2016. http://www.nsf.gov/sbe/sbe_2020/2020_pdfs/Chilton_Elizabeth_297.pdf.

CLA Roadmap. 2016. "Shattering Expectations: The Case for Liberal Arts." Accessed 16 October 2016. http://roadmap.cla.umn.edu.

Derry, Linda, and Maureen Malloy, eds. 2003. *Archaeologists and Local Communities: Partners in Exploring the Past*. Washington, DC: Society for American Archaeology.

Guantánamo Public Memory Project. 2013. "Guantánamo Public Memory Project." Accessed 15 February 2016. http://gitmomemory.org/.

Harrison, Rodney. 2013. *Heritage: Critical Approaches*. New York: Routledge.

Hayes, Katherine, Greg Donofrio, Patricia Emerson, Tim Hoogland, Phyllis Mauch Messenger, Kevin P. Murphy, Patrick Nunnally, Chris Taylor, and Anduin Wilhide. 2019. "Challenging the Silo Mentality: Creating a Heritage Studies and Public History Program at the University of Minnesota and the Minnesota Historical Society." In *History and Approaches to Heritage Studies*, ed. Phyllis Mauch Messenger and Susan J. Bender, 127–49. Tallahassee, FL: University Press of Florida.

Heritage Collaborative. 2016. *University of Minnesota Graduate Program in Heritage Studies and Public History Proposal to add a new Master's Program and graduate minor.* Manuscript on file, Institute for Advanced Study, University of Minnesota, Twin Cities.

Heritage Education Partnership. 2013. *Heritage Education Partnership Between the University of Minnesota and the Minnesota Historical Society.* Document on file, Institute for Advanced Study, University of Minnesota, Twin Cities.

Heritage Partnership. 2014. *University of Minnesota/Minnesota Historical Society Heritage Partnership Proposal for FY15 Continuation.* Document on file, Institute for Advanced Study, University of Minnesota, Twin Cities.

———. 2015. *Proposal to the Heritage Partnership Program, Arts & Cultural Heritage Fund, FY16 MNHS/UMN Heritage Studies Partnership Program.* Document on file, Institute for Advanced Study, University of Minnesota, Twin Cities.

Heritage Studies Collaborative. 2014. *IAS Heritage Studies Collaborative Final Report.* Manuscript on file, Institute for Advanced Study, University of Minnesota, Twin Cities.

Hines, Rachel. 2015. "A Home Worth Fighting For: The Evictions at The Bohemian Flats." *Open Rivers: Rethinking the Mississippi,* no. 1. Accessed 1 February 2016. http://editions.lib.umn.edu/openrivers/article/a-home-worth-fighting-for-the-evictions-at-the-bohemian-flats/.

Humanities Action Lab. 2015. "States of Incarceration: A National Dialogue of Local Histories." Accessed 16 February 2016. http://humanitiesactionlab.org/.

Immigration History Research Center. 2009. "Minnesota 2.0 Project Collection (Digital Archive)." Accessed 15 February 2016. http://archives.ihrc.umn.edu/vitrage/all/ma/ihrc3908.html.

———. 2011. "Sheeko: Somali Youth Oral History, Collection." Accessed 15 February 2016. http://archives.ihrc.umn.edu/vitrage/all/sa/ihrc3926.html.

Kowalczyk, Stefanie. 2015. "An Enchanted Landscape: Remembering Historic Swede Hollow." *Open Rivers: Rethinking the Mississippi,* no. 1. Accessed 1 February 2016. http://editions.lib.umn.edu/openrivers/article/an-enchanted-landscape-remembering-historic-swede-hollow/.

Little, Barbara J. 2009. "Forum: What Can Archaeology Do for Justice, Peace, Community and the Earth?" *Historical Archaeology* 43(4): 115–19. doi: 10.1007/BF03376772.

———. 2010. "Epilogue: Changing the World with Archaeology." In *Archaeologists as Activists: Can Archeologists Change the World?,* ed. M. Jay Stottman, 154–58. Tuscaloosa, AL: The University of Alabama Press.

Little, Barbara J., and Paul Shackel. 2014. *Archaeology, Heritage, and Civic Engagement.* Walnut Creek, CA: Left Coast Press.

Messenger, Phyllis Mauch. 2016. *MNHS/UMN Heritage Partnership Interviews.* Manuscript on file, Institute for Advanced Study, University of Minnesota, Twin Cities.

Messenger, Phyllis Mauch, and George S. Smith, eds. 2010. *Cultural Heritage Management: A Global Perspective.* Gainesville, FL: University Press of Florida.

Minnesota Historical Society. 2010. "Minnesota: State of Innovation. A Twenty-Five Year Vision, Framework, Guiding Principles, and Ten-Year Goals for the Minnesota Arts and Cultural Heritage Fund." Accessed 14 February 2016. http://www.mnhs.org/achf/docs_pdfs/ACHFFinal.pdf.

———. 2015. "Historic Fort Snelling: A National Historic Landmark." Accessed 15 February 2016. http://www.historicfortsnelling.org/.

Moberg, Laurie. 2015. "'Remembering the Bohemian Flats': An Exhibit and a Practice of Public Memory." *Open Rivers: Rethinking the Mississippi*, no. 1. Accessed 1 February 2016. http://editions.lib.umn.edu/openrivers/article/remembering-the-bohemian-flats-an-exhibit-and-a-practice-of-public-memory/.

Rubertone, Patricia E., ed. 2008. *Archaeologies of Placemaking: Monuments, Memories, and Engagement in Native North America*. Walnut Creek, CA: Left Coast Press.

Sabloff, Jeremy A. 2008. *Archaeology Matters: Action Archaeology in the Modern World*. Walnut Creek, CA: Left Coast Press.

Schofield, John, ed. 2014. *Who Needs Experts? Counter-mapping Cultural Heritage*. Surrey, England: Ashgate Publishing Limited.

Smith, George S., Phyllis Mauch Messenger, and Hilary A. Soderland, eds. 2010. *Heritage Values in Contemporary Society*. Walnut Creek, CA: Left Coast Press.

Sørenson, Mary Louise Stig, and John Carman, eds. 2009. *Heritage Studies: Methods and Approaches*. New York: Routledge.

Stottman, M. Jay, ed. 2010. *Archaeologists as Activists: Can Archeologists Change the World?* Tuscaloosa, AL: The University of Alabama Press.

Teaching Heritage Collaborative. 2012. *IAS Teaching Heritage Collaborative Final Report, May 24, 2012*. Manuscript on file, Institute for Advanced Study, University of Minnesota, Twin Cities.

University of Minnesota Twin Cities Strategic Plan. 2014. Accessed 16 October 2016. http://strategic-planning.umn.edu/sites/strategic-planning.umn.edu/files/strategicplan_umtc_final_1.pdf

CHAPTER 6

Gathering Public Opinions about Archaeology and Heritage in Belize
A Drive toward Better Local Access and Programming

Geralyn Ducady

Introduction and Project Background

In June 2016, I traveled to Belize and gathered 210 opinion questionnaires from local citizens in each of Belize's six districts, along with a number of informal interviews. Goals of the project were to better understand how citizens view local archaeology, identity, and their relationship with archaeology and Maya heritage. Research results will prove to be useful to the Belize Institute of Archaeology (IA)[1] and archaeologists who work in the area. Knowledge gained will serve as a guide when developing new public programs or point out areas where outreach is needed. This project will be a first step in gauging community interest and future involvement between archaeologists and community stakeholders. The research will also be a model for archaeologists in the fields of public archaeology and heritage education that can be conducted in other regions of study.

    In the spring of 1999, as an undergraduate at Boston University, I spent a semester in Belize with the Xibun Archaeological Research Project (XARP) under the leadership of Patricia McAnany, now at the University of North Carolina, Chapel Hill and Executive Director of InHerit: Passed to Present.[2] During the field school season, we worked alongside local men and women who were hired to clear the jungle and cook for us; they sometimes took part in the excavations. Since most of us working on the project were outsiders from the United States, I began to wonder what interest and knowledge local people had about archaeology. For my final term paper project, I opted not to analyze potsherds or stone tools from our excavations. Instead, I conducted a survey in the local community at a pub along the Western Highway and at a bus station in the city of Belmopan to find out what residents thought about local archaeology and archaeologists. The results of this survey were published in *Sacred Landscape and Settlement in the Sibun River Valley: XARP 1999 Archaeological Survey and Excavation* (Dion 2002).

Beginning in 2006, Patricia McAnany formed the Maya Area Cultural Heritage Initiative (MACHI) that later became InHerit: Passed to Present. These initiatives focus on working with Indigenous communities in Central America to strengthen links between them and their ancient Maya heritage. Some of the goals include building knowledge of and pride in Indigenous identity and training Indigenous communities in heritage management. These goals are reached through educational programming in schools, community mapping, radio-*novelas*, and other community outreach programs (McAnany 2016).

When she was a PhD student of Dr. McAnany, Claire Novotny included members of the primarily Indigenous village of Aguacate in Southern Belize in her archaeological research in addition to conducting nearby archaeological survey and excavations for her dissertation work. In this experiment in social archaeology, she included members of the community from the start. She consulted with community members throughout the project, hired local men to work on the project, conducted tours at the sites, and helped start a local heritage center containing objects from the sites. She has yet to conduct formal evaluations with participants to determine if views of archaeology and heritage have changed as a result of her project (Novotny 2015).

Both programs mentioned above focus on including Indigenous peoples in archaeological research and heritage management. In 2016, the Belize National Institute of Culture and History (NICH) published a document they call their National Culture Policy. The National Culture Policy aims to build a national heritage for all Belizeans to identify with, even those who do not identify as Indigenous. Along with this, educational programming sponsored by the IA focuses on building this national identity.

For archaeologists in the United States who work in areas around the world, there has been a movement over the past decade toward involving communities, Indigenous and otherwise, in the education and management of their local heritage (Atalay 2006; Atalay et al. 2014;

Lea and Thomas 2014; McAnany 2014). For the past five years, education committees at the Society for American Archeology (SAA) and at the Archaeological Institute of America (AIA) have pushed to professionalize scholars who focus on public archaeology and heritage education in the field of archaeology through workshops and conferences at annual meetings, of which I have been a part. A special volume on archaeology education was published in November 2016 by the SAA's journal *Advances in Archaeological Practice*.

At Dr. McAnany's suggestion—given the recent work in public education in Belize and the focus on heritage education in the profession of archaeology as a whole—I returned to Belize in 2016 and conducted a follow-up to my initial 1999 survey. I gathered information from those who identify as Indigenous as well as those who identify as one (or more) of Belize's many other ethnicities; participants had to be residents of Belize. I also expanded my research area to include all six districts of Belize, hoping to be able to compare results by district.

I pursued this project when I was employed as the Curator of Programs and Education with the Haffenreffer Museum of Anthropology, Brown University. Although I am no longer employed there, I remain connected to the Museum as an Education Program Affiliate. Under the direction of Director Robert Preucel, the Haffenreffer Museum sponsored my research and travel. Dr. McAnany and her organization supported the project by connecting me with Claire Novotny, who was then InHerit's Program Director and who works closely with the IA.

In this chapter, I will highlight some parts of the trip where particular lessons were learned and explain the methodology used that may guide other archaeologists interested in conducting similar research in other areas. I will also examine research results and provide conclusions that may help guide archaeology educational programming in the area.

About Belize

Located south of Mexico and east of Guatemala, Belize has the honor of being both on the Caribbean coast and a part of rain-forested Central America. At only 8,800 square miles, it is slightly larger than New Jersey (Peedle 1999). It was the only English colony in Central America and called British Honduras until 1973; Belize gained its independence from Britain in 1981. The modern-day country is broken up into six districts: Belize, Cayo, Corozal, Orange Walk, Stann Creek, and Toledo (Twigg 2006).

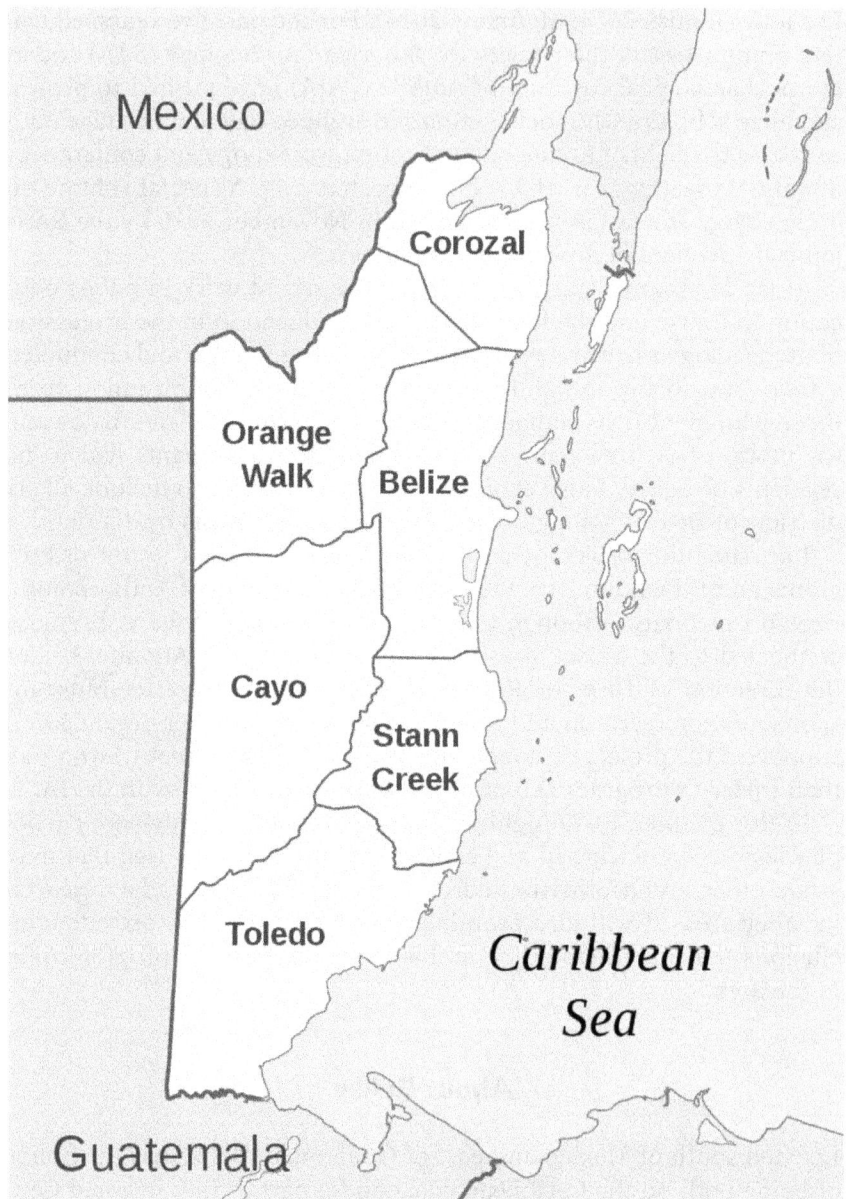

Figure 6.1. Map of the districts of Belize. Wikimedia Commons.

Belize is comprised of many ethnic groups, and, despite its small size, population make-up varies district by district. Mestizos make up almost half of the population (52.9 percent). They are descendants of both Mexicans and Maya who fled into Belize during the Mexican Caste War in the 1800s. Many are bilingual English/Spanish speakers with some speaking only Spanish. Creoles make up the next largest ethnic group (26.0 percent). They are of mixed African and white ancestry whose ancestors were brought to Belize during the transatlantic slave trade. Most speak English and a separate Creolized language. The Maya make up 11.3 percent of the population and are of two distinct groups, the Ketchi (or Q'eqchi K'iche') and the Mopan, and they speak different languages. The Garifuna (or Garinagu) make up 6.1 percent of the population. Their ancestors were runaway slaves from St. Vincent who created a distinct Garifuna culture and language and are of African and American Indian descent. Some scholars consider the Garifuna an Indigenous group. Mennonites (3.6 percent) began coming to Belize from Canada and Mexico in the 1950s; they maintain an agrarian lifestyle, are orthodox Protestants, and speak a German dialect. East Indians make up 3.9 percent of the population, Caucasians 1.2 percent, Chinese 1.0 percent, and 1.2 percent and 0.3 percent as "other" or "not stated." (According to the 2010 census, there were 324,528 people living in Belize.) Language popularity and ethnic concentrations vary by district (The Statistical Institute of Belize 2013, 20; Twigg 2006, 14–16).

Roman Catholicism makes up 40.1 percent of the population and is the most popular religion. However, many Christian-based religions can be found in the area. I noticed that even the small villages had up to four churches, and some of the schools are Roman Catholic or Methodist. There are about 100 males to every 100 females, and the median age is twenty-one years old (The Statistical Institute of Belize 2013).

Setting up in Belize

Claire Novotny and I took the same connecting flight to Belize and met for the first time on the plane. By the time we got through customs and picked up the rental car, we headed straight to the office of the IA in Belmopan to obtain my permit. While speaking with other archaeologists, I learned about recent politically charged events and land rights issues related to archaeology in Belize. In fact, there was a fairly recent incident in the village of Santa Cruz (Toledo District) that had a lot of people on edge. The incident involved the destruction of archaeological ruins and resulted in unresolved ethnic tensions that are beyond the scope of my ability to describe without appearing to take sides ("PM Says 'Outrageous'; Mayans Say 'Justifiable'" 2015). In addition, another site that was recently destroyed in the Orange Walk District (Noh Mul) has also politicized archaeology. It is not uncommon for construction projects to clash with archaeological preservation and stones from temples are often used for road fill (Parks 2016). I wondered if these events would affect what I would hear or read from survey participants.

After our meetings, Dr. Novotny and I checked into our hotel and then chatted over dinner. The first place I was to gather surveys was in the village of Aguacate where Dr. Novotny had done her work and where she had hoped the results I gathered would help her in her community work in the village. I expressed concern over visiting Aguacate, which is not far from Santa Cruz. What if people shared something that could get them in trouble politically? My surveys and research protocol had gone through the approval process of the Brown University Human Research Protection Program and were completely anonymous. But, since it is a small community, and it would be easy for someone to figure out I visited there, I was worried someone might figure out who said what, or that I might get the community in trouble. As I will explain soon, though, members of the community had similar concerns.

Lessons Learned in a Small Maya Village

The next day, I followed Dr. Novotny in my rental vehicle down to Punta Gorda. Here, we split, and I continued down a five-mile dirt road to the small Maya village of Aguacate close to the Guatemalan Border where I participated in a homestay program set up by the village council chairman where I was placed with a family for the duration of my stay. Before making the trip to Belize, Dr. Novotny had contacted the chairman to inform him of my wish to conduct surveys and interviews. He was interested in the project, but upon arrival, informed me that I would need permission from the Alcalde, the traditional leader of the village[3] before I could talk to people. Additionally, village council elections were to be held Sunday and he might no longer be chairman. The Alcalde was out of town that day, however. The next day, Dr. Novotny and the village's new Heritage Committee hosted a community

Figure 6.2. Community children look closely at a feature at Kaq Ru Ha. Photo courtesy of the author.

gathering to celebrate the inauguration of the village's Heritage Center that will house artifacts and research papers associated with the nearby archaeological site called Kaq' ru Ha', which was the subject of Dr. Novotny's PhD dissertation. At the celebration, I approached the Alcalde who included members of the Heritage Committee in the conversation. They were interested in the project but said I would have to make a proposal in front of the council since decisions are made communally and not by any one individual. They invited me to speak after the council elections the next day.

I arrived at the tail end of the elections where the Alcalde introduced me to the group in Q'eqchi' Maya. I stated my purpose, then everyone spoke to each other in Q'eqchi'. I could not understand what was being said, but I could tell by the tone of the conversation that people were concerned. They ultimately decided to not allow me to survey members of the village, and their concerns were expressed to me in English. I was not surprised by most of the concerns that were raised since I suspected they might be of issue. One reason was that they frequently get researchers coming to the village who do not get permission, gather information from people, and leave without ever sharing their research results. One gentleman asked about compensation, which I cannot provide through the IRB protocol. Another was worried they had no control over what I would write and I could thus give them a bad reputation. These reasons point to the feeling that they are being used for others' research gains. Another interesting concern was that they were used to researchers being university students and they did not understand why I was doing research; I am "just a worker." In addition, because I had to get a permit from the IA, there was concern that I was in fact working for the government. In light of what happened in nearby Santa Cruz, people were concerned I was there to uncover negative sentiments. They suggested I come back with a written proposal and contract that stated I would share my results in the end. Although legally I could have spoken to people in public areas, I wanted to respect the wishes of the community council. I had suspected that doing research in a small community like this would require several trips to build rapport and gain permission before returning to conduct the research. Unfortunately, I did not have the funding to be able to do extensive research like that. Given that Dr. Novotny had worked with the village for several years, she and I both mistakenly thought that if she introduced me to them then I could skip rapport-building.

Of note, however, was Dr. Novotny's efforts to include the community in her research and her aide in helping them form a Heritage Committee and Heritage Center where artifacts from her excavations and where copies of her research articles, reports, and dissertation are housed for community members to have access to them. During the ceremony at the archaeological site to celebrate the opening of the Heritage Center, Dr. Novotny led community members around the site and explained the ruins. We discovered a looter's hole. One gentleman turned to me and said that it was a shame since the site and its history belongs to the community, not for one individual's profit. He also pointed out that not everyone in the community agreed with preservation or perhaps people from neighboring communities did not feel as connected to the site. There was also a sense that the archaeologists should police archaeological sites.

Unfortunately, there are hundreds and hundreds of sites across Belize making it impossible for the IA to monitor all of them. Archaeologists who come to Belize to conduct their research do not have the funding for security in perpetuity. In helping to form the Heritage Committee, Dr. Novotny aimed for villagers to feel a sense of pride and ownership for the site with one byproduct being that Committee members would monitor the site. However, even they cannot police it at all times.

From Town to Town

I next visited the larger town of Punta Gorda. I first reached town in the late afternoon and felt a bit down from not yet having collected any surveys. I checked in to my hotel room and headed to the town center. It was a hot, sweaty, and sunny afternoon. No one in the town center would talk to me. I went back to my room to cool off and sulk a bit. I then went into the lobby and chatted to the hotel security guard who was a local female college student. She suggested that many people might think I am trying to test them and may feel embarrassed by their lack of knowledge. She gave me some tips on approaching people and filled out a survey herself. I went back into town in the early evening and finally was able to get some people to speak to me and fill out surveys. The next days were better, and I was finally rolling.

Some towns proved easier than others. Dangriga Town is a largely Garifuna community that does not get a lot of tourists. I had a difficult time there at first because most people were less receptive to tourists and they are also a community that has been over-researched. There was a group from a US university staying in my hotel that was also conducting surveys in town. More people were willing to talk to me on my last day; perhaps because they were used to seeing me in town.

San Antonio Experience

In the middle of my trip, I stayed at the small Mestizo town of San Antonio Rio Hondo in the Orange Walk District, a few miles outside of Orange Walk Town. The town sits on what is known as Albion Island, and is located between two channels of the Rio Hondo River. I was interested in staying there because there is an archaeological site near the village and a cenote.[4] I was hoping to see if survey answers differed for those who lived near an archaeological site from those who did not, and to compare thoughts of those in a Mestizo village to those in the Maya village I visited earlier.

There, I stayed in a room rental with a family in the village. Due to an emergency situation that I helped out with, the pouring rain, and a migraine on my part, my research day was cut short. By the time I set out for Orange Walk Town to conduct surveys, I only had a couple of hours before the shops closed. I quickly went up and down the main streets and around the main plaza to get surveys. It was pouring on and off, and I sprinted through puddles and tucked the surveys under my rain jacket. I had placed all surveys and recording equipment in plastic zip-lock bags in my backpack. Although I did not get as many surveys as I had hoped, that was the most surveys I had gathered in a period of two hours. In the village of San Antonio, I got only a handful of surveys, and I did not get a chance to visit the archaeological site. It was located some ways into the jungle, and no one wanted to lead me through the mud and rain on the hike there.

I considered stopping in Orange Walk Town again the next morning before heading to my next destination, but I unfortunately awoke to another downpour. It was a bit of a drive to the next destination, and I wanted to take my time on the wet roads. The next town also had a bridge crossing the river and dirt roads. I wanted to get there with time to make sure things were not washed out and with time to flag someone down in the daylight if I got stuck in mud.

Crooked Tree

My next stop was in the Creole village of Crooked Tree, located within the Belize District just south of the Orange Walk District line. Although I already had stops in the Belize District planned for my trip, I added Crooked Tree to my itinerary when I learned about the work Dr. Alicia McGill was doing there. An archaeologist currently teaching in a public history program at North Carolina State, she did her graduate school archaeological work in the nearby archaeological site of Chau Hiix under the direction of Dr. Anne Pyburn (Provost Professor of Anthropology, Indiana University, Bloomington) and has returned to the village to focus on community archaeology projects. She has worked in the area for several years and led several school and community programs there and in a neighboring village (McGill 2014). Most recently, she and her students conducted surveys in town and, when I arrived, were preparing to open a community exhibit about the local archaeology in the Audubon Society building. Aside from being next to a major archaeological site (not open to the public), the village of Crooked Tree is also a wildlife sanctuary on an island in the middle of a lagoon, and is reachable by car on one road. The Audubon Society office is the first building as you enter the village and the village's dirt roads are the trails. The village is well known to birders and attracts hundreds of bird-watchers every year. I arrived in the off-season and was the sole occupant at the inn I stayed at.

While staying in the village, I took a day to visit Chau Hiix. To get to the village of Crooked Tree, you head west from the Northern Highway and cross a man-made land bridge over a lagoon. Chau Hiix is located on the other side of the village island across another lagoon. I took a two-hour trip by horse from where I was staying in the village to the site, with a guide who is a former bushman by trade. I say former because, as he explained, it is a lost art since young people are no longer learning the trade. Bushmen have a deep understanding of the rainforest, know its dangers and provisions, and are skilled with a machete to clear paths and swaths of land.

 Archaeologists in the area often hire bushmen to guide them to sites and clear the sites so the archaeologists can do their work. In fact, my guide had worked on the site of Chau Hiix for years when Dr. Pyburn was doing archaeological investigations there. He was knowledgeable of the archaeological process, methodology, and information about the site itself. Aside from bushmen, cooks are needed to feed the crew, and often a handful of people are hired to help with the excavation. My guide also helped with the excavation of the site, and had a sense of pride over it. All archaeologists are required to acquire a research permit from the IA. As a part of the permit, the IA requires that archaeologists hire a number of local people to work on the sites. This serves the purpose of bringing income to the local community, educating the community about the archaeology in their area, and (it is hoped) instills a sense of pride and connection to local heritage.

 Although the inhabitants of Crooked Tree Village are largely Creole and are not direct ancestors of the Maya, but because they grew up having a Maya archaeological site in their "backyard," they did feel connected to the history and felt it to be a part of their heritage. The older generation referred to Chau Hiix as "Indian Hill" and spoke about their grandparents playing on "Indian Hill." People also recalled being hired to work on the site while the archaeological work was being done in the 1990s. Not only do they see the site as their heritage, but as a source of work and income. Many people expressed their wish that the work was still available as a source of income. Although an archaeological project may last a decade or more, it does end at some point, leaving people without that source of income. When I attended the Belize Archaeology and Anthropology Symposium at the end of my trip, a discussion about this very issue came up during one of the sessions. Archaeologists expressed concern about suddenly dropping that source of income for villagers when a project ends. They also acknowledged that community members who worked on the sites now have another set of skills; they have learned how to do archaeology and they have learned about the archaeology. But, once the project is over, there is not a way for them to apply those skills elsewhere. Archaeologists at the conference were discussing ways to help villagers apply their new skills or find similar work on another project, perhaps through a certificate program.

My guide informed me that when the work stopped, guards were hired to "police" the site. A guard would stay at the site for two weeks at a time and then rotate with another. Unfortunately, money ran out to hire guards, and the guards did not like the isolation of the position. He told a story of one who had seen ghosts and heard voices. During my tour of the site, we discovered a looter's hole. A building that served as Dr. Pyburn's laboratory had been broken into long ago as well.

Chau Hiix is difficult to reach, is not kept clear of the rainforest, and is not manicured like some of the tourist sites. Therefore, tourism for the site is not a source of income for the community, and they rely mostly on wildlife tourism as an Audubon sanctuary and popular location for birders. The site is even difficult to reach for those who live there, and members of the community talk about not having visited since the archaeological work stopped. Dr. McGill's work to open a community exhibit[5] in town is a great way to show the eco tourists the rich heritage of the village, and to allow villagers and the younger generation of villagers to learn about the history of their area.

Tourist Sites

I also visited a number of archaeological sites open to tourists during this research trip. The ones I visited were each very different in their manner of education and preservation, and all are managed by the IA.

To visit the Actun Tunichil Muknal (ATM) archaeological site you are required to go with a licensed tour group. Incidentally, I saw a number of tour guides at the Belize Archaeology and Anthropology Symposium that I attended at the end of my trip, demonstrating tour guide commitment to learning and keeping up to date on what is going on in the field. The ATM site is miles off the main road, and, once parked, the tour group must hike a few miles, including wading through a few rivers, to the entrance of a cave where there was more wading in water, hiking through the cave, and climbing high ladders. The IA decided to keep the artifacts *in situ* rather than collect them. This served to allow the site to become a major tourist destination. It is rare to visit a site with artifacts still in place. This is also why one must go with a licensed tour guide. Not only will the guides keep you from getting lost in the cave, but they are also trained to protect the artifacts and to keep people on the marked path away from them. The $160 BZD per person per

Figure 6.3. Artifact "display" at the Marco Gonzalez archaeological site. Photo courtesy of the author.

trip is out of the price range for most Belizeans, and this trip is geared for tourists. All of the members of my tour group were tourists from other countries.

Another site I visited was the Marco Gonzalez site at the southern end of the Island of Caye Ambergris. One does not need a tour guide to enter, and little hiking is needed. The IA charges Belizeans a lower fee to enter the park than tourists from other countries, making it more feasible for local people to visit. The site was recently opened to the public and is undergoing excavations and preservation efforts. Artifacts found in previous excavations are displayed on tables with basic interpretation and exposed to the elements, and there are still artifacts scattered throughout the site. Interpretive signs throughout the site along with a paper guide we were handed explained the patterns of the ruins and also medicinal plants and trees. The site was fairly clear, but the rainforest was allowed to encroach upon the site. Most of the Belizeans who live in the town of San Pedro on Ambergris Island did not grow up there and live there for jobs in the tourism and hospitality industry. A few were knowledgeable of the archaeology of the Island as there are sites throughout.

Figure 6.4. The author at Cahal Pech archaeological site. Photo by Angela Dion, used with permission.

I also visited Cahal Pech which is a Classic period site located within the town of San Ignacio. The road and parking abut the site. It also has a lower fee for Belize citizens. It is a well-groomed site. It is cleared of the rainforest, level, and the pyramid structures and other ruins have been re-built. It is easy to get to and easy to walk around once in the park. Cahal Pech is representative of the condition of most of the major tourist sites in Belize that attract visitors because they are well-groomed, contain larger pyramids, and the ruins are re-built so that people have a better understanding of what they looked like in ancient times and can be in awe of their grandeur.

Survey Analysis

Methodology

I developed survey questions with the intention of gaining insights into people's knowledge, thoughts, and feelings toward archaeology and foreign archaeologists, and their connections to heritage and ethnicity. Although English is the national language, many citizens speak

Spanish as their main language. I therefore had Nicole Larrondo, an education outreach intern at the Haffenreffer Museum of Anthropology, translate the survey instrument into Spanish so that I may include Spanish-speakers in my research as well. My goal was to gather at least fifty paper surveys in each of Belize's six districts for a minimum of three hundred surveys. With at least fifty surveys in each district, I would be able to compare results across the different regions. I also intended to conduct a number of recorded interviews with people who demonstrated that they wished to share more than the written survey would allow or have a deeper conversation. However, due to reasons explained above, my goal numbers turned out to be ambitious. I ended up with more samples from some districts over others and with a total of 210 surveys. No participants were comfortable with being recorded, but I did have a handful of informal interviews. I spent four weeks in Belize and had one to three days in each location. Sampling was random and collections took place at public locations. Although I conducted the surveys face-to-face, the responses were anonymous. Most participants filled out the surveys on their own, but others preferred that I read the questions to them and fill out their answers for them. No identifying information is associated with the surveys. Participants were informed that they could skip questions they were not comfortable with or end participation at any time. Completed surveys were kept with me at all times during the trip. I do not plan to share completed surveys with other scholars, but plan to share only the final results and report.

Results

Open-ended questions and "other" questions that appear at the end of a checklist were coded and the coded responses were added to the data table for frequency and cross-tabulation. Coded responses and certain multiple-choice answers may add up to more than 100 percent of those surveyed since people could give or choose more than one answer to a question. Since the number of surveys collected in each district varied significantly, I do not think comparison in answers between districts is valid despite my original intentions to do so, even if considering overall difference in population distribution across districts. Cross tabulations were calculated and are available, however.

I completed 210 surveys throughout the country of Belize. Although I set out to collect an equal number of surveys from each of the six districts, that did not prove to be feasible due to ease or difficulty working in some areas or the variations in local population densities. I collected

73 (34.8 percent) surveys in the Belize District, 53 (25.2 percent) in Cayo, 36 (17.1 percent) in Toledo, 19 (9.0 percent) in Corozal, 15 (7.1 percent) in Orange Walk, and 14 (6.7 percent) in Stann Creek. Seven of the surveys were taken in Spanish. Although I had a Spanish version of the survey instrument, not being able to engage in initial conversations with people in Spanish to talk to them about the survey and the project made it difficult to convince Spanish speakers to take the survey. For the handful who did take the survey in Spanish, the participant either had a friend translate for me or the person spoke some English but felt more comfortable answering the Spanish survey. Given my limited Spanish speaking abilities, I was not able to conduct any interviews with Spanish-only speakers.

Eighty-seven participants were college educated (41 percent), 71 (34 percent) participated in high school as their highest form of education, 11 (5 percent) completed secondary school as their highest form of education, and nine (4 percent) completed only primary school. Participants varied in age from eighteen to seventy-seven. One hundred ten (52.4 percent) of the participants were female, 82 (39.0 percent) were male, and 18 (8.6 percent) did not respond. Seventy-four respondents (35.2 percent) chose more than one category, 46 (21.9 percent) identify

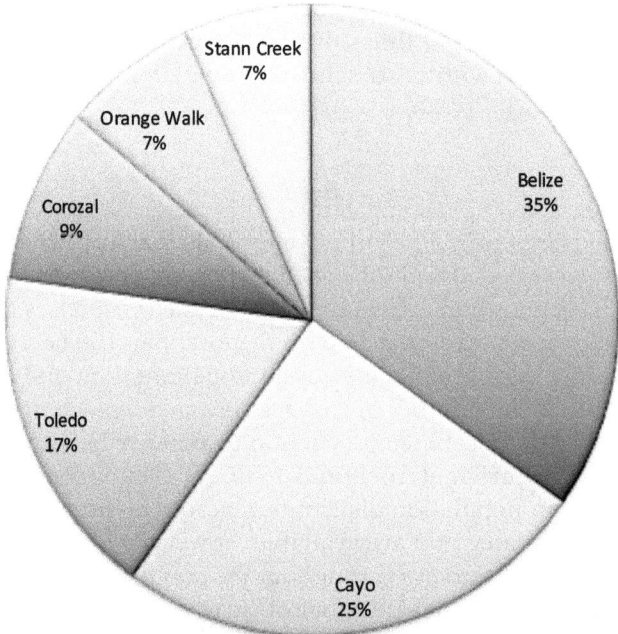

Figure 6.5. Percentage of surveys from each district. Courtesy of the author.

as Mestizo, 24 (11.4 percent) identify as Creole, 19 (9.1 percent) as Maya (Ketchi, Mopan, or Yucatec), 13 (6.2 percent) as Garifuna, six as East Indian/Hindu (2.9 percent), five (2.4 percent) as white, three (1.4 percent) as African, one (0.5 percent) as Mulatto (written in), and one (0.5 percent) as Asian. I was unable to get any Mennonites to take the survey.

I did not ask people about their religion, but as mentioned earlier, even the small villages had up to four churches (Roman Catholic, Methodist, Evangelical, Mennonite). A few people commented to me that they believed people in the villages were so divided and unable to work together because of the waves of different religious groups that have established themselves over time. In almost every area I was staying, there was also a church youth group of missionaries from the United States.

Question one was set up on a Likert scale with one being "not at all familiar" and seven being "very familiar." The question asked how familiar people were with archaeology. Fifty-nine (28.1 percent) said they were very or mostly familiar with archaeology. Twenty-two (10.5 percent) said they were "mostly not familiar" or "not at all familiar," with the rest falling in between or with no answer. The most frequent answer was "somewhat familiar" at 65 (31.0 percent). The results may be slightly skewed in the positive because a number of people who refused to take the survey did so because they "did not know anything about it" despite me telling them that answering that they were not familiar was helpful to my results. Another possible error with this question became apparent when people took the survey verbally. Some of them misunderstood the word "familiar" and thought I was asking about family.

Along the same vein, on a five-point Likert scale, participants were asked if they knew much about the archaeology in Belize. The most frequent answer was "a little," number three on the scale at seventy-one responses (33.8 percent). 41.4 percent claimed they know "a lot" or "some" while 23.8 percent claimed they know "not much" or "nothing."

When asked how they feel about archaeology in general, the majority of participants (74.8 percent) answered "positive" or "mostly positive." No one answered in the negative, except for one who responded "somewhat negative" and said, "they [archaeologists] should work with the people of Belize." Others repeat the sentiment of wanting local archaeologists and wanting more collaboration from foreign archaeologists in later questions. Many respondents (31.4 percent) noted in the comments that understanding heritage is a factor for feeling positive about archaeology. One respondent wrote, "I believe this takes a very vital role in our country since it was [sic] what is left of our ancestors. It gives us the pride of commemorating our history." Eighteen respondents mentioned the importance of archaeological tourism and jobs for the Belize economy. This also comes up in other subsequent questions.

When asked if they feel a personal connection to local archaeological sites, 87 said "yes," 80 said "no," and 36 said "not sure," with the rest not responding. Some reasons for saying "no" were that they were not Maya and do not feel connected to that heritage ("Cause I'm not Mayan I guess"), and because they have never been or have not frequently been to archaeological sites ("Because I've only been to two sites in my lifetime living here in Belize").

When asked how participants feel about foreign archaeologists working on sites in Belize, 47.7 percent answered "positive" or "mostly positive" with only 4.3 percent answering "mostly negative" or "negative." Reasons for negative or even marking "no opinion" include the belief that archaeologists steal artifacts and do the work for their self-benefit. Reasons for marking in the positive range include 35 people who noted that foreign archaeologists have more education and experience, 32 who say archaeologists help them learn about their heritage, 10 who say they help the outside world learn about Belize, and 5 who note that archaeologists provide jobs for locals. Some who chose "no opinion" had both negative and positive reasons in their comments. Eighteen respondents (8.6 percent) noted that they have worked on a dig or have worked or currently work as tour guides in archaeological parks, and they thus may have a better opinion and understanding of archaeology.

When asked if they believe it is important to preserve archaeological sites, 92.9 percent responded "yes." Nine did not answer the question, five said they were "not sure," and one answered "no" with no reasoning. Of the folks who said "yes," 71 spoke to the importance of heritage and identity ("Those sites are who we are!"), 28 noted that it was important to preserve the past for future generations ("For the benefit of our children and our children's children"), and 25 noted the importance of sites attracting tourists as an economic boost for the country (". . . it [is a] good money making venture in tourism").

When asked if they believe it is okay for citizens who are not archaeologists to take artifacts from archaeological sites, 82.9 percent said "no," 6.7 percent were not sure, and 4.8 percent said "yes" (5.7 percent did not respond). Those who said it is not okay understood the criminality of it and that "most people take to sell. We lose that component of history that we could learn a lot from. We [should] put it in [a] museum for all humanity to benefit, especially local people."

Reasons that some said that it is okay stems from the mistrust of archaeologists. "Because archaeologist [sic] themselves remove artifacts without our knowledge and if they can do this then why questions [sic] our citizens?"

When asked how often they visit archaeological sites, 60 percent marked "once a year or less" and 26 percent marked "never." The few who went more often lived near easy-to-reach sites or work at or have worked at sites. Forty-two respondents said they do not have time outside of work to go. Thirteen mentioned that admission is too expensive. Sixteen noted that the sites are too far away and they do not have access to transportation to get there. Indeed, during my trip, I had to limit my stops at sites due to time constraints. I passed side roads to many other sites, but they were down dirt roads that could be seventeen or more miles off the highway. Eighteen participants noted they only went when they were school age and were brought during field trips. Ten noted they go only when friends or family are in town visiting.

When asked how participants feel about tourists coming to Belize to visit sites, 85.2 percent felt "positive" or "mostly positive." Some had no opinion or did not answer and only one person marked in the "negative" range. Sixty-three people noted that tourism makes the country known around the world and helps people to learn about the country, ten mentioned that outsiders can appreciate the beauty of the country, and 53 mentioned tourism's importance to the Belizean economy. Tourism is a big economic resource for Belize. People come not only to visit the archaeology, but for eco-tourism in the rainforest and along the coast. It is a popular destination for diving and snorkeling. And, it being an English-speaking country that is both in Mesoamerica and in the Caribbean, it attracts tourists from other English-speaking countries.

When asked how they have learned about the past cultures of Belize, 84.3 percent note they learned about them in school, 50 percent said from television, 46.2 percent from the internet, 35.7 percent said it is common knowledge, 34.8 percent from the radio, 31.9 percent from newspapers, 27.6 percent from magazines, and 27.1 percent from attending public lectures. In the "other" category, 10 people noted that they learned about past cultures from their elders, 5 mentioned from reading books, and 5 noted through visiting archaeological sites.

When asked how they learned about new archaeological discoveries, 62.4 percent from television news, 40.5 percent from the internet, 35.7 percent from radio news, 34.3 percent from the newspaper, 30.5 percent said from school, 17.1 percent from museums, 10 percent from magazines, 8.6 percent from public lectures, and 8.1 percent said it was common knowledge.

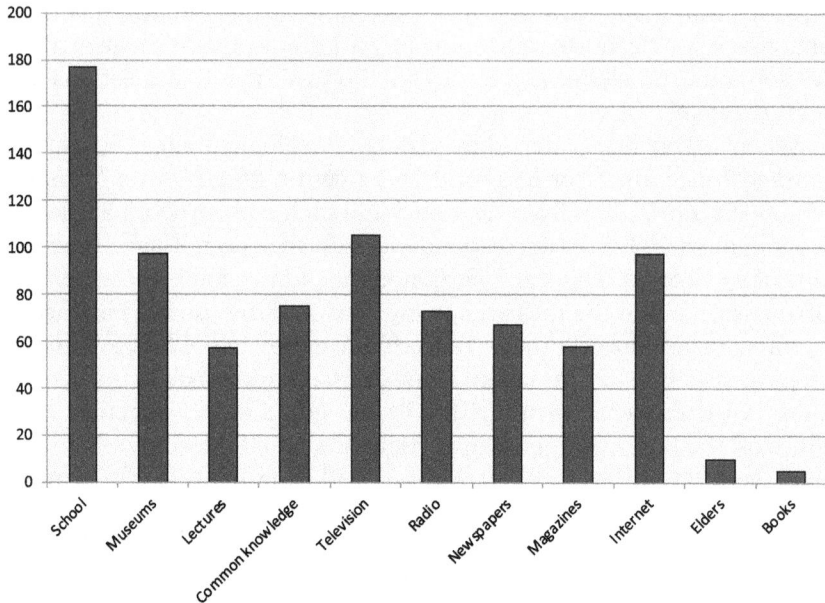

Figure 6.6. Survey result: How have you learned about the past cultures of Belize? Courtesy of the author.

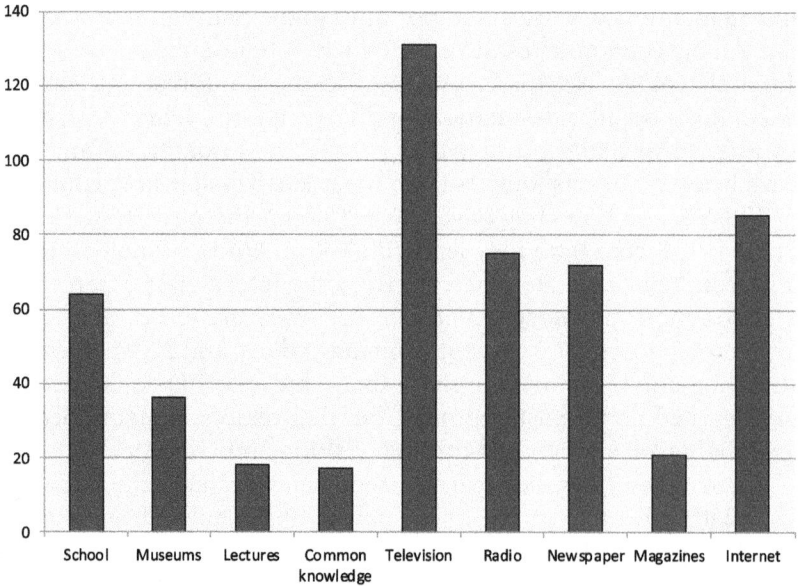

Figure 6.7. Survey result: How have you learned about new archaeological discoveries in Belize? Courtesy of the author.

When asked if they believe it is important to understand and learn about ancient Maya culture, 85.6 percent said "yes": "It is our history, our culture;" "It makes us who we are! It's a part of our identity when it comes to our culture, ethnicity, and heritage;" "They are a part of our Belizean History." The rest were not sure or did not answer. No one marked "no."

When asked what kind of outreach programs about history or archaeology they would be likely to participate in, 61.9 percent said tours, 35.7 percent said workshops, 27.6 percent said lectures, 25.2 percent said fairs, and 16.2 percent said performances.

66.2 percent of respondents marked that they believe ancient Maya history is a part of their family's history. 12.4 percent said "no" and 13.3 percent said they were not sure. The rest left the question blank. Similarly, 57.6 percent of the people believe that the archaeology of Belize is a part of their family's history. 13.8 percent said "no" and 19.5 percent were not sure.

When asked how proud people were of their ethnic identity, 87.7 percent said they were very or mostly proud. Some people did not answer and no one answered in the negative. People boasted their pride in their ethnicity ("Because I am proud to be Black and Creole and Belizean at the same time;" "Because I am who I am"). A Garifuna man says, "we are the only black people in America which still have our language and culture alive." A Mestizo says "[I'm proud] Because I'm a

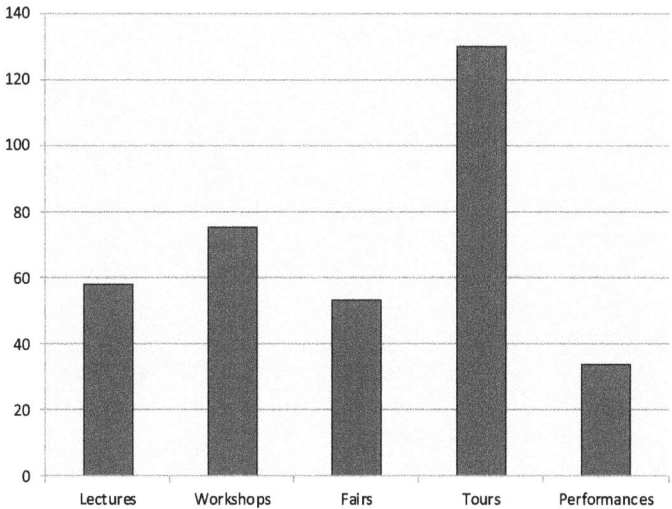

Figure 6.8. Survey result: What kind of outreach programs about history or archaeology would you be likely to participate in? Courtesy of the author.

full Mestizo." A Maya, "cause im [sic] a 100 percent Maya person." And others, "Because I am Creole!!" "My culture is diverse and beautiful, and so is my country." Two participants checked off "a little proud." One commented, "I don't quite see much point of finding pride in it because we're all the same species."

A majority of respondents (84.3 percent) said they are comfortable sharing their ethnic background with other Belizeans. 59.5 percent of respondents say they are comfortable identifying themselves anywhere. Of those who say there are certain places where they feel more comfortable (18.1 percent), a handful note that those places are regions where more people of a similar ethnic background live or frequent. Some mentioned they feel uncomfortable outside of their region or when they encounter racist people.

Lastly, I asked if respondents believed that contemporary Maya people are descendants of the ancient Maya. 63.3 percent said "yes," 5.7 percent said "no," and 20 percent were not sure. Those who were not sure said things like, "Maybe, but so long ago, doesn't really count. Genes far away from people who did (the temples). Mixed now with other genes now." Those who say "no" point out that the Maya in Belize are all from Guatemala or other places and are thus not connected to the ancestors in Belize. (In their history of colonization, the Maya of Belize were pushed into the high mountains in the sixteenth through eighteenth centuries; not all the Maya left during this period. Migrations into Belize occurred in the late nineteenth and twentieth centuries when people were escaping the Caste Wars in Mexico and taxation in Guatemala [Twigg 2006, 28–29]).

Informal Interviews

Although not one wanted to be recorded, I did have a number of longer conversations with people who did not want to fill out a survey but were happy to speak to me. In the survey answers, ethnic or racial tensions did not surface although I was trying to extract that with some of my questions. However, in some of these longer and deeper conversations, those tensions did come out. One gentleman in the Toledo District who identifies as Garifuna said that he did not even want to see the survey because he knows it will be about "Indians," and he is not interested. "Everything is Maya, Maya, Maya. Even when I lived in the States, that's all that was promoted about Belize was the Maya . . . because that's where the money is." He wants to learn more about what is being done in Garifuna archaeology and heritage. He knows there are a few archaeologists who study Garifuna sites, and he wants to see that promoted more.

A gentleman in the Toledo District who identifies as Creole spoke to me for almost an hour about land rights and indigeneity. He claims that the Maya in Belize are not Indigenous (to Belize) because they moved there from Guatemala or Mexico and are not connected to the ancient ruins in Belize. He says they receive benefits and land rights as Mayas but he does not because he is Creole even though his ancestors have been in Belize longer. "Black people can't live in their villages," he says and may be alluding to the recent incidents in Santa Cruz village, "Instead of creating unity, they are creating divisions. 'That's my community. You can't be there.'" Although his grandmother and aunt were Maya, since his grandfather was black, he is deemed Creole and has no Indigenous rights.

In the Belize District, two ladies, on separate occasions, who identify as Creole noted that they do not like going to certain villages because some people speak only Spanish. "If they are Belizean, they should be able to speak English." Also in the Belize District, a Rastafarian gentleman said he felt uncomfortable going to places like San Pedro (a tourist town located on Caye Ambergris) because he fears people "might take me for someone else violent."

Also on two separate occasions, a Caucasian male from the Orange Walk District and one from the Belize District had conversations with me where they expressed that villagers were lazy, wanted hand-outs, and did not want to work. This repeats similar remarks I heard from a Caucasian female in the Cayo District when I first surveyed people in 1999.

A Creole man in the Corozal District, where there is a mainly Mestizo population, exclaimed "did you notice there aren't many black people in this town?" He said that the Hispanics believe they are above the black people and make it difficult for black people to get ahead. He cannot get things approved due to politics.

In another long conversation, a gentleman from the Belize District wished for more help from the IA to train local people to be able to give tours to lesser known archaeological sites. He also noted that the youth do not care to learn about their heritage, including things like the medicinal value of the plants in the rainforest.

Comparison to 1999 Cayo District Results

In the small survey I conducted in 1999 in the Cayo District as an undergraduate student, some of the same themes had emerged back then. Forty-seven of the fifty people surveyed (94 percent) felt positive about archaeology with some of them writing of its value to the economy in the form of tourism while others wrote about the importance of understanding the past.

One of the people who had negative feelings about archaeology said it was because Belizeans are not encouraged to participate in the field. Seventy-eight percent felt positive about non-Belizeans working on archaeological projects in Belize and thought so because they believed foreign archaeologists are better educated. However, like in my recent survey, some people expressed worry that artifacts were being taken out of the country or that reports were not being shared with Belizeans. And, again, many expressed that more Belizeans should participate in archaeological projects.

Ninety-eight percent of those surveyed in 1999 reported that past cultures were important to understand and sites preserved. Participants noted that knowledge of the past helps people appreciate what they have or that past cultures may have something to teach about sustainability. Television was noted as the most popular means of finding out about local archaeology, just as it was in the 2016 survey. And again, public lectures were listed as the least popular medium for learning about local archaeology (Dion 2002).

In both the 1999 and 2016 project, I was unable to convince Mennonites to take the survey. In 1999, I had more males than females take the survey, and I had noted that oftentimes, when I approached a woman whose husband was present, she would defer to him to take the survey. In the recent 2016 project, I ended up with more females than males. I did not encounter women deferring to their husbands this time. Some of the reasons I ended up with more females this time may be researcher bias; perhaps I inadvertently approached more women since I am a woman. I also approached people in plaza and shop areas, where there may have been more women.

Recommendations

For much of my trip, I believe I would have done better in some towns if I had stayed two or three more days to allow people to get to know me. I unfortunately did not have the time to stay longer. I recommend to researchers who want to collect information in a large area to try to fund a longer trip or several trips in order to spend more time in each area of study.

Another general tip for researchers is to not let your nerves get to you. Each time I started in a new town, I found I felt nervous going up to talk to people. I felt like an outsider and just another researcher. But, even though some places were easier than others, everyone was friendly and kind, and many were eager to talk. I had to constantly work up my nerve.

The sun would set around six, and I was told driving at night was dangerous and I should not go out at night alone. I had to thoughtfully plan when I should leave one area for the next. I needed time in case I got lost or had car trouble, and I had to arrive at my destination with time to get dinner while it was still light. I was subject to a harmless form of catcalling throughout my trip, and I even sometimes used it as an opportunity to get someone to fill out a survey. However, I arrived at one town just before sunset and by the time I was ready for dinner, I had to walk a couple of blocks to the nearest eatery in the dark. That time, I experienced some aggressive street calls. In addition, I opted to carry my laptop with me at all times since I was warned that keeping it in the car or my rooms was not secure. Carrying my laptop in a backpack on me at all times for weeks at a time in the heat was strenuous and brought on back issues. Other researchers may wish to invest in a tablet to work from to lighten the load.

About a third of the way through my trip, I experienced mental fatigue from collecting surveys. Although I learned a lot, I grew tired of asking people the same questions whether it was taking a survey verbally or giving my spiel when asking people to write the survey themselves. There were days I was asking thirty or more people. This is something other researchers should consider when organizing such research. Either plan several breaks throughout the trip, plan to collect surveys over a number of different trips, or hire additional surveyors to help.

Conclusions

This short project should be considered the beginning of a possible larger project. Despite gathering a small number of surveys from the population and the short research period over a large area, what was learned can be applied to bigger projects or expanded upon if someone would like to take a closer look at each community or District. Outside of the survey results, general conversations with people and experiences in different locations, even if some of those experiences contained setbacks, added qualitative value to the results.

During my trip, there were new discoveries at the archaeological site of Xunantunich in San Ignacio. In general conversation, people would mention that they had heard about it on the radio or saw it on the television news. People also mentioned the destruction of Noh Mul that was on the news again when suspects were sentenced for the crime. And, people did know about the recent issues over the destruction of a site in the village of Santa Cruz that I mentioned earlier. The IA is doing a good job of making sure major discoveries are in the news to keep archaeology and its importance in the minds of citizens.

Most citizens feel positively about archaeology. They believe the ruins of the ancient Maya are a part of their national heritage. They are proud that many people from around the world want to come to Belize to see its beauty and explore the archaeological sites. There are unfortunately obstacles that keep most citizens from the opportunity to visit the sites themselves. Many people say they do not have enough time outside of work to be able to make the trip. Many people do not have their own vehicles and public transportation does not go to the far, off-the-main-road sites. It is too expensive for an average family to rent a car or take taxis. For many, even the admission fees at the archaeological parks are cost-prohibitive, especially if trying to go with families. Those who live closer to sites remember going with their school on field trips, but those farther away did not even have that opportunity.

The IA does much community outreach. They host archaeological fairs in town centers, have information booths at other town events, and communicate through news channels and social media. Although they offer reduced admission rates for citizens, the rates are still unfortunately high for many and it can be difficult for people to travel to the sites. Perhaps the IA could find grants to host events where buses could pick people up from town centers and hold tours to and at local sites. As noted in the survey results above, the type of educational program most people were interested in was tours. People would like to go to the places to learn about heritage rather than hear about the sites at a lecture.

Most of the archaeologists that work in Belize are from other countries. They usually fund their research and travel through grants. Archaeologists could include in their funding requests opportunities for community involvement. That could include bussing to sites, school programs, and community fairs. Efforts by archaeologists and the IA could help bring more people who otherwise would not be able to afford the opportunity to the sites.

Many surveyed also mentioned the lack of local archaeologists and attribute that to the lack of formal education in that area of study. The

IA, with the help of practicing archaeologists should push for archaeological study at the local colleges. Practicing archaeologists could serve as guest lecturers and incentives can be made for academics to remain in Belize to teach at the colleges. In addition, internships and apprenticeships can be set up for local students of archaeology to work alongside practicing archaeologists. Scholarships can be set up to send promising students to universities in the United States and Europe with the stipulation they return to Belize for their archaeological work.

In addition, there was some criticism that most archaeology is done on ancient Maya sites. Although there are a few archaeologists doing work on colonial sites and sites for groups of other ethnic backgrounds, the IA could provide incentives for more scholars to pursue those under-researched areas and encourage more community outreach in those subject areas. Belizeans can learn more about and be proud of the history of the many ethnic groups that have contributed to and make up the country.

Acknowledgments

I would like to thank Dr. Robert Preucel and the Haffenreffer Museum of Anthropology, Brown University for funding and supporting this research. I also thank Dr. Patricia McAnany for the project idea and for providing support through InHerit: Passed to Present by connecting me to InHerit staff that work in the area. I especially thank Dr. Claire Novotny who was working for InHerit at the time of this research. She helped me shape my proposal, answered numerous questions, connected me to the Director of the Institute of Archaeology in Belize, and is probably the only reason I was able to secure a research permit. She also guided me and served as a contact during my time in Belize and introduced me to community members. Staff members at the Brown University Human Research Protection Program were friendly and helpful in ensuring my research was sound. A big thank you to Nicole Larrondo for translating my surveys and consent forms into Spanish and a thank you to Daniel Denci for translating Spanish survey answers into English. Thank you to Dr. John Morris of the Institute of Archaeology at the National Institute of Culture and History for the research permit and research tips. I give a huge thank you to Dr. Christy DeLair for helping me formalize my research plan, reviewing my proposals, answering many questions, and offering encouragement throughout the process of this project. And, finally, I wish to thank my husband

Larry and daughter Leona for holding down the fort and keeping the cat alive while I was out of the country.

Geralyn Ducady, MA, Director, Newell D. Goff Center for Education and Public Programs, Rhode Island Historical Society, and Educational Affiliate, Haffenreffer Museum of Anthropology, Brown University.

Notes

1. Belize Institute of Archaeology (IA) website: http://www.nichbelize.org/ia-general/welcome-to-the-institute-of-archaeology.html.
2. InHerit: Passed to Present website: http://in-herit.org.
3. Alcaldes are traditional Maya leaders who also serve as adjudicators in village disputes. The chairman heads the village council—institutions that were set up by the British government when Belize was a colony. Villages thus have two leaders.
4. A collapsed section of limestone bedrock, or sinkhole, that exposes the water table. Usually circular.
5. Over one hundred people attended the exhibit opening and it was generally well-used by the community. Unfortunately, a fire destroyed the building in May 2017.

References

Aguacate Homestay Program. 2015. Accessed 19 August 2015. http://aguacate-belize.com.
Atalay, Sonya. 2006. "Indigenous Archaeology as Decolonizing Practice." *American Indian Quarterly* 30(3&4): 280–310.
Atalay, Sonya, Lee Rains Clauss, Randall H. McGuire, and John R. Welch. 2014. "Transforming Archaeology." In *Transforming Archaeology: Activist Practices and Prospects*, ed. Sonya Atalay, 7–29. Albuquerque, NM: Left Coast Press.
Dion, Geralyn. 2002. "Belizean Perspectives on Archaeological Research." In *Sacred Landscape and Settlement in the Sibun River Valley: XARP 1999 Archaeological Survey and Excavation,* Occasional Publication No. 8, ed. Patricia A. McAnany, 219–27. Albany, NY: Institute for Mesoamerican Studies, State University of New York.
Lea, Joanne, and Suzie Thomas, eds. 2014. *Public Participation in Archaeology.* Suffolk, England: Boydell & Brewer.
McAnany, Patricia. 2014. "Transforming the Terms of Engagement Between archaeologists and Communities: A View from the Maya Region." In *Transforming Archaeology: Activist Practices and Prospects*, ed. Sonya At-

alay, Lee Rains Clauss, Randall H. McGuire, and John R. Welch, 159–78. Albuquerque, NM: Left Coast Press.

———. 2016. *Maya Cultural Heritage: How Archaeologists and Indigenous Communities Engage in the Past.* New York: Rowman & Littlefield.

McGill, Alicia Ebbitt. 2014. "Situating Public Archaeology in Crooked Tree, Belize." In *Public Participation in Archaeology,* ed. Joanne Lea and Suzie Thomas, 129–38. Suffolk, England: Boydell & Brewer.

National Institute of Culture and History and Government of Belize. 2016. *Belize National Culture Policy 2016–2026: Our Cultures, Our Values, Our Identity, Our Prosperity.* Accessed 16 October 2018. https://www.dgft.gov.bz/wp-content/uploads/2017/08/Copy-of-National-Cultural-Policy-Final-Policy-Document-1.pdf.

Novotny, Claire. 2015. "Social Identity Across Landscapes: Ancient Lives and Modern Heritage in a Q'eqchi' Maya Village." PhD diss., University of North Carolina, Chapel Hill.

Parks, R. 2016. "$24,000 for destroying ancient Mayan temple Noh Mul." *Amandala,* 23 April. Accessed 11 November 2016. http://amandala.com.bz/news/24000-destroying-ancient-mayan-temple-noh-mul/.

Peedle, Ian. 1999. *In Focus Belize: Guide to the People, Politics, and Culture.* Brooklyn, NY: Interlink Publishing Group, Inc.

"PM Says 'Outrageous'; Mayans Say 'Justifiable.'" 2015. *7NewsBelize,* 23 June. Accessed 11 November 2016. http://www.7newsbelize.com/sstory.php?nid=32845.

The Statistical Institute of Belize. 2013. *Belize Population and Housing Census 2010: Country Report.* Belmopan: Statistical Institute of Belize. Accessed 11 November 2016. http://www.sib.org.bz/Portals/0/docs/publications/census/2010_Census_Report.pdf.

Twigg, Alan. 2006. *Understanding Belize: A Historical Guide.* Madeira Park, BC: Harbour Publishing.

CHAPTER 7

Archaeology for a Lifetime
Reaching Older Generations through Adult Education Programs

Katherine M. Erdman

Introduction

With more sites around the world coming under threat from war, development, or neglect, it is critical to open a dialog with our communities to convey why the past is worth saving. To do so, we need to appeal to audiences of all ages through different means. Where do we begin? As the preceding chapters have shown, it is possible to connect with younger members of the public by incorporating archaeology into their curricula and through service learning, internships, or educational camps. Adults with children in school may even encounter archaeology by proxy and therefore, continue to be exposed and learn about the discipline. However, once connections to formal schooling have long passed, archaeologists have limited opportunities to engage and share knowledge about archaeology and preservation with the public; the dialog stalls. How then, do we reach older generations, who may be decades out of formal schooling, to inspire and foster a love of archaeology?

An overlooked opportunity for reaching the public is through community education courses. *The Condition of Education 2007* report shows that in 2005, 44 percent of adults (individuals sixteen years or older) in the United States enrolled in a community education program, and 21 percent enrolled in a course for their own personal interest (National Center for Education Statistics 2007, 31). When we examine the demographics of enrollment, we see that participants between the ages of fifty-five and sixty-four make up 20.7 percent of the total and those aged sixty-five or older make up 18.8 percent. This is a largely untapped generation of learners with whom archaeologists might connect.

Educating adult and senior learners has the potential to make broad impacts in the community and in the wider world of archaeology and preservation. There are some things we must consider about the process. This chapter will explore how one might do this through a community education program and consider the different learning styles between older and younger generations of learners. Using survey data I gathered in the fall of 2015 from participants enrolled in an adult education course focused on archaeological ethics and heritage, I offer some thoughts on how archaeologists can most effectively engage with older generations of learners and consider how we may continue to foster a dialog with them going forward.

Continuing Education for Adults and Seniors

There are a lot of great programs for children which can excite a passion for archaeology, but what about older generations? How might we appeal to the more experienced generations in our society and convey the importance of archaeology for the future? Teaching adult education programs is an overlooked, though highly effective, venue for opening a dialog with the public, and more importantly, one's local community. This interpersonal approach ensures the transmission of accurate information and heightens the effectiveness of the learning experience by directly connecting audiences to an expert in the field (Erdman, Introduction).

There are many types of informal educational programs for adults each with their own nuances of meaning and implications, e.g., community education or enrichment, lifelong learning programs, and non-university credit continuing education programs (Jarvis 2010, 56). Here I group a variety of these educational programs under the term "adult education" for simplicity. These types of programs are designed to appeal to lifelong learners, or those seeking to learn outside of formal university settings. Let us consider the benefits to these courses and things to keep in mind when teaching adults and seniors.

Why You Should Consider Teaching Adult Education Courses

There are many advantages to leading adult education programs as an instructor. Many communities across the country already offer some type of adult education. Since many of these are established programs, they may have county and state funding to ensure their continuation in addition to the fees paid by participants. As funding is a rare and precious resource for most archaeologists, teaching within an established organization, i.e., state or community supported enrichment programs, liberates us from having to seek financial support for archaeology-specific education programming. This option is particularly helpful for those looking to make an impact in their community or to meet outreach guidelines for research grants.

Funding for these establishments also pays for specialized administrators who take care of enrollment, finances, and finding locations for classes. There are often quarterly or seasonal course catalogs or advertisements distributed around the community, which is incredibly helpful for reaching audiences who may not have previously considered learning about archaeology while simultaneously providing a new learning opportunity for those who are already passionate about the subject. Administrators also handle the financial side of these programs, including determining and collecting course fees. Most programs have fees, which naturally exclude some from participating; however, the cost is usually very affordable to encourage participation. In sum, offering an archaeology course within one of these programs puts a low or non-existent financial and administrative burden on the instructor and has the potential to reach many participants within the community.

When designing a course, there is the opportunity to be creative allowing for almost infinite topics. For established professionals, it is easy to develop an adult education course using materials and research that one regularly discusses, or one can pick some aspects of their research to examine in a different way or even explore new themes for future research. These courses are also great opportunities for graduate students to gain practice as instructors, interpreters, or education coordinators, and to start organizing future classes or to learn how to present their research to public audiences. In addition to course creativity and development, older learners are challenging and require an instructor to think on their feet; it is a very different dynamic from university students (see below). These experiences are beneficial for all levels and types of professionals. Teaching to an engaged audience helps one flesh out the structure of a course or program, experiment with new ideas, and receive real time feedback about the presentation of new materials.

Organizing and teaching such courses is low commitment, yet has the potential for big payoffs. Some programs have particular requirements for the number of sessions or weeks for each class, while others leave it up to the instructor to decide. My experiences have varied; I have taught two-hour sessions once a week for two to three weeks, while others have been one and a half hour sessions once a week for six to eight weeks. For an experienced instructor, little preparation time is needed to plan lectures or find relevant readings, especially if one is talking about his or her own research. Compared to university courses which may meet up to three times a week, the schedule and preparation required for adult education classes is liberating.

There are also many benefits for learners who participate in adult education programs. These programs make both local and international archaeology visible within the community and have the potential to make lasting impacts. There is repeated contact between students and instructors, sometimes for several weeks at a time, which fosters a continued dialog about archaeology. Because a class meets multiple times, an instructor or a student may follow-up on a particular idea or clarify a point made in a previous week. Repeated contact, or knowing there will be another meeting, also helps keep archaeological issues more alive in the minds of the students. Headlines about archaeology stand out more when it is something they are regularly thinking about. These courses also offer a connection between these groups; archaeologists are reminded of topics that concern the community, while the community is made aware of the challenges or issues facing archaeologists.

One of the greatest benefits to teaching adult education courses is the peace of mind that comes from knowing we can easily and efficiently counteract many of the inaccurate and pseudo-archaeologies presented in popular media with actual facts about our discipline (Pagán 2015). It is incredibly satisfying to hear, "I thought it was always X, but now I see it is Y," or "Wow! Our ancestors were more capable than I gave them credit for," or "I found X information so interesting that I shared it with my friends." Responses such as these have encouraged me to continue working with adult learners.

Finally, as an adult education instructor, archaeologists can help their students become more involved in archaeology. We know better than most when archaeological programs or public events are happening in our community. Word of mouth is a great way to advertise these and encourage greater attendance or participation in local and national archaeology organizations. Similarly, it is easy to point to additional resources, such as book recommendations, scholars to follow, or quality documentaries, so that students can continue to learn and further explore a topic on their own. Encouraging adult learners to continue exploring these materials creates a network of community and global activists and advocates who feel personally connected to the past and invested in its future.

Teaching Adults vs. University Students

Before plunging headfirst into the world of adult education, we must consider our audience and who they are as learners. For some archaeological educators, our teaching backgrounds may be more connected to university students or working with younger school groups where teacher-directed learning is the standard. Adult education, however, is often student-directed or a combination of teacher- and student-directed learning (Merriam 2001).

Modified over the years, the principle of andragogy, the process of adult learning using techniques that are most effective for adult education, refers to all types of adult education, such as training for work or continued voluntary education (Holton, Swanson, and Naquin 2001, 127). While learning is not one size fits all, scholars have identified several characteristics common to adult learning which are summarized as the following (Knowles, Holton, and Swanson 1998):

1. Adult learners need to know why they need to learn something;
2. They prefer to self-direct their own learning;
3. Experiences of the learner are an important resource for future learning;
4. Adults are ready to learn when they need to accomplish a task or solve a problem;
5. Learning is a way of developing problem-based skills to grow as a person and are less likely to be content-oriented; and
6. The desire to learn is internally motivated.

Characteristics two and four are unlikely to manifest within an archaeology-focused adult education course since there is no opportunity for the students and instructors to discuss the learning agenda in advance nor is it likely that they are taking this type of course to accomplish work-related tasks. The other characteristics, however, are highly likely to play a role in the classroom and should be explored further.

The motivations for enrolling and excelling in a course differ between adults and traditional students. Adults often voluntarily seek out experiences and learn a subject to please themselves (internally motivated), whereas for younger students it may be more obligatory (e.g., a school outing, they must go to college, the class fulfills a requirement).

University students may be driven to learn so that they may receive a better grade in their course (externally motivated), unlike adult students who do not receive grades.

Since adult learners come to such courses voluntarily, they may already have some knowledge of or interest in archaeology, which they are looking to advance. For younger students, it may be their first archaeology course and may need foundational information presented more thoroughly. Adults bring a lot of life (and travel) experience with them to the classroom, which influences their approach to learning and radically shapes the classroom. In some of my archaeology courses, for example, adults contributed their memories of visiting a site and their interpretations drew on perspectives from their past work experience as a possible way of solving or approaching a challenge. On the other hand, university students rely less on life experiences, since theirs are more limited, and discussion must sometimes be prompted by the instructor who pulls in outside examples.

Adults can be highly critical learners. When presented with new information, they approach it with a skeptical eye evaluating and critiquing it almost immediately. They look at the big picture—they want to know *why* what they are learning matters and where it fits into their lives or the wider world of knowledge; they want to know the mechanisms behind the idea presented and want to interpret it for themselves. Their orientation toward problem-centered learning is also apparent here. When presented with challenges, many adult and senior learners want to know what archaeologists are doing to solve them or what support is needed to figure out solutions. University students tend to be more trusting and accepting of what is shared with them because we, as instructors, are an authority. They are more prone to ask *what*—they want to build their knowledge base with specific facts and content and are less likely to consider the broader implications of the knowledge in the world.

Considerations for the Classroom

For adult and senior students to get the most out of such courses, we must keep in mind a few points that will enhance their learning experience. As Holton et al. describe, "preparing learners" is critical (2001, 124). As with most learning experiences, it is important for the student to know the organization and direction in which the class is headed. This helps them to recognize the structure of each class and what they can expect to learn from it. I have organized some courses based on theme, while others have been organized temporally or geographically, which I often indicate in the title and course description and outline on the first day. The specific classes within that course tend to follow a regular pattern as well, or if it differs, I am sure to state what they can expect that day. Ultimately, I want to demonstrate that these topics are easy and fun to explore, thus sparking a desire to pursue the topic after the course has ended and to set them upon a strong foundation for further exploration.

Likewise, the "learning climate" must foster effective learning (Holton et al. 2001, 124). It is sometimes not possible for the instructor to select a classroom that meets all of their needs, but we can control the attitude and atmosphere. While information sharing will likely be more one-sided, opening the content for relaxed and welcoming discussion between other learners and the instructor is vital. Adult learners bring many experiences to the discussion which also influences their perspectives on the subject (Jarvis 2010, 125). Being respectful of their interpretations, even if they are misguided, is necessary for continuing and guiding a discussion to the desired conclusion. The dialog must be collaborative, not preachy, and encourage continued reference to the facts presented. Discussion should also be balanced; there will inevitably be a few students who will want to control the conversation and this is where the instructor should intervene to allow others a chance to speak if necessary.

Another important factor to enhance the learning climate is consideration of the physical limitations of the students. On more than one occasion I have had senior learners approach me and thank me for offering a break so that they can stretch their legs or get some coffee during a long class. I have also had a student become upset and drop a class because I did not offer a transcript of a video I showed; it had not dawned on me I might have someone hard of hearing in my class. Likewise, I have found that larger fonts and clean and contrasting colors help aging eyes stare at a screen for longer periods.

Coming away from these courses with strong foundational knowledge and skills for discussing the materials empowers adult learners to continue exploring topics on their own in a way that appeals to their desire for individual growth (Holton et al. 2001, 131).

Adult and Senior Engagement in Action

I began teaching adult and senior learners across the Twin Cities metro in 2012. I have worked with two organizations specializing in adult education, the University of Minnesota's Osher Lifelong Learning Institute (OLLI) and the 728 ISD's (intermediate school district) Active Minds program.

Based in Minneapolis and St. Paul, Minnesota, OLLI describes itself as "a vital community of older adults who are brought together by their intellectual curiosity and love of learning," and maintains the motto, "a health club for the mind" ("Osher Lifelong Learning Institute" 2016). Founded in 1995, the organization today has over a thousand members who participate in volunteer-led courses on a variety of subjects. Participants come from diverse backgrounds, but are primarily well-traveled and highly educated, many of whom are retired professors from the University of Minnesota. Instructors are equally diverse and may include retired professors, local experts, or graduate students who are offered a stipend and the title of OLLI Fellow to teach a course; I first connected with the organization in this latter role and continued as a volunteer.

The Active Minds program, located about forty minutes northwest of Minneapolis, is designed "for the adult looking for intriguing topics, in-depth dialog and new topics to explore" ("Active Minds" 2016). The organization is nestled within the Community Education branch of the county's ISD, the latter of which supports youth through adult programs for local residents. Participants in the Active Minds program are primarily retirees coming from more diverse educational and professional backgrounds than those in OLLI. Instructors for the courses are academic leaders and subject-specific experts or hobbyists. I was recruited to Active Minds by its program director because of my experience as an OLLI Fellow.

Throughout my work with these organizations during and after my doctoral program, I developed a variety of courses based on my own research and topics I was exploring or wanted to have prepared for the future. Courses included the following: "Religion in the Roman Provinces," "Exploring Prehistoric France" (aka, "The Archaeology of Wine and Cheese"), "Art of the Paleolithic," "The History and Practice of Archaeology," "The Peoples of Iron Age Europe," and "Evidence of Rituals from Ancient Europe."

My style of instruction and class organization changed as I gained more experience. The greatest influences, however, were the behaviors and learning styles of my adult and senior students in the classroom. All of my courses focus on lectures and image-heavy PowerPoints with site examples, artifacts, or important tables and graphs. As I do not have required readings for the classes, only suggested readings, the lecture component is vital for discussion. I quickly realized the teacher-directed classroom I was accustomed to with university students was not ideal for adult learners. I needed to focus less on information transmission and more on using the materials from the lecture as a springboard for discussion leading to a teacher- and student-directed learning environment.

In later courses, I started to promote deeper discussion by problematizing possible or existing interpretations of materials and asking for connections to the modern world to contextualize the significance of an issue. I encouraged learners to draw on their own experiences or backgrounds when arguing their perspective and to determine if it accurately fits with the materials presented. Throughout the lecture and discussion, I referenced additional reputable resources, namely books or scholarly websites, which allow them to pursue a topic in greater depth. For some classes, I created free Weebly websites with additional images, links to interactive archaeological information, lists of suggested readings, and relevant documentaries to encourage independent learning after the conclusion of the course.

Some students continued learning by enrolling in new classes I offered or in courses offered by other archaeology instructors. There are several archaeologists who regularly offer courses in the OLLI program and the students regularly tell us how much they enjoy the diverse archaeological courses we offer. Repeatedly enrolling in one to two archaeology courses annually shows there is a high demand for the subject.

Contested Archaeology and Cultural Heritage

In the fall of 2015, I offered a course titled "Contested Archaeology and Cultural Heritage" through both OLLI and Active Minds. The course examined several ethics-based issues and threats facing archaeology today. I was motivated to offer such a course because of my own frustrations with current events. At the time, the media was actively covering the destruction of famous archaeological sites by ISIS. During the broadcasts showing videos and images of sites being blown up or artifacts in museums destroyed and the aftermath of these events, archaeologists were rarely interviewed. Our voices were not reaching the public, which made it difficult for those outside of archaeology to understand the gravity of the situation. I wanted to contextualize this destruction for the public and discuss what it means for the study of our past and its future; I wanted them to hear from an archaeologist, not a reporter or politician. Reflecting further on issues of preservation, I realized there are many threats to our collective archaeological heritage, some rooted in recent historical events, of which the public likely knows little. My primary teaching goal was to have students come away with an understanding of the challenges and complexities facing the study and preservation of archaeological sites and materials. Many of these issues are not black and white; they are connected to broader political, economic, historical, and social matters across the world (Contreras 2010; Davis 2011; Matsuda 1998; Smith 2005).

The format of the courses varied slightly based on the parameters of the organizations. For OLLI, I offered a seven-week course which met once a week for an hour and a half and had a regular attendance of about twenty-eight to thirty-two participants out of the thirty-eight who had enrolled. For Active Minds, I offered a two-week course which met for two hours and had only three participants (this attendance is normal as most of their programs average less than ten participants). The OLLI course proved more conducive for discussion partly because of the additional time allotted for the class and partly because of the group size; each class was a combination of teacher- and student-directed learning. The Active Minds group, being smaller and the class more condensed, was less focused on discussion and more teacher-directed to ensure the main topics and points surrounding them were covered.

While the length of the courses varied between each program, they covered the same topics, but to varying depths. From my previous experiences working with older adults, I know they enjoy complicated issues that can be debated and I selected topics with this in mind. Since there were no required readings for the course, I focused on examples which the students may have already encountered in popular media or could easily find additional information on. I also developed a multimedia course website where they could find relevant articles, books, and videos organized by themes and examples as well as links to advocacy organizations working to protect world archaeological heritage.

During each class, I emphasized at least one theme and one case study and pulled in others when possible. I introduced a topic by presenting the facts and the main points of view for each side using a combination of lectures, summary videos, and/or recorded interviews to appeal to different learning styles. I then opened the floor for discussion where we examined why these issues were problematic, the broader conditions or events surrounding them, and debated what could be done to resolve the conflicting opinions or prevent repeating the same mistakes in the future.

My lectures were geographically biased focusing on examples in the Middle East, Europe, and North America, partly because I am most familiar with these and also because they tend to be reported on by the popular press allowing students to seek out additional information independently. Week One provided a brief introduction to archaeology and a list of threats to archaeological heritage, to which we returned each subsequent week. I briefly described each issue and why it was problematic, and demonstrated how historically rooted actions by some antiquarians led to the commodification of the past for subsequent generations citing examples of recent television shows like *American Diggers* (example of suggested reading: Felch and Frammolino 2011). Week Two built on this idea as we explored the problems of acquiring and owning the past using the example of the Elgin Marbles and the recent attempts by Greece to have them returned from England. I emphasized the importance of archaeological and cultural contexts and how collecting can limit our access to and knowledge of the past (example of suggested reading: Waxman 2008).

Weeks Three and Four examined the threat war poses to archaeological sites and artifacts while focusing on the 2003 looting of the National Museum of Iraq in Bagdad and then on the effects of ISIS today. I presented the timeline of events leading up to the looting of the museum, how it happened, what was lost, political and legal responses to the destruction, and side effects this had across the region (examples of suggested reading: Bogdanos and Patrick 2005; Rothfield 2008). We looked at how it opened up a door to subsequent destruction and looting of archaeological sites and materials, from which ISIS was happily indulging and profiting (example of suggested reading: "Special Issue: The Cultural Heritage Crisis in the Middle East" 2015). I contextualized these events and the broader social, economic, and political factors that allowed them to happen and that also make them hard to stop, such as the limitations of international laws for protecting these sites and the extreme economic disparity in some regions that promotes looting. Week Five followed up on what happens to artifacts when looted from war-torn areas concentrating on the black-market sales of antiquities by groups like ISIS, as well as who buys them (examples of suggested reading: Felch and Frammolino 2011; Waxman 2008). I described how these markets work, what laws exist to prevent or stop such sales, and what is done when an object is determined to be illicit, like some of those from the Getty Museum and other institutions across the United States.

In Week 6, I focused on the issues of modernization and construction, such as dam building and urban development, which threaten archaeological sites around the world. We looked at what happens to materials found during these projects or by chance, particularly those whose ownership and rights are contested by indigenous groups and researchers, such as Kennewick Man (example of suggested reading: Rasmussen et al. 2015). We examined NAGPRA (Native American Graves Protection and Repatriation Act) and indigenous rights and if it is possible to for scientists and descendant communities to compromise on such matters.

In our final session, I had the group revisit the themes and case studies from the previous classes and had them summarize, in their own words, why these issues are problematic and what we all stand to lose. I then talked about other challenges and threats that will become more problematic in the near future, such as a lack of funding to protect sites as well as global climate change. We concluded on a more positive note by identifying what can be done on various levels to ensure the past is preserved for future generations.

Archaeological Heritage Survey

On the first and last days of class, I asked the students to participate in a brief voluntary and anonymous survey, the results of which would be presented at a national archaeology conference, i.e., the 2016 Society for American Archaeology's annual meeting in Orlando, Florida. The objective of these surveys was to determine what people knew about archaeology and heritage preservation before coming into the class and what they take away from it. Is a course like this an effective approach for educating the public about archaeological heritage? Are there better ways we can reach the public? Are there issues within archaeology and heritage preservation that might offer opportunities to open a dialog between professionals and nonprofessionals?

Both surveys included multiple-choice, with the option to circle all answers that apply (note that some response totals may exceed 100 percent for this reason), and short-answer questions. Each survey was one page with questions on the front and back sides. I kept them relatively short to ensure greater participation; having offered questionnaires to adult students in previous classes, I noticed many are unwilling to participate if it is too long. While it would have been ideal to keep the survey results from each class independent to illustrate potential differences, there were not enough data for this; the qualitative and quantitative responses from each class are therefore combined and presented in the subsequent analysis and discussion. Enrollment totaled forty-one participants between the Active Minds and OLLI courses, though some were absent the day(s) the surveys were administered or abstained from participating. The small sample size means these data are exploratory. They also do not represent the general population of adult and senior learners, but rather, a limited demographic as described above, and the results are specific to this particular course and learning environment. However, the data are informative for gauging learning and outcomes one might expect when offering a similar course.

Survey One: Before the Class

The first survey, offered at the start of the first session, had ten questions total, four on the front and six on the back (see chapter appendix). I collected thirty-two surveys between the two classes, however, only thirty-one participants answered questions on the front side and only twenty-nine answered questions on the back. It seems likely they did not realize there were two sides or I did not communicate the instructions clearly enough.

The first survey had two parts, "Background Knowledge" (Questions 1–5) and "Your Experiences" (Questions 6–10). In the "Background Knowledge" section of the survey, I wanted to gauge the participants' basic understanding of archaeology and heritage and to determine where knowledge gaps occur. As some of the course participants likely had some exposure to archaeology already, they may represent a more informed public than if one were to survey random people on the street. With this in mind, it seems more likely that if their answers demonstrate gaps in basic archaeological knowledge, these are likely points that the general public may also be unaware of. In the "Your Experiences" section, I wanted to get a feel for the respondents' first-hand experiences with archaeology. I wanted to see if this exposure was self-directed, and what, if any, archaeological learning opportunities were available to them. I hoped this may offer insights into the ideal method or life-stage to reach all ages of the public about archaeology as well as those specific to older generations.

Questions One and Two asked students to identify the primary subject of archaeological inquiry and what archaeologists do with artifacts when they find them. The answers showed that many of the participants (n=28) have a good understanding that archaeology focuses primarily on the study of past societies through their material culture, rather than the history of the earth (n=2), the written texts from a society (n=4), dinosaurs (n=2), or all of these things (n=4). They also identified that, unlike Indiana Jones, archaeologists do not sell their artifacts or keep them (both had n=0 responses) or bring them home to study (n=8), but in fact take them to museums for further study (n=22).

In Question Three, when asked why preserving information about past cultures and societies is important, the main types of responses can be summarized as follows: (1) we will repeat the past if we do not learn from it, (2) we can only understand the present by learning who we are and where we came from, and (3) our history is a precious resource. These are traditional sorts of statements often used to validate studies of the past and demonstrate that they recognize the past has value in the modern world. While most of the responses focused on using the past to understand our present, a few of the following quoted responses also convey the notion that the future of humanity and the world lies in the past: "To teach children so they don't have to learn it again by themselves"; "To know where we are going, we study where we have been"; and "It is especially important to understand in these times of changing climate/threat to the planet. We need to take action/educate others for preserving the beauty and human history of life on earth." There is a sense of responsibility, necessity, and urgency that people should understand the past for it has inherent value in the modern world and its future.

Question Four asked respondents to identify activities that were problematic for preserving archaeological heritage. This question was designed to be more difficult than the others as some of these activities may be acceptable or permitted in some parts of the world, while discouraged in others; responses strongly erred on the side of caution. Twenty-five identified that buying artifacts from galleries and dealers is problematic. Almost a third of the responses also found that collecting projectile points on private land (n=13), visiting archaeological sides during excavations (n=10), and using a metal detector (n=10) threatened archaeological preservation.

In the final question in the "Background Knowledge" section, of the twenty-nine total responses, almost half (n=13) of the responses identified that archaeological sites are under threat around the globe. Others specified (n=9) that the Middle East is a high-risk area (no doubt from recent events), as well as sites in Africa (n=5) and North America (n=4).

In the "Your Experiences" section of this survey, I wanted to get a feel for the respondents' exposure to and experiences with archaeology. Responses to Question Six showed that most first learned archaeology at some point during their formal education (elementary school, junior high/high school, and college/university); one person responded they learned about archaeology only after formal schooling and for three students, it was their first experience with it. In Question Seven, almost half of the respondents (n=12) reported they learned about heritage or conservation efforts while learning about archaeology; the other half (n=11) said they did not learn about this idea or could not recall (n=5).

Question Eight asked where the respondents get their information about archaeology. Most of the students rely more on traditional media sources—documentaries and television (n=25), newspapers (n=22), and popular texts and magazines (n=18)—to learn about archaeology. Some participate in courses or public lectures (n=14) and/or follow online news (n=11); few seek out professional journals and books (n=4) or blogs (n=3), and three reported other sources including museums, field trips, or travel. It is worth noting here that most of the respondents learn about archaeology passively. Stories or information about archaeology are casually found while channel surfing, opening a newspaper, or flipping through *National Geographic*. While they are interested in the topic, it seems they are not actively searching for primary sources, like scholarly texts. Some do seek out interpersonal learning experiences through lectures and visiting places where history is found, but for some, this may be limited due to physical or financial constraints. These are observations we need to keep in mind when trying to determine the best methods for reaching adult and senior learners and will be discussed below. It is also likely that this trend may change with future adult and senior generations who may be more connected to online digital content.

Question Nine inquired as to why students wanted to take this course. The primary motivations for most can be summarized as: (1) curiosity and general interest in archaeology, (2) current news about site destruction in the Middle East and issues of repatriation in Greece and North America, (3) an interest in traveling and visiting sites, and (4) relating to children or relatives who work in this or similar fields. A few quotable responses hint at something else: "Interested in controversies in archaeology. Curious about how museums and other institutions of 'victors' came to own, control, and interpret other people's cultures and contribute to ethnocide"; "Have always been skeptical of the popular interpretations of archaeological sites"; and "History is suspect—looking backward to justify the present. I am interested in writing a historical novel that presents a non-traditional point of view." Such responses demonstrate a critical view of history. These participants are skeptical and hint at wanting to know the "real truth" about our past, or perhaps this is the influence of sensationalized television promoting alternative archaeological interpretations. Other motivations for taking the class were a bit lighter in tone ("Always a nerd" and "I wanted to do this but in the 1960s my brother got a Master's. I was told I need to type."), and suggest this course allowed them to fulfil an inherent desire they have for the discipline.

The final question in the first survey asked what students hoped to learn from this class. Most hoped to leave with a better understanding of current issues and archaeological ethics. These answers point to a reaction about what they are seeing in the news; they want to understand the situation and to know the perspectives of professionals. Others wanted to have a better understanding of archaeology and how archaeologists interpret sites, one specified wanting to learn about the resources available for continued learning, and another blatantly stated, "I have no agenda."

Survey Two: After the Class

The second survey had six questions total, three on the front and three on the back (see chapter appendix). I collected only fifteen surveys between the two classes; all fifteen participants answered questions on the front side while only twelve answered questions on the back. Fewer wanted to participate in this survey partly because the survey was offered at the end of the class, and partly due to an unseasonably warm November day. With the second survey, I wanted to determine what information students took away from the course, which they see as the greatest threats to archaeological heritage, and possible solutions to these issues.

Question One repeated a question from the first survey asking where archaeological sites were threatened. It was clear half (n=8) still understood that archaeological sites around the globe are under threat, though the Middle East (n=8) really stood out as the most endangered. This was perhaps because of my teaching bias or because of its continuous coverage in the news; however, an overemphasis on certain regions would not explain why Central America (n=4) would stand out on the second survey when I did not offer examples of threatened preservation from this region, and while I did talk about destruction of sites in North America, on the second survey no one specifically identified this location as having threatened sites. In fact, I expected all participants to circle all regions of the world as in danger rather than still selecting particular ones. For future courses, it appears I would need to offer more balanced examples to achieve this result, repeatedly emphasize the types of threats that occur globally, and/or include a map showing affected areas.

In Question Two, all participants circled "All of the Above" identifying a lack of interest in the field, religious/political extremism, war, lack of funding, climate change, illicit antiquities sales, and collecting as problematic issues facing archaeological materials today. I started each class with this list; repeatedly emphasizing these points weekly was demonstrably effective.

Similar to a question from the first survey, Question Three asked, what is archaeology's greatest contribution to understanding the present and future of humanity? Many of the positive attitudes toward archaeological knowledge resurfaced in the answers (e.g., it helps us understand who we are, it helps us learn from the past/not repeat mistakes), but an additional point emerged in some of the comments—archaeology tells us about our shared human history! Comments in the survey and during our final in-class discussion illustrated there was a feeling that we must support areas where the population cannot protect their own heritage for it is part of our heritage too; it appears the course may have inspired a few advocates for archaeological preservation.

In Question Four, most participants saw ignorance or lack of education, war, and lack of funding as the greatest obstacles for protecting archaeological materials; however, responses in Question Five suggest effectively protecting archaeological heritage could be brought about through better international and domestic laws to protect archaeological materials from looting, illicit sales, and war, and through interpersonal educational programs for all ages.

Finally, Question Six wanted to know how we can bring more attention to archaeology and the importance of preserving the past. The main suggestion was education, broadly speaking, but some specified the following potential approaches: "Some short funky TED talks? It is a conundrum"; "Bring it into the schools. Make it real to children. Educate adults! Do we have a Ministry of Culture in our government?!"; "Offer education activities for people who travel to or near archaeology sites—cruises, tours, travel companies"; and "Use speakers who have lived through events." These specific ideas emphasize a preference for interpersonal educational opportunities that stress showing over telling to make the past come alive. Combining the overall comments from Questions Five and Six, the message from adult and senior learners to archaeologists seems to be introducing archaeology at a young age is vital, and fostering its relevance throughout one's life is more likely to produce passionate advocates among the general public.

Discussion

The results of the 2015 Archaeological Heritage Survey offer some insights into how we might reach and continue to inspire archaeological learning in adults and seniors. Thinking back to the principles of adult learning, the survey also illustrates some of these points in action.

Responses from the first survey showed that most students had some exposure to or knowledge about archaeology during their formal education. Most understood that archaeology examines the material culture of past societies and that archaeologists act responsibly with the materials they recover during excavation, i.e., they are not selling artifacts. Their answers also demonstrate that, from this previous exposure, they already recognized the inherent value archaeology offers the world (e.g., a way of understanding the present, shows us past mistakes, etc.). This information is useful for preparing programs for adult learning. We cannot assume everyone will have a strong grasp of archaeology or its worth, however, it is likely that the majority of participants will already have a sense of its importance. As an instructor, you may not have to dedicate as much time to building a basic archaeological foundation because many students may already have this; you can move on to some of the more detailed or challenging topics that will be new to them or incorporate fundamentals into these discussions. After taking the class, when asked about the value of archaeology on the second survey, a new point emerged—archaeology represents our shared human history. I made this point a few times while talking about why we should care about sites in the Middle East being destroyed, but the students really took it to heart because they could contextualize the information and saw for themselves why preserving sites matters. In many ways, adult and senior learners just "get it"; they see why they need to know something, we do not have to preach it to them.

This ability to see the value of archaeology is rooted in their own experiences. Unlike many younger students, older learners come to the classroom with a lifetime of knowledge. This may present itself as life lessons rooted in personal triumphs or failures, e.g., learning from their own mistakes; as memories, such as traveling to places or encountering something that connected them with the past; or as facts rooted in studying a particular subject. As new material is presented during a class, older students bring that time-depth with them and it often manifests as peer-to-peer directed learning. As they discuss and share with the class their impressions of a site they visited twenty years ago which has since been destroyed by war, others gain access to that exclusive first-hand knowledge and use that to shape how they view the present. This form of shared or collective knowledge and experience further enhances their connection to the past and shows, rather than tells, how quickly we can lose history when not preserved or protected.

Connecting to their own experiences in a more meaningful or fulfilling way, was one of the motivators for taking the class. All of the participants voluntarily enrolled in the class, but for a variety of personal reasons. Some wanted to better understand current events they were following in the news, others wanted to get at the "real truth" of history. For many, they wanted to understand sites they visited or read about as a way of reliving and understanding them more profoundly. Others simply wanted to connect with others who are also passionate about archaeology or so that they could relate to family who work in the discipline.

Another motivation for enrolling in the class was to develop the skillset to understand problems facing archaeological preservation today. From the news, many knew of site destruction in war-torn areas, but did not necessarily know until after the class that archaeological sites around the globe face a variety of physical threats or the contexts that allow such things to begin and flourish. While I did not market this as a skill-building course, in many ways it ended up being that, partly because the students drove it that way. Responses from the first survey told me they wanted to learn how to think like an archaeologist—specifically to better understand current events and archaeological ethics. They asked questions about why and how we interpret materials and how we assess ethical situations. Many identified in the first survey that buying artifacts from dealers was problematic but wanted insights into the process that led to it happening in the first place. Most importantly, they wanted to know how to take what they learned in this class and apply it to other situations or contexts, as one would when developing any skill.

Students also wanted to know how to stay informed and how to help protect the past. Interestingly, in the first survey the majority of participants reported getting their archaeological news and information from television or the newspaper and other traditional media (see Erdman, Introduction). However, when asked on the second survey how to educate and foster an interest in archaeology and preservation amongst the public, students pushed for interpersonal learning experiences, and starting these at a younger age, as being the most effective. This is an interesting paradox that we can think about in several ways.

As discussed in the Introduction to this volume, traditional media has its vices and virtues. It is relatively accessible either for purchase or through libraries. Printed materials, in particular, are effective for conveying a lot of information and are useful for educating the reader on a subject. Traditional media also often lack connection, whereas this is one of the greatest strengths of interpersonal experiences. When a member of the public interacts with an expert in the field of archaeology or gets to see and touch an artifact, the past becomes more real. While interpersonal communication may be less accessible overall and may not be able to convey the same quantity of information as traditional media, it offers the participant sensory information that cannot always be conveyed through text or photos.

We may also consider that interpersonal learning becomes more meaningful because it is less accessible than traditional or digital media; it is a special experience. Not many people can recall "that time when I read that archaeology book," but many can remember the experience of going to a museum and seeing an object on display or a special exhibit about mummies. Experiences are not common; they are not our everyday. Interpersonal experiences lead to more meaningful and longer lasting learning because they stand out in our memories. Connected to this is the value of peer-to-peer and intergenerational learning. In many ways, hearing about someone else's experiences gives us a point of reference to history; this is how history comes alive. Sharing that experience gives it value and motivates one to embrace and protect the past so that it can be shared with another generation.

A final point to consider is the preference of adult and senior learners for traditional media and interpersonal approaches over digital media. Are we looking at an actual rejection of the more impersonal digital world, or is this a generational preference? While more research would be needed to conclude anything definitive on this matter, it is something worth examining. The current generation of adult and senior learners prefer traditional methods for learning, but will subsequent generations feel the same when they reach that age? Will my generation, the last to remember life before the internet, prefer digital media over print or interpersonal experiences, or is there something inherent that comes with age that encourages direct interaction and contact? We cannot assume the learning preferences for the current senior generation will hold true for subsequent generations; effective and preferred teaching methods will have to be reassessed regularly over time.

Conclusions

The answers to the challenges facing archaeology will not be easily fixed. It will require the combined efforts of archaeologists and those outside of the discipline to introduce change. There was a consensus amongst my students that the best chance for protecting archaeological heritage is to incorporate it more rigorously into K–12 curricula or at least develop interpersonal opportunities, such as archaeology summer camps or special classroom programs, for young students. Fostering a love of (or at least a respect for) archaeology at a young age is vital for the future of heritage preservation as these children will one day be making policies that affect sites and artifacts and determining funding for such projects.

In addition to engaging young people, we must not forget adults and seniors. Working with lifelong learners through community education programs can be a refreshing opportunity to open dialogs with captive and passionate audiences who are willing to engage in critical debate. My students embrace the opportunity to ask professionals more about particular topics and cultures. They want to know what inspires us and to hear about our research and what we do (including the mundane). Many joked that they are living out their dreams vicariously through my experiences. Being an archaeologist is a fascinating and mysterious career path that almost always sparks an interest in those outside of the discipline that professionals often take for granted.

Another benefit to working with adult and senior learners is that they are already in positions to promote change and have the time or financial means to become advocates for archaeological heritage. Many, as retirees, could get involved as volunteers if we offer opportunities for participation. Through their life and career experiences, they often bring alternative and thoughtful perspectives and practical solutions to some of our most difficult issues. Developing connections with professionals or retirees who have backgrounds in law, primary or secondary education, nonprofits, journalism, or social justice, for example, all have the opportunity to contribute knowledge, resources, and professional networks that can help advance and foster an interest in archaeological stewardship amongst the general public. Traditionally an active voting demographic, they can also support archaeological interests at fundamental levels. They are advocates willing to get involved with local and national archaeology chapters, to find new events and opportunities to participate in the community, and to share information they learn from such courses with others.

It is critical to share what we know with those who are willing to listen and to encourage younger generations of archaeologists to be active in sharing their knowledge with the general public. Finding audiences who are receptive to accurate information about contemporary issues facing in our field is vital to its future. We need to take advantage of the fact that archaeology is one of those rare disciplines that captivates nonprofessionals enough to bring them back into the classroom through adult education programs. Opportunities to share our knowledge with such audiences should be welcomed, not viewed as a burden, because these are the people that will make our efforts of preserving the past easier and more successful.

Katherine M. Erdman, PhD, Visiting Scholar, University of Minnesota.

Appendix: Archaeological Heritage Survey 2015

Archaeological Heritage Survey 2015: Part I

Instructions
This survey is voluntary and anonymous. The qualitative and quantitative data gathered from these questions will be presented by your instructor, Katherine Erdman, at an archaeology conference in April 2016. The aim of this survey is to see what non-professionals know about archaeology and heritage preservation prior to the course.

Part I: Background Knowledge (prior to this course). Please circle all that apply.

1. Archaeology is the study of . . .
    a. The history of the earth
    b. Past human societies through written materials
    c. Past human cultures through material remains
    d. Dinosaurs and extinct animals
    e. All of these

2. When archaeologists find something, they . . .
    a. Get to keep it
    b. Take it to a museum
    c. Can sell it to fund their next excavation
    d. Bring it home to study

3. Why is preserving information about past cultures and societies important?

4. Which activities are problematic for preserving archaeological heritage?
    a. Buying copies of objects from the museum gift shop
    b. Collecting projectile points on family property
    c. Buying artifacts from galleries and dealers
    d. Visiting archaeological sites during an excavation
    e. Using a metal detector

5. Where are archaeological sites currently under threat?
    a. Africa
    b. Asia
    c. Australia
    d. Central America
    e. Europe
    f. Middle East
    g. North America
    h. South America

Part II: Your Experiences

6. When did you first learn about archaeology?
    a. Elementary school
    b. Junior high/High school
    c. College/University
    d. After formal schooling
    e. Never, this is my first class

7. Did you also learn about cultural heritage, heritage management, or archaeological preservation?
    a. Yes
    b. No
    c. Do not recall

8. Where do you get your information about archaeology?
    a. Scholarly journals and books
    b. Popular texts and magazines
    c. Newspapers
    d. Online news sites
    e. Blogs

f. Courses and public lectures
   g. Documentaries and television
   h. Other:

9. Why were you interested in this course?

10. What do you hope to take away or learn from this course?

Source: Courtesy of the author.

Archaeological Heritage Survey 2015: Part II

Instructions
This survey is voluntary and anonymous. The qualitative and quantitative data gathered from these questions will be presented by your instructor, Katherine Erdman, at an archaeology conference in April 2016. The aim of this survey is to see what non-professionals have learned about archaeology and heritage preservation after taking the course.

1. Where are archaeological sites currently under threat?
   a. Africa
   b. Asia
   c. Australia
   d. Central America
   e. Europe
   f. Middle East
   g. North America
   h. South America

2. What are some of the major threats to archaeology today?
   a. Lack of interest in the field
   b. War
   c. Climate change
   d. Collecting
   e. Religious/political extremism
   f. Lack of funding
   g. Illicit antiquities sales
   h. All of the above

3. What do you think is the greatest contribution archaeology can make to understanding the present and future lives of humans?

4. What do you see as the greatest obstacle to protecting archaeological heritage?

5. What suggestions do you have for improving the protection of archaeological heritage?

6. How can we bring more attention to archaeology and the importance of preserving the past?

Thank you very much for your participation!

Source: Courtesy of the author.

References

"Active Minds." 2016. *ISD 728 Community Education.* Accessed 23 May 2016. https://www.728communityed.com/registry/classlist.asp?catID=22055.

Bogdanos, Matthew, and William Patrick. 2005. *Thieves of Baghdad: One Marine's Passion for Ancient Civilizations and the Journey to Recover the World's Greatest Stolen Treasures.* New York: Bloomsbury Publishing.

Contreras, Daniel A. 2010. "Huaqueros and Remote Sensing Imagery: Assessing Looting Damage in the Virú Valley, Peru." *Antiquity* 84(324): 544–55. http://works.bepress.com/daniel_contreras/10/.

Davis, Tess. 2011. "Supply and Demand: Exposing the Illicit Trade in Cambodian Antiquities through a Study of Sotheby's Auction House." *Crime, Law and Social Change* 56(2): 155–74. doi:10.1007/s10611-011-9321-6.

Felch, Jason, and Ralph Frammolino. 2011. *Chasing Aphrodite: The Hunt for Looted Antiquities at the World's Richest Museum.* Boston: Houghton Mifflin Harcourt.

Holton, Elwood F., Richard A. Swanson, and Sharon S. Naquin. 2001. "Andragogy in Practice: Clarifying the Andragogical Model of Adult Learning." *Performance Improvement Quarterly* 14(1): 118–43. doi:10.1111/j.1937-8327.2001.tb00204.x.

Jarvis, Peter. 2010. *Adult Education and Lifelong Learning: Theory and Practice,* 4th ed. London: Routledge.

Knowles, Malcolm S., Elwood F. Holton, and Richard A. Swanson. 1998. *The Adult Learner,* 5th ed. Houston, TX: Gulf Publishing.

Matsuda, David. 1998. "The Ethics of Archaeology, Subsistence Digging, and Artifact Looting in Latin America: Point, Muted Counterpoint." *International Journal of Cultural Property* 7(1): 87–97.

Merriam, Sharan B. 2001. "Andragogy and Self-Directed Learning: Pillars of Adult Learning Theory." *New Directions for Adult and Continuing Education* 2001(89): 3–13. doi:10.1002/ace.3.
National Center for Education Statistics. 2007. *Condition of Education 2007*. Washington, DC: US Department of Education. Accessed 17 January 2017. https://nces.ed.gov/pubs2007/2007064.pdf.
"Osher Lifelong Learning Institute." 2016. *Osher Lifelong Learning Institute, Regents of the University of Minnesota*. Accessed 23 May 2016. http://olli.umn.edu/.
Pagán, Eduardo. 2015. "Digging for Ratings Gold: American Digger and the Challenge of Sustainability for Cable TV." *The SAA Archaeological Record* 15(2): 12–17.
Rasmussen, Morten, Martin Sikora, Anders Albrechtsen, Thorfinn Sand Korneliussen, J. Víctor Moreno-Mayar, G. David Poznik, Christoph P. E. Zollikofer, et al. 2015. "The Ancestry and Affiliations of Kennewick Man." *Nature* 523(June): 455. http://dx.doi.org/10.1038/nature14625.
Rothfield, Lawrence. 2008. *The Rape of Mesopotamia: Behind the Looting of the Iraq Museum*. Chicago: University of Chicago Press.
Smith, Kimbra L. 2005. "Looting and the Politics of Archaeological Knowledge in Northern Peru." *Ethnos* 70(2): 149–70. doi:10.1080/00141840500141139.
"The Cultural Heritage Crisis in the Middle East." 2015. Special issue, *Near Eastern Archaeology* 78(3). http://www.jstor.org/stable/10.5615/neareastarch.78.issue-3.
Waxman, Sharon. 2008. *Loot: The Battle over the Stolen Treasures of the Ancient World*. New York: Times Books.

PART III

THE FUTURE OF ARCHAEOLOGY, EDUCATION, AND PRESERVATION

CHAPTER 8

Best Practices in Archaeology Education
Successes, Shortcomings, and the Future

Jeanne M. Moe

Introduction

At this writing, I can count a little more than thirty years of experience in archaeology education. My interest and involvement in archaeology education began when I was a graduate student in the Department of Anthropology at the University of Utah in the mid-1980s. Whenever the department got a call from a school requesting an archaeologist to come to the classroom, I always volunteered. Perhaps, I should not have volunteered because it took a lot of time away from my studies and other projects, but I could not leave it alone. It was far more challenging than I thought it would be and, while I could not put my finger on it, I knew that I was missing some piece of knowledge or experience that would make my lessons work well in a classroom. Even as inexperienced as I was, I could see that the students were not learning as much as I had hoped they would and I sensed that they might have been confused. In other words, there was much more to it than I thought and I wanted to know more about it.

The field of education so intrigued me that I discontinued my graduate work in archaeology and transferred to the Department of Education at the University of Utah. Even with a secondary teaching certificate under my belt, I still realized that I was missing some important aspect of education and teaching for conceptual understanding.

After graduate studies in both archaeology and education, I landed a job with the Bureau of Land Management (BLM) at the Utah State Office in Salt Lake City. As the assistant cultural resources program lead for the state, I responded to all of the requests for archaeology education in local classrooms. I honed my skills and my presentations improved, but persistent questions kept bothering me. What do young people really understand about archaeology? Are they learning something of value or am I confusing them? How can I better engage them in active learning about science and archaeology?

In early 1990, I found myself in the right place at the right time. The 1988 amendments to the Archaeological Resources Protection Act (ARPA) gave the federal land managing agencies their marching orders to create educational programs that would teach the public about "the significance of archaeological sites and artifacts on public lands and the importance of protecting them" for present and future enjoyment and for their scientific value (16 U.S.C. § 470). In partnership with Utah Interagency Task Force on Cultural Resources, the BLM spearheaded a project to bring archaeology education to the state. With my credentials in both archaeology and education, I landed a spot on the project team. Our effort became the Intrigue of the Past Archaeology Education Program and our main education product was *Intrigue of the Past: Investigating Archaeology* (1992). In 1992, we presented *Intrigue of the Past* to our colleagues at the Society for American Archaeology (SAA) conference in Pittsburgh, Pennsylvania. Many wanted to join with us to create archaeology education programs for their states. In 1993, Project Archaeology was born out of the Intrigue of the Past program and the BLM's new national Heritage Education Program. In 2001, program operations moved to Montana State University (MSU) under a partnership agreement and are jointly sponsored by the BLM and MSU.

Fast forward to 2018. I have been the national lead for Project Archaeology since 1994. While I have learned a great deal, I still have far to go. The most important thing I have learned is the value of research in developing and delivering high-quality educational materials so that they will be used effectively by teachers in their classrooms. We should know what students know and understand about archaeology before proceeding with expensive and/or time-consuming projects.

From my thirty plus years in archaeology education, I can conclude one thing: education is hard. People construct knowledge for themselves and we cannot place the correct knowledge in anyone's brain. Just because we teach some piece of content, and even if we teach it well, we cannot know what learners understand unless we ask them—

and ask them we must. Alarmingly, we may even be starting new misconceptions or perpetuating erroneous preconceptions without even knowing it.

At this point in my career, I am much more an educator than an archaeologist. I have worked primarily in formal education, i.e., teachers and their students, but at Project Archaeology we are frequently asked to provide informal learning opportunities for local school children and youth groups. Although I recently earned a doctoral degree in curriculum and instruction, I need to know even more about the huge and diverse field of education. Because education changes frequently and sometimes rapidly, I must be able to follow the latest trends and predict the future needs of both classroom teachers and informal educators. The task is almost overwhelming, but it is essential that we all persevere for archaeology education to ever hold a significant place in modern education. The remainder of this chapter will focus on my personal experiences with archaeology education in formal school settings, largely through Project Archaeology, the program that I helped develop and have managed since 1994.

Formal Education

In January 1990, two BLM archaeologists and two local educators on contract to the BLM, began our research for what became Utah's Intrigue of the Past Archaeology Education Program. We examined all of the existing archaeology education materials that we could find and several conservation education programs including Project WILD (www.projectwild.org) and Project Learning Tree (www.plt.org). We decided to model an archaeology education program after these two successful programs. Both programs were based on solid educational research at the time, provided supplementary science and social studies curricula to educators, and allowed for maximum flexibility in both classrooms and informal settings. Based on our research, our earliest conclusions were:

—Classroom teachers do not have time to add anything new to their already packed curricula; our materials would have to help them teach what they were already required to teach.

—Archaeologists cannot do the job of educating the public alone; we must have help from both formal and informal educators.

—The participation of descendant communities is essential for creating accurate, inclusive, and culturally sensitive educational materials.

Based on our findings and classroom testing in the 1990–91 academic year, we created and published *Intrigue of the Past: Investigating Archaeology* in 1992. We delivered the materials to Utah teachers and informal educators through professional development workshops. With the help of a grant from the Utah Humanities Council, the program took off statewide. Between 1992 and 2000, fourteen other states adopted the curriculum and began offering a revised version of the first activity guide, *Intrigue of the Past: An Activity Guide for Fourth through Seventh Grades* (Smith et al. 1993). The national program became known as Project Archaeology in 1994 and the program has been established in thirty-eight states and remains active in thirty-three states (www.projectarchaeology.org/state-programs). An additional six states are currently developing new programs.

Early formative assessment of the *Intrigue of the Past* activity guide showed that non-native public school students connected with the descendants of Native Americans who lived in Utah through a series of lessons on rock art and the prevalence of vandalism at these important sites. When asked what they would remember in a year after instruction in archaeology, many students replied (paraphrased from written questionnaires), "Vandalism of archaeological sites hurts the living descendants of precontact peoples." We knew that we had something. Archaeology seems to be uniquely qualified to teach deep understanding of other cultures. Perhaps by stepping into the past, cultural differences become less threatening and learners can more easily concentrate on our commonalities.

While we were pleased with our successes, we soon realized that teachers "cherry picked" the lessons (Ellick 1997; Moe and Letts 1998; Rees 2000). It was and still is a standard practice, however we suspected that students might not make the conceptual links we were hoping for or may not relate the concept taught to archaeology. For example, on a couple of occasions I observed teachers teaching the lesson on classification. In both cases, the teachers had the students classify the doohickey kits (collections of modern artifacts) and never related them to archaeology and how archaeologists use classification in archaeological inquiry. The objects then were just a bunch of stuff, not connected to archaeology nor to science or history.

The Basics of Human Cognition

If we want to be good educators, we need to know something about how people learn and, in some cases, why they do not learn. Just because we "do" archaeology education does not mean that people actually learn what we want them to learn. The field of human cognition is huge and the following is a brief overview and its relevance for archaeology education.

In 1969, cognitive psychologist David Ausubel famously said, "the most important factor influencing the meaningful learning of any new idea is the state of the individual's existing cognitive structure at the time of learning (Ausubel and Robinson 1969, 143). Ausubel's pioneering research on cognitive structures and assimilation of knowledge has guided decades of development and refinement of educational theory and practice, especially in science (Mintzes and Wandersee 2005; Novak 1977, 1993; von Glaserfeld 1989). Clearly, learners construct their own knowledge. We cannot directly transfer what is in our brains to the brains of our learners and therefore "knowledge" may change a bit in the process. If pre-existing knowledge is correct, learners will be in a good position to acquire new knowledge and subsume it into existing cognitive structures. By contrast, brain research clearly shows that misconceptions, unless they are identified and dispelled, can halt learning and the acquisition of new ideas (Bransford, Brown, and Cocking 2000). For example, in the United States and Canada, 95 percent of the population conflates archaeology and paleontology; they think they are one and the same (Ramos and Duganne 2000). Using a course pre-test and post-test, Lauren Ritterbush, professor at Kansas State University (2008, pers. comm.), found that students can persist in conflating the two disciplines even after an entire semester of an undergraduate introductory course in archaeology.

Science educators Mintzes and Wandersee (2005) estimate that about 3,500 articles on science education research had been published at the time of their writing. They make twelve knowledge claims based on these studies. Some of these claims, summarized below, are relevant to archaeology education:

—Learners are not "empty vessels" or "blank slates." Learners bring a diverse set of ideas about natural objects and events to formal science education. Often these ideas are incompatible with those offered by teachers and textbooks and they are often tenacious and resistant to change by traditional teaching strategies.

—As learners construct meaning, knowledge they bring with them interacts with knowledge presented in formal instruction. The result can be a diverse set of learning outcomes. Because of limitations in formal assessment strategies, these unintended outcomes may remain hidden from teachers and from students themselves. Unintended outcomes are products of a diverse set of personal experiences, including direct observation of natural phenomena and events, peer culture, everyday language, and the mass media as well as formal instructional intervention.

—Successful science learners (and all learners) possess a strongly hierarchical, cohesive framework of related concepts and they represent those concepts at a deeper, more principled level. Understanding and conceptual change are epistemological outcomes of the conscious attempt by learners to make meanings. Successful learners make meanings by restructuring their existing knowledge frameworks through cognitive processes. Instructional strategies that focus on understanding and conceptual change may be effective tools. Similarly, strategies that focus on misunderstandings and misconceptions may be particularly effective tools. (Mintzes and Wandersee 2005, 76)

Research clearly shows that without conceptual understandings of both process and content, learning is likely to be superficial and unlikely to be retained after the learning event (Bransford et al. 2000; Moe 2011, 2016). To develop competence in inquiry and mastery of a discipline, ". . . students must (a) have a deep foundation of factual knowledge, (b) understand facts and ideas in the context of a conceptual framework, and (c) organize knowledge in ways that facilitate retrieval and application . . . Deep understanding of subject matter transforms factual information into usable knowledge" (Bransford et al. 2000, 16). For example, historical knowledge is much more likely to "stick" if students build the knowledge themselves through examination of primary resources such as photographs, artifacts or objects, census records, and diaries and formulating robust interpretations based on the evidence that they have analyzed (Henderson and Levstik 2016). Additionally, learners need built-in opportunities to evaluate the efficacy of their own interpretations and to make adjustments based on new or better evidence (Bransford et al. 2000). Hence, concentrating solely on archaeological processes, particularly excavation, to the exclusion of real content will probably make learners think that archaeology is fun and engaging, but it is esoteric and does not contribute important knowledge about the world.

In summary, the implications of learning research for teaching any inquiry-based subject including science and history are threefold:

1. Teachers must draw out and work with the preexisting understandings that their students bring with them.
2. Teachers must teach some subject matter in depth, providing many examples in which the same concept is at work and providing a firm foundation of factual knowledge.
3. The teaching of metacognitive skills should be integrated into the curriculum in a variety of subject areas. (Bransford et al. 2000, 19–21)

All of these implications are relevant and instructive for archaeology education and I will return to them below.

The University of Kentucky Research

Assessment data collected by researchers at the University of Kentucky confirmed our misgivings that upper-elementary aged students might be confused about the relationship between the archaeological record (sites and artifacts) and past human cultures (Levstik, Henderson, and Schlarb 2008; Henderson and Levstik 2016). The fifth-grade students in the Kentucky study learned about archaeology in the classroom using *Intrigue of the Past* and other localized educational materials. As part of their five-week unit on archaeology, they spent one day excavating nineteenth-century slave quarters at the Ashland Estate in Lexington. They enjoyed finding artifacts that someone had touched long ago and engaged enthusiastically in speculating about the lives of these people. The Kentucky researchers found, however, that using objects as evidence was challenging for students. For example, when some students uncovered strips of metal in the slave quarters, they thought that they had uncovered the remains of the Underground Railroad not understanding that "railroad" was a metaphorical term for the escape of enslaved Africans. When asked to explain the lifeways of past peoples, students rarely used artifacts as evidence for their interpretations; they were more likely to revert to familiar historical narratives.

The Kentucky researchers found that the use of the word "story" for interpreting archaeological data was problematic (Henderson and Levstik 2016, 508–9). Students seemed to think that there was only one story that could be derived from a set of archaeological data and the story often took a narrative form. Instead, of developing multiple evidence-based interpretations, students wanted to tell "the whole story" of the past.

While students understood the importance of context in archaeological inquiry, they were often unable ". . . to explain the role context plays in more firmly establishing an artifact's meaning while still allowing multiple interpretations of the lifeways surrounding its use" (Henderson and Levstik 2016, 509). Despite their inability to use context in interpretations, students understood that undisturbed context was an important aspect of preserving sites and artifacts for archaeological inquiry. Artifacts out of context prevented archaeologists from telling the "real story" and they could make only "educated guesses." In summary, students did understand that leaving artifacts in context was important, but they did not really understand why.

Project Archaeology: The Next Generation

By the early 2000s with about ten years of experience under our belts, several surveys on teacher use of our curricular materials, and some of the preliminary results from the Kentucky research, we launched the next generation of Project Archaeology. When we began in Utah in 1990, we never intended to be a national program, but by the turn of the century we had programs in fifteen states and were working with several more states and regions to develop and implement programs. Because of our growing national reach, we knew that Project Archaeology materials needed to meet national education standards and at the same time allow teachers to localize archaeology to meet their state and district requirements.

Since 2001, all Project Archaeology curriculum guides have been developed using the Understanding by Design (UbD) curriculum development model (Wiggins and McTighe 1998, 2005). The materials are designed to guide students from Point A to Point Z for conceptual understanding of archaeological inquiry, the content of the archaeological record, and the importance of protecting archaeological sites. Adopting UbD was one of the best decisions that we have made. The model forces curriculum designers to formulate the Big Ideas or Enduring Understandings that we want people to remember long into the future before designing specific activities that might be fun or interesting. It also forces curriculum designers to outline the evidence of understanding before launching into topics and learning procedures. In other words, how will we know that the students understand? Hence, assessment of learning outcomes is built into the curriculum from the beginning. In many ways, UbD resembles a good archaeological research design beginning with important questions and defining evidence to answer those questions and build knowledge toward important understandings of the human past.

All Project Archaeology materials teach four enduring understandings:

1. Understanding the past is essential for understanding the present and shaping the future.
2. Learning about cultures, past and present, is essential for living in a pluralistic society and world.
3. Archaeology is a systematic way to learn about past cultures.
4. Stewardship of archaeological sites and artifacts is everyone's responsibility.

Similarly, we chose broad themes in archaeology and found authentic data to teach the big ideas or enduring understandings (Erickson 2001). The main Project Archaeology themes are shelter, subsistence, and migration, and a total of four major curriculum guides targeted at grades 3–8 will cover the three themes. At this writing, two of the four guides have been completed and two are under development:

—*Project Archaeology: Investigating Shelter* (Letts and Moe 2009, reprinted in 2012). The guide for grades 3–5 provides the conceptual tools of archaeological inquiry, an investigation of a shelter using authentic archaeological and historical data, and the laws and principles of stewardship. To date, sixteen regional and historic shelter investigations are available to educators and several more are in production.
—*Project Archaeology: Investigating Nutrition* (Agenten, Letts, and Moe 2015). The guide for sixth grade provides the conceptual tools of archaeological inquiry, an investigation of changes in human nutrition at two Neolithic sites on the upper Euphrates River, and the laws and principles of stewardship.
—*Project Archaeology: Investigating Food and Land* (in production). The guide for grades 4–6 will provide the conceptual tools of archaeological inquiry, an investigation of the relationship between people and their environments using archaeological data, and the laws and principles of stewardship. The first investigation will focus on Great Basin foragers and additional investigations are planned for farmers of the Southwest and the Southeast, hunters of the Great Plains, and as many other regions as possible.
—*Project Archaeology: Investigating Migration* (in production). The guide for grades 7–8 will provide the conceptual tools of archaeological inquiry, an investigation of human migration using GIS technology and other primary sources, and the laws and principles of stewardship. The first investigation will focus on the Overland Trail in southern Wyoming and future investigations will focus on other trails across the nation as well as peopling of the Western Hemisphere and precontact migrations within North America.

Additional themes such as artistic expression, the ethics of human subjects research, and sense of place, are emerging as we work on new curricular materials. For example, *Project Archaeology: Investigating Rock Art* (Moe, Agenten, and Letts 2018) focuses on artistic expression on rock faces across North America. Three curricula (*Investigating Fort Meade* [Alegria, Francisco, and Moe 2012]; *Investigating Garnet, a Historic Mining Town* [Alegria et al. 2017]; and *Changing Land, Changing Life* [Doyle, Alegria, and Moe 2016]) focus on the archaeology and history of specific places. *Investigating the First Peoples, a Clovis Child Burial* (Agenten, Alegria, and Doyle 2014) focuses on the ethics of human subject research in archaeology and includes both scientific and descendant community perspectives.

Beginning in 2001, we used the current national standards in social studies (National Council for the Social Studies 1994) and science

(National Research Council 1996) to develop all new Project Archaeology materials. The science standards called for inquiry-based learning across the sciences and the social studies and history standards called for the use of primary sources including artifacts, oral history, and maps in building interpretations about past lifeways and cultures. Our first major curriculum unit, *Project Archaeology: Investigating Shelter*, was published in 2009. We welcomed the advent of the Common Core State Standards (CCSS) in 2010 (Common Core State Standards Initiative 2017); our emphasis on inquiry-based learning, the exclusive use of authentic archaeological data, reading and analyzing primary documents, and the development of evidence-based interpretations fit perfectly with the Common Core. In fact, we were thrilled! It seemed like educational standards had finally caught up to us. In 2015, Stella Estrada, the president of the California Council for the Social Studies said, "Project Archaeology is the Common Core" (Stella Estrada 2015, pers. comm.).

Project Archaeology has engaged descendant community members since 1990, when curriculum and program development first began. Members of each of Utah's tribes were invited to review our early drafts of the activity guide and we implemented their suggestions as much as we possibly could, including the elimination of unacceptable portions of the draft. Over the years we have tried to increase the participation of descendant communities through curriculum development workshops and by including the voice of a descendant in every curriculum piece (e.g., *Investigating Shelter*). In Kentucky and Montana, archaeology educators were able to collaborate with community members who actually lived in the structures under archaeological investigation (Henderson et al. 2016) or remembered the home when their grandparents still lived there (Thompson et al. 2009). The results are pure educational gold. For example, students in Utah who investigated the archaeology of the Tinsley Homestead in Montana, thought that Jackie Thompson, great-great-granddaughter of Lucy and William Tinsley was "a rock star" (Samantha Kirkley 2013, pers. comm.). Similarly, students in rural Kentucky who "met" the poor African Americans and Euro-Americans living in urban shotgun houses during the mid-twentieth century, identified with them and longed to live in a happily integrated neighborhood like Davis Bottom (Henderson and Levstik 2017). We have tried to increase "participation" to full "collaboration" as encouraged by Chambers and Shackel (2004) and have achieved good results with a curriculum project on the Absaroka Agency or Second Crow Agency, where the Crow Indians made the transition from hunting and gathering to settled reservation life in the late 1800s

(Alegria and Moe 2017). Through a series of community meetings, Crow tribal members outlined the enduring understandings for the unit, led the development of the curriculum unit, and helped assess student learning outcomes (Doyle, Alegria, and Moe 2016).

In early archaeology education efforts, content and process were rarely linked (Henderson and Levstik 2016, 506). While archaeology is an excellent tool for inquiry-based instruction and critical thinking, it rarely appears in public school instruction (Smardz and Smith 2000), possibly because of the lack of connection between content and process. Using authentic data in curricular materials is difficult, but I do not think it is possible to teach for conceptual understanding without authentic content. Similarly, the use of authentic archaeological sites and artifacts (although we are forced to use maps and artifact illustrations in the classroom) creates a compelling lesson in the importance of context and the need to leave artifacts in place to develop a comprehensive interpretation of the site. We are shooting ourselves in the foot if we teach the process of excavation exclusively and omit robust interpretations of the data and compelling stories of past human lives.

With the adoption of UbD and formative assessment of all new curricular materials, we have noticed an improvement in conceptual understanding of archaeological inquiry, interpretation of archaeological evidence, the importance of stewardship, and personal responsibility for the protection of archaeological sites (Brody et al. 2014; Henderson and Levstik 2017; Moe 2011, 2016). Although we do not have good comparable data from earlier efforts, the research data show positive and generally consistent results across a variety of classrooms and geographic areas.

Formative assessment of *Project Archaeology: Investigating Shelter* between 2005 and its first publication in 2009, shows that students increased their knowledge of the importance of archaeological stewardship and their personal responsibility for protecting archaeological sites and artifacts following instruction (Moe 2016). Lesson Nine of the guide (Letts and Moe 2009) focuses specifically on preservation laws including the National Historic Preservation Act (NHPA) and the Archaeological Resources Protection Act (ARPA), and provides personal guidelines for visiting or discovering an archaeological site. Additionally, we think that the inclusion of authentic data from real archaeological sites increases students' emotional investment in preservation and protection (Henderson and Levstik 2017). In 15 fourth and fifth grade classrooms from California to the District of Columbia, students clearly demonstrated increased awareness of the need to protect archaeological sites and what they might do to help (Moe 2016). While instructional pre-tests showed that they had a pretty good idea that taking things from archaeological sites was probably not a good idea even before instruction, their answers on the post-test were more specific and diverse, and showed a greater understanding of the reasons for protection.

A case study conducted with 27 fifth grade students, investigated conceptual understanding of five science inquiry concepts and related skills: observation, inference, context, classification, and evidence (Moe 2011, in press). Understanding of these concepts was completely idiosyncratic. When asked in an interview, all of the students in the study, except one, retained some notion of each one of the concepts following instruction with *Investigating Shelter*. Only three students, however, showed no sign of confusion or misunderstanding of any of the five concepts. For example, approximately one-third of the students confused and even conflated classification and context, thinking that they were basically the same thing. The study was encouraging because it showed that it is possible to teach the fundamentals of scientific and historical inquiry through archaeology, but it was also sobering in that it clearly demonstrated how easy it is to perpetuate existing misconceptions or even to start new misconceptions. The study showed that it is essential to identify misconceptions and dispel them before learning can continue and, most importantly, misconceptions can become teachable moments.

Emphasis on conceptual understanding and authentic content have certainly helped students build more robust interpretations of the past (Brody et al. 2014; Henderson and Levstik 2017). Recent assessment of student learning outcomes in rural Kentucky schools showed that, ". . . students had little difficulty in using multiple material culture and documentary sources to build evidence-based historical interpretations or in connecting their study to a preservation ethic" (Henderson and Levstik 2017, 7). Based on all of our assessment research gathered through pre-tests and post-tests, interviews with students, and examination of student homework and other documents, we have found that students are generally in favor of preserving the archaeological evidence of past people's lives. While students can usually identify their own personal responsibility in protecting archaeological sites, i.e., leave artifacts in place, do not damage structures, contact an archaeologist or the authorities, they are not as sure of what to do in the face of development that will destroy archaeological sites or entire historic neighborhoods (Henderson and Levstik 2017). Regrettably, this portion of the curriculum is often omitted due to time constraints in the classroom. Students in our studies probably did not yet have enough information or opportunity to think in terms of their own civic agency in confronting civic problems related to historic preservation and finding solutions.

Practical Implications for Archaeology Education

With nearly thirty years of experience and research, we can formulate some practical recommendations for developing archaeology education materials and teaching archaeology (Moe 2011; Henderson and Levstik 2016).

Provide teachers with the materials and professional development that they need to be successful in the classroom—no more, no less. We begin every curriculum development project by asking two questions: (1) What do we want students to understand and remember twenty years from now (the Enduring Understanding)? and (2) What do teachers need to guide students to that Enduring Understanding? For example, there is no point in including a lesson on stratigraphy, if the students do not need it to analyze the data, answer the guiding questions, build evidence-based interpretations, and reach the desired Enduring Understanding. Teachers are busier than ever and we are not doing them any favors by giving them everything we know about an archaeological site or archaeological processes. Similarly, lots of ancillary materials such as explorations of related topics, might be both overwhelming (too much time) and intimidating (too difficult to understand and incorporate into instruction). These materials might be included as extensions to learning, but I would discourage adding too much to a publication just because teachers may think that they have to do it all. If they think it is too much, they may decide that they simply do not have the time to do any of it. Know your audience and what their needs are; do not get caught up in your own agenda or particular interest.

What students already know and the misconceptions they may harbor are of paramount importance in any educational endeavor including archaeology (Davis 2005; Henderson and Levstik 2016; Moe 2011). It is essential to identify misconceptions and they can usually be used as "teachable moments" or opportunities to explore concepts and content more deeply. For example, as an archaeology educator you will almost certainly have multiple opportunities to help learners of all ages progressively differentiate between archaeology and paleontology. You can begin with the knowledge the person has (archaeology and paleontology both deal with "old stuff" and they look similar in photographs of excavations) and help him or her understand that paleontology is limited to animals and plants while archaeology studies humans.

Use metaphors carefully (Henderson and Levstik 2016). The idea that archaeology can tell us "the story of the past" is a compelling idea for learners of all ages, but we must guide them to the possibility of multiple evidence-based interpretations of the archaeological record. While it is tempting to get children thinking in terms of story and narrative, we must show them that it is not that simple and that we can never know the "real" or "complete" story of the past. This can also be an advantage because it opens opportunities for personal agency in interpreting the archaeological record, rather than relying on historical narratives provided by the experts. It is one of the reasons that children and adults find archaeology fascinating; they get to interpret the evidence for themselves.

Archaeology provides an excellent lens for inquiry-based learning in social studies, history, and science (Davis 2005; Henderson and Levstik 2016; Letts and Moe 2009, 2012; Moe 2011). With archaeology, educators can guide the "uncovering" of knowledge and conceptual understanding by marrying process and content through the study of authentic archaeological data. Just as questions guide archaeological research, good questions should always guide learning. Knowledge that learners build themselves and integrate into their own existing cognitive structures will be retained far longer than "covering" information from a textbook to be regurgitated for a test. As archaeology educators, we can provide teachers and students with the means to uncover important concepts in science and history and compelling knowledge about the lives and cultures of people who lived in the past. Learners need built-in time for self-reflection on their own learning process (Bransford et al. 2000; Wiggins and McTighe 2005). For example, learners should have the opportunity to evaluate the validity of their own interpretations and adjust them as needed.

While archaeology may provide an avenue for people to interpret the archaeological record themselves, we also want them to produce robust interpretations based on real evidence. Not all interpretations are good. Using objects or artifacts to produce interpretations of the human past is challenging (Henderson and Levstik 2016). Even trained archaeologists cannot always provide a "perfect" interpretation of a particular artifact or site and our interpretations certainly change with new evidence, new questions, and new analytical procedures. Nevertheless, we want people to produce the best possible interpretations based on the evidence they have at hand and be able to evaluate potential flaws in their own arguments, holes in the data that may skew an interpretation, and recognize that more than one inference may be drawn from the same observation based on prior knowledge or bias (Letts and Moe 2009, 2012; Moe 2011).

Conclusions

Since the beginning of my career as an archaeology educator, we have come a long way. Through the efforts of many professionals throughout the United States and Canada, we have developed a good foundation of solid curricular materials with case studies to demonstrate their efficacy for teaching students and their value for educators. Thirty-some years down the road, we find that our early conclusions still hold.

First and foremost, we still need the help of educators and our first charge is to be ever mindful of their needs. We must continually strive to give classroom teachers and informal educators what they need to be successful—no more, no less. Other archaeology educators have confirmed our early conclusion and added suggestions for better serving educators *through* archaeology (e.g., Bartoy 2012). Too much information is just as bad as not enough. Similarly, we must remain cognizant of the fact that education changes constantly. We must be willing to change with it, learn to anticipate future trends, and be ready to fulfill the next set of requirements. What may have worked well for the past five or ten years, may not work at all next year.

To take it a step further, archaeologists need to become educators or at least well versed in the salient features of education such as: human cognition and constructivism, the ins and outs of assessing student learning outcomes and publishing the results, and how to deliver adequate teacher pedagogical content knowledge through compelling professional development. If we are serious about educating the public, we do not need doctoral degrees in archaeology. We need doctoral degrees in education.

Lastly, collaboration with descendant communities is a moral imperative of our time and for our entire profession. Archaeology education is no exception. At Project Archaeology, we have established many lasting professional relationships and friendships with descendant community members through collaboration on curricular materials (Alegria and Moe 2017). Happily, collaboration also helps us produce better educational materials that are more compelling for both teachers and students (Brody et al. 2014; Henderson and Levstik 2017).

The Future of Archaeology Education

Yes, we have come a long way, but we have far to go (King 2016). While we have increased our reach to both formal and informal educators, we have barely made a dent in the huge potential population of educators both nationwide in the United States and globally. To become major players in K–12 education we will need to research the efficacy of archaeology in improving student learning outcomes, publish our results in education research journals, and present at education conferences. In short, we will need to become "educators" rather than "archaeologists."

We need to decide as a profession what we want our citizenry to know and remember about archaeology long into the future. In 2010, Project Archaeology and Montana State University conducted a Delphi survey of 125 archaeologists, informal educators, and other related professions to formulate a national vision for archaeological literacy (Fisher et al. 2011). Results from this study need to be published. Franklin and Moe (2012) published "A Vision for Archaeological Literacy" based on papers presented in a symposium at the 2008 Society for American Archaeology conference. While we have made some progress in producing a series of national "standards" or "benchmarks" for archaeological literacy, we need to build on our existing work and complete the process. A set of national benchmarks would provide a foundation for assessing learning outcomes across all education programs and projects.

At Project Archaeology, we would like to apply for a series of grants from the Institute of Educational Sciences (IES) at the US Department of Education to prove the worth of archaeology education as an intervention that will promote conceptual understanding of important themes and help students perform better on tests. Successful grants from the IES pave the way for broad implementation of curricular materials nationwide. Archaeology is a small profession and we cannot hope to crack the educational establishment without a solid research base and backing from high level administrators.

Archaeology education needs to become more of a business and cannot rely on the efforts of volunteers nor can we expect much success if we are dependent solely on the time that individual archaeologists can devote to education. While I would like to see all archaeologists involved in promoting, funding, and delivering archaeology education to the public, the task is beyond our abilities as a small profession. Project Archaeology is developing a business model for producing, marketing, and distributing all products. The goal is professionalization and sustainability and it is built into everything we do. While we are making tremendous strides in developing high-quality educational materials that serve educators and their students well, marketing and distribution of our products remain a huge challenge. Classroom teachers have even less time for new curricular materials than they did in the early 1990s. Additionally, we are competing with huge textbook companies who have legions of sales representatives. Many other small educational organizations with goals of conserving soil and water or solving world hunger and many others have missions as important and compelling as our own.

Recent research (Brody et al. 2014) clearly demonstrates that archaeology is an effective but under used tool for engaging underserved audiences in science education. Science educators constantly struggle to make science relevant to cultural groups such as African American or Native Americans (Key 2003). Archaeology provides a way for African American or Native American school children to learn about their own culture and history through science inquiry. Research results are very promising and funding can probably be found for using archaeology to help underserved audiences engage with classroom science.

We need more research on what teachers need to be successful with archaeological education in their classrooms; this is commonly known as teacher pedagogical content knowledge. At Project Archaeology, we have begun to research the needs of teachers, what they learn through professional development, and how we might better help them to be successful (Agenten, Hartshorn, and Moe 2017). Much more research is needed. Similarly, while we pride ourselves on the inherently interdisciplinary nature of archaeology, we also need to recognize that integration of traditional school subjects may be confusing and intimidating for both teachers and students (Moe 2017). We need to assist teachers and students with integrating subjects through archaeology by first grounding them in the disciplines in question (most likely history and science) and showing them how these school subjects can be integrated to build robust interpretations of the past.

Much of archaeology education is conducted in informal settings such as museums, science learning centers, and on the ground at archaeological sites and this will probably continue. While informal education can be engaging and provide access to sites and artifacts unavailable in the classroom, it is also very difficult to assess what people actually learn from these experiences. Many variables, prevalent to both the learner and the venue, come into play and make assessment very complicated (e.g., Falk, Brooks, and Amin 2001; Falk and Storksdieck 2005). Additionally, it is difficult to obtain even very basic data in informal settings (Schields, Malo, and Tramel 2017). We do know that there is a huge potential for starting and/or perpetuating misconceptions, e.g., archaeology and dinosaurs are the same (Schields et al. 2017). That said, I applaud all efforts to gather data on informal learning in archaeology because informal venues will certainly remain important places to reach a diversity of audiences and provide engaging learning opportunities. I am certain that we will improve both our programs and their assessment in the coming years. In many cases, informal venues can provide powerful enhancements to classroom learning.

Despite the difficulties with assessing the efficacy of archaeological learning in informal settings, we have some good informal venues and audiences built for archaeology education; we should concentrate on these audiences. For example, the Boy Scouts of America have offered an Archaeology Merit Badge since 1997. As of 2016, 170,968 boy scouts have earned the badge and many thousands more will earn it in the coming years. Similarly, the Girl Scouts of Utah are developing Archaeology Camps and Archaeology Patches and more than one hundred girl scouts have attended these high-quality learning events since 2015. Girl Scout leaders in other states have requested assistance in establishing similar programs. The interest is there and we have an opportunity to fill a need.

The field of archaeology education needs to become a valued and respected part of the profession. The Society for American Archaeology has been supportive of public education since the inception of the Public Education Committee (PEC) in the early 1990s. The Heritage Education Network (THEN) recently formed as a nonprofit organization to help coordinate heritage and archaeology education efforts across all organizations and is open to all interested individuals. The scenario would be ideal if all professionals in the field of archaeology supported public education in some way. Not every archaeologist needs to be an educator, but the entire profession needs to assist those who work with the public either financially or through in-kind support. The very existence of archaeology depends upon an informed and supportive citizenry.

To be taken seriously by educators, we need more advanced degrees in education rather than in archaeology. Similarly, we need better ways to intersect with teachers, administrators, and educational researchers, and perhaps, better ways to form strong national, state, and local level partnerships with educational organizations. We will need to build a solid research base through Department of Education, National Science Foundation, and National Endowment for the Humanities grants and publish our results in peer-reviewed educational journals.

Archaeology is the only way to examine the deep history of humankind and to provide information on long-term changes in the human condition (Trigger 2008). For example, no other discipline can speak to global and regional changes in climate and their effect on cultures and history as well as archaeologists can. Climate change is undoubtedly one of the most important and compelling issues of our time and we certainly have the information to guide the conversation to possible solutions and necessary human adaptations to a changing world. Historical archaeology can also illuminate the lives of past peoples such as enslaved African Americans who are only scantly represented in historical documents (Heath 1999). In short, archaeology provides the framework on which to attach much of the work of other social scientists, including historians and cultural anthropologists, and may even inform the work of sociologists, economists, and psychologists. As applied anthropologists, we certainly have much to contribute to modern education by providing engaging curricula and instruction in scientific and historical inquiry and deep understanding of cultural differences and similarities.

In thirty plus years, archaeology educators and educational researchers have clearly demonstrated that we can greatly increase knowledge about stewardship and personal responsibility for protecting archaeological sites and artifacts through high-quality instructional materials. While there is a clear overlap between the laws that protect archaeological sites, the goals of archaeologists to retain intact sites for future research, and educational requirements for citizenship education, we must remember that stewardship education must be part of larger pieces that include compelling inquiry-based instruction, critical thinking, the inclusion of descendant communities, and the building of civic agency among students. If we play our cards right, it seems that we can have it all. We can provide students with life-changing educational experiences, help teachers fulfill literacy requirements in science and social studies, and employ education to help protect the archaeological record for all to learn from and enjoy long into the future.

Jeanne M. Moe, EdD, BLM Project Archaeology Lead.

References

Agenten, Courtney L., Crystal B. Alegria, and Shane M. Doyle. 2014. *Project Archaeology: Investigating First Peoples, the Clovis Child Burial.* Bozeman, MT: Montana State University/Project Archaeology.
Agenten, Courtney L., Tony Hartshorn, and Jeanne M. Moe. 2017. "Putting Project Archaeology Workshops to the Test." Paper presented at the 82nd Annual Society for American Archaeology Conference, Vancouver, BC, Canada, 30 March 2017.

Agenten, Courtney L., Cali A. Letts, and Jeanne M. Moe. 2015. *Project Archaeology: Investigating Nutrition.* Bozeman, MT: Montana State University/Project Archaeology.

Alegria, Crystal B., Kathleen J. Francisco, and Jeanne M. Moe. 2012. *Project Archaeology: Investigating Fort Meade.* Bozeman, MT: Montana State University/Project Archaeology.

Alegria, Crystal B., and Jeanne M. Moe. 2017. "Descendant Communities and Curriculum Development: Working Towards a Culturally Relevant Development Process." Paper presented at the 82nd Annual Society for American Archaeology Conference, Vancouver, BC, Canada, 30 March 2017.

Alegria, Crystal B., Tim Ryan, Courtney Agenten, and Terri Wolfgram. 2017. *Project Archaeology: Investigating Garnet, a Historic Mining Town.* Bozeman, MT: Montana State University/Project Archaeology.

Ausubel, David P., and F. Robinson. 1969. *School Learning: An Introduction to Educational Psychology.* New York: Holt, Rinehart, and Winston.

Bartoy, Kevin M. 2012. "Teaching *through* Rather *than* About: Education in the Context of Public Archaeology." In *The Oxford Handbook of Public Archaeology,* ed. Robin Skeates, Carol McDavid, and John Carmen, 552–65. Oxford, UK: Oxford University Press.

Bransford, John D., Ann L. Brown, and Rodney R. Cocking, eds. 2000. *How People Learn: Brain, Mind, Experience, and School,* expanded edition. Washington, DC: National Academy Press.

Brody, Michael, Jeanne M. Moe, Joelle Clark, and Crystal B. Alegria. 2014. "Archaeology as Culturally Relevant Science Education: The Poplar Forest Slave Cabin." In *Public Participation in Archaeology,* ed. Suzie Thomas and Joanne Lea, 89–104. Woodbridge, UK: The Boydell Press.

Chambers, Erve J., and Paul A. Shackel, eds. 2004. *Places in Mind: Public Archaeology as Applied Anthropology.* London: Routledge.

Common Core State Standards Initiative. 2017. *Common Core State Standards for English Language Arts & Literacy in History/Social Studies, Science, and Technical Subjects.* www.corestandards.org

Davis, M. Elaine. 2005. *How Students Understand the Past: From Theory to Practice.* Walnut Creek, CA: AltaMira Press.

Doyle, Shane M., Crystal B. Alegria, and Jeanne M. Moe. 2016. *Changing Land, Changing Life: Investigating Archaeology in Absáalooke Homeland.* Bozeman, MT: Montana State University/Project Archaeology.

Ellick, Carol J. 1997. *New Mexico Project Archaeology: Program Evaluation,* Technical Report 97–16. Tucson, AZ: Statistical Research.

Erickson, H. Lynn. 2001. *Stirring the Head, Heart, and Soul: Redefining Curriculum and Instruction,* 2nd ed. Thousand Oakes, CA: Corwin Press.

Falk, John H., Pauline Brooks, and Rinoti Amin. 2001. "Investigating the Role of Free-Choice Learning on Public Understanding of Science: The California Science Center L.A.S.E.R. Project." In *Free-Choice Science Education: How We Learn Science Outside of School,* ed. John H. Falk, 115–32. New York: Teachers College Press.

Falk, John, and Martin Storkesdieck. 2005. "Using the Contextual Model of Learning to Understand Visitor Learning from a Science Center Exhibition." In *Science Learning in Everyday Life,* ed. Lynn D. Dierking and John H. Falk, 744–78. Wiley Periodicals, Inc. www.interscience.wiley.com.

Fisher, John W. Jr., Helen Keremedjiev, Michael Brody, and Jeanne M. Moe. 2011. "Archaeological Science for All: Archaeology and Science Education." Paper presented at the 76th Annual Society for American Archaeology Conference, Sacramento, CA, 1 April 2011.
Franklin, M. Elaine, and Jeanne M. Moe. 2012. "A Vision for Archaeological Literacy." In *The Oxford Handbook of Public Archaeology*, ed. Robin Skeates, Carol McDavid, and John Carmen, 566–80. Oxford, UK: Oxford University Press.
Heath, Barbara J. 1999. *Hidden Lives: The Archaeology of Slave Life at Thomas Jefferson's Poplar Forest.* Charlottesville, VA: University of Virginia Press.
Henderson, A. Gwynn, and Linda Levstik. 2016. "Reading Objects: Children Interpreting Material Culture." *Advances in Archaeological Practice* 4(4): 503–16.
———. 2017. "Investigating a Shotgun House: Piloting a New Project Archaeology Shelter Investigation." Paper presented at the 82nd Annual Society for American Archaeology Conference, Vancouver, BC, Canada, 30 March 2017.
Henderson, A. Gwynn, M. Jay Stottman, Robin L. Jones, and Linda S. Levstik. 2016. *Investigating a Shotgun House.* Project Archaeology: Investigating Shelter Series No.12. Bozeman, MT: Montana State University/Project Archaeology.
Key, Shirley Gholston. 2003. "Enhancing the Science Interest of African American Students Using Cultural Inclusion." In *Multicultural Science Education: Theory, Practice, and Promise*, ed. S. M. Hines, 87–101. New York: Peter Lang.
King, Eleanor M. 2016. "Systematizing Public Education in Archaeology." *Advances in Archaeological Practice* 4(4): 415–24.
Letts, Cali A., and Jeanne M. Moe. 2009. *Project Archaeology: Investigating Shelter.* Bozeman, MT: Montana State University/Project Archaeology.
———. 2012. *Project Archaeology: Investigating Shelter* (second edition). Bozeman, MT: Montana State University/Project Archaeology.
Levstik, Linda S., A. Gwynn Henderson, and Jenny S. Schlarb. 2008. "Digging for Clues: An Archaeological Exploration of Historical Cognition." In *Researching History Education: Theory, Method, and Context*, ed. Linda S. Levstik and Keith C. Barton, 392–410. London: Routledge.
Mintzes, J. J., and J. H. Wandersee. 2005. "Research in Science Teaching and Learning: A Human Constructivist View." In *Teaching Science for Understanding: A Human Constructivist View*, ed. J. J. Mintzes, J. H. Wandersee, and J. D. Novak, 59–92. Burlington, MA: Elsevier Academic Press.
Moe, Jeanne M. 2011. *Conceptual Understanding of Science through Archaeological Inquiry.* EdD diss., Montana State University.
———. 2016. "Archaeology Education for Children: Assessing Effective Learning." *Advances in Archaeological Practice* 4(4): 441–53.
———. 2017. "Archaeological Inquiry and Integrating Science and Social Studies: A Research Opportunity." Paper presented at the 82nd Annual Society for American Archaeology Conference, Vancouver, BC, Canada, 30 March 2017.
———. In press. "Archaeology in Schools: Student Learning Outcomes." In *Archaeologists and the Pedagogy of Heritage: Theory and Practice*, vol. 2, ed.

Phyllis Mauch Messenger and Susan J. Bender. Gainsville, FL: University Press of Florida.

Moe, Jeanne M., Courtney L. Agenten, and Cali A. Letts. 2018. *Project Archaeology: Investigating Rock Art.* Bozeman, MT: Montana State University/Project Archaeology.

Moe, Jeanne M., and Cali A. Letts. 1998. "Education: Can It Make a Difference?" *Common Ground: Archaeology and Ethnography in the Public Interest* 3(1): 24–29.

National Council for the Social Studies. 1994. *Expectations of Excellence: Curriculum Standards for Social Studies, NCSS Bulletin 89.* Silver Spring, MD: National Council for the Social Studies.

National Research Council. 1996. *National Science Education Standards.* Washington, DC: National Academy Press.

Novak, Joseph D. 1977. *A Theory of Education.* Ithaca, NY: Cornell University Press.

———. 1993. "Human Constructivism: A Unification of Psychological and Epistemological Phenomena in Meaning Making." *International Journal of Personal Construct Psychology* 6: 167–93.

Ramos, M., and D. Duganne. 2000. *Exploring Public Perceptions and Attitudes about Archaeology.* Washington, DC: Society for American Archaeology.

Rees, Diane A. 2000. *Does Archaeology Have a Place in the Precollegiate Curriculum of Colorado?* Master's thesis, School of Archaeological Studies, University of Leicester, UK.

Schields, Rebekah, Erika Malo, and Nichole Tramel. 2017. "Archaeology Fairs: Measuring Informal Learning." Paper presented at the 82nd Annual Society for American Archaeology Conference, Vancouver, BC, Canada, 30 March 2017.

Smardz, Karolyn, and Shelley J. Smith, eds. 2000. *The Archaeology Education Handbook: Sharing the Past with Kids.* Walnut Creek, CA: AltaMira Press.

Smith, Shelley J., Jeanne M. Moe, Kelly A. Letts, and Danielle A. Paterson. 1992. *Intrigue of the Past: Investigating Archaeology.* Salt Lake City, UT: Bureau of Land Management.

———. 1993. *Intrigue of the Past: A Teacher's Activity Guide for Fourth through Seventh Grades.* Dolores, CO: Anasazi Heritage Center, Bureau of Land Management.

Thompson, Jackie, Dan Kinsey, Crystal B. Alegria, Jenny Nagra, and Arianne Adams. 2009. *Investigating a Historic Farmhouse.* Project Archaeology: Investigating Shelter Series, No. 6. Bozeman, MT: Montana State University/Project Archaeology.

Trigger, Bruce G. 2008. *A History of Archaeological Thought,* 2nd ed. Cambridge, UK: Cambridge University Press.

von Glaserfeld, Ernst. 1989. "Constructivism in Education." In *The International Encyclopedia of Education, Supplementary volume 1,* ed. T. Husen and T. N. Postlethwaite, 162–63. Oxford, New York: Pergamon Press.

Wiggins, Grant, and Jay McTighe. 1998. *Understanding by Design.* Alexandria, VA: Association for Supervision and Curriculum Design.

———. 2005. *Understanding by Design,* 2nd ed. Alexandria, VA: Association for Supervision and Curriculum Design.

CHAPTER 9

Navigating Heritage Stewardship in the Digital Age

Jodi Reeves Eyre and Leigh Anne Ellison

Introduction

Digital access to archaeological, cultural, and historical information can inspire and support public interest in cultural heritage. As Katherine M. Erdman illustrates in the introductory chapter to this volume, we must engage a diverse audience when promoting an appreciation and respect for cultural heritage. When you form a connection with something, it becomes worth saving and protecting. From providing access to local, historical documents in an online repository to using 3D scans to create replicas of destroyed international cultural heritage sites, a plethora of digital tools exist that can be used to promote the stewardship of cultural heritage.

But, where to begin? From digitizing and photographing existing collections, to creating born digital materials in the field, from open access publishing to social media, "digital cultural heritage" encompasses a diverse landscape. One must consider required resources, ethical and compliance issues related to digital cultural heritage, and what tools and methods will meet one's goals in inspiring and developing interest, maintaining that interest, and promoting long-term preservation and stewardship of digital materials.

In *Mobilizing the Past*,[1] Morag M. Kersel admits in "Response: Living a Semi-digital Kinda Life" to being "often lost in the platforms, programs, and terminology used by the authors. Clearly there is a new language associated with digital technologies with which I am unfamiliar. In addition to the technical terms and programs I noted new 'buzzwords' like granular, workflow, and born digital, which appear in almost every chapter" (2016, 476). Despite ourselves being actively engaged in promoting digital preservation and curation, we often also find the wider realm of digital cultural heritage, especially the more technical aspects of digital preservation and repository development, daunting. This feeling of being "lost" in this digital reality has motivated us to conclude this volume by exploring its landscape. The hope is to provide guidance for archaeologists, educators, and others interested in cultural heritage stewardship who are new to using digital tools, or have some experience but want to begin to apply tools more systematically.

In writing this final chapter, we relied heavily on inspiration from the previous chapters in this volume. They did not disappoint. Our fellow authors are dedicated to cultural heritage stewardship, especially that of archaeology, and have been open and candid about their experiences and lessons learned, particularly in the field of education. What was lacking was extensive discussion of digital methods, whether they employed digital means to collect cultural heritage data, digitized resources, or used digital media in the classroom or in outreach. Three chapters mention digital cultural heritage, Chapter 2, Chapter 5, and Chapter 8. This may be because some digital tools are now so integrated into archaeological and cultural heritage practice that there is no perceived need to explicitly describe them. This is likely true for the routine use of computers, word processors, digital photography, etc. However, the explicit, thoughtful use of digital tools can add to the breadth, depth, impact, and documentation of cultural heritage stewardship programs.

In this concluding chapter, we explore the challenges and opportunities of utilizing digital tools as part of cultural heritage stewardship using real life examples, several pulled from our fellow authors from this volume. In this process, we hope to provide resources for navigating the digital cultural heritage landscape, depending on your needs. Finally, we look at ways of gauging the impact of using digital tools to promote cultural heritage stewardship. In a world where cultural heritage stewardship is a difficult field to navigate, digital considerations can make it harder but, perhaps, even more exciting and engaging for a wider, more diverse audience.

What Is Digital Cultural Heritage?

For a field dedicated to preserving the past, heritage stewardship relies heavily on modern innovations. As mentioned above, digital cultural heritage or digital archaeology[2] can be a confusing and daunting area for the uninitiated.

Ashley Richter notes that "Digital Archaeology is a delightful phrase that has several different meanings," before listing three main divisions:

1. Digital Archaeology is the study of the archaeological past using technology.
2. Digital Archaeology is a practice.
3. Digital archaeology is also "Virtual Archaeology and CyberArchaeology": Virtual archaeology involves the reconstruction of archaeological visuals. So all those snazzy re-imaginings of ancient cities on history documentaries or in video games fall into the virtual archaeology category. CyberArchaeology is more or less where one takes the digital archaeological data into a virtual immersive environment. (2014)

There are also ways of using the term "digital archaeology" that are less related to normal archaeological practice, such as digital archaeology as digital forensics: recovering data and information from digital devices (for an example of this usage, see Graves 2014).

More useful is the UNESCO Charter on the Preservation of Digital Heritage (2003, Article 1):

The digital heritage consists of unique resources of human knowledge and expression. It embraces cultural, educational, scientific and administrative resources, as well as technical, legal, medical and other kinds of information created digitally, or converted into digital form from existing analogue resources. Where resources are "born digital," there is no other format but the digital object.

Digital materials include texts, databases, still and moving images, audio, graphics, software, and web pages, among a wide and growing range of formats. They are frequently ephemeral, and require purposeful production, maintenance, and management to be retained.

Many of these resources have lasting value and significance, and therefore constitute a heritage that should be protected and preserved for current and future generations. This ever-growing heritage may exist in any language, in any part of the world, and in any area of human knowledge or expression.

For the most part, here we use digital cultural heritage as a catch-all term covering the use of digital tools to promote public interest around cultural heritage (such as the use of blogs, social media, etc.), digital objects created from cultural heritage materials such as 3D scans and photographs of collections, digital publication of cultural heritage data and information, preservation and curation of digital cultural data and information, use of digital tools to manage and visualize data, and the collection of digital data in the field. Cultural heritage refers to archaeological remains, as with many of the chapters of this book, as well as other cultural items and actions still in use or that have a role in their communities. You do not need to do all of these things to do digital cultural heritage, but you should be aware of the potential implications.

To this end, we promote the idea that digital cultural heritage can be seen as a landscape. You just need to find your place, or your project's place, within it. The following sections include examples of how digital tools are used in cultural heritage stewardship. With these examples, we hope to promote some simple examples of how tools, methods, and considerations coming out of digital archaeology can be integrated into cultural heritage stewardship in general and for engaging the public specifically.

Goals

In any landscape, you encounter barriers and challenges on your journey. It can be intimidating to contemplate the required resources, the ethical and compliance issues related to digital cultural heritage, selecting an approach for inspiring and developing interest, maintaining that interest, and promoting long-term preservation and stewardship. Instead of referring to resources, ethics and compliance, interest, and preservation as challenges or barriers, here we refer to them as a set of goals or destinations that people aim for as they navigate the use of digital tools within cultural heritage stewardship. This positive spin is more than semantics. After all, we should want to create projects that are ethically sound and engage interest in communities. As part of stewardship, we should want to use the resources we have access to thoughtfully and ensure the preservation of cultural heritage materials.

Resources

The most obvious challenge to digital cultural heritage, especially the preservation of digital materials, is cost, considered both in terms of time and money.

A curator for the archaeological collection at a state museum wants to create an Instagram account to share photographs of artifacts from the collection, as well as photographs of the preservation and curation process. This level of digital engagement seems simple enough and may not take up much of the curator's time. However, the curator needs to set up an account (and make sure the account complies with any institutional rules and marketing requirements), identify items or processes of interest to the public, take the photographs, draft captions, include important keywords to increase the image's audience (usually in the form of hashtags), and do all of these often enough to cultivate an interested audience—another goal. Hopefully the interested audience will respond to posts, but this requires more engagement from the curator. Is it worth it? The institution likely has its own social media presence, but, as campaigns such as #AskACurator, attest, people are interested in hearing from, and engaging with, experts. How do you evaluate the resources needed for such a project with the potential outcomes?

A first step is to establish your short-term and/or long-term goals. Next, you should evaluate existing resources. This process identifies resource gaps, both for your short-term goals and for your long-term goals. You can then begin to address these gaps with basic additional resources with minimal access threshold. This is a cyclical process, and you will need to reevaluate resources throughout the project.

> Existing resources may include:
> —Current staff and current, reliable volunteers with needed skills
> —Existing, popular digital platforms (Facebook, Twitter, Instagram, etc.)
> —A small amount of money in an established budget
> —Existing collaborative networks.
>
> Basic additional resources may include:
> —Recruiting new volunteer(s) with a specific skill set
> —Using professional development funds for current staff to gain a needed skill or experience
> —Running a pilot project
> —Outsourcing complex, but short-term tasks.

In 2015, EXARC, the ICOM Affiliated Organization representing archaeological open-air museums, experimental archaeology, ancient technology, and interpretation, was preparing for a major revamp of their organizational website. In addition to information about EXARC, the website was a major access point for resources including back issues of the *EXARC Journal*, a skills marketplace, and a bibliography of topical publications. The bibliography in particular, which was searchable and had over 11,000 entries gathered by EXARC Director, Roeland Paardekooper, was a popular resource. There were some resource challenges with the bibliography, however. The bibliography took up a lot of server space and content management relied on one individual. There was also a desire to add value to the bibliography by including access to the resources themselves.

Reeves Eyre had been a member of the EXARC Secretariat for several years and had volunteered as an editor for the *EXARC Journal*. During this period, she was transferring out of her editing role, but wanted to remain involved. To Reeves Eyre, the challenges facing the bibliography were actually opportunities to create a digital collection of experimental archaeology materials. Together with Paardekooper and fellow Secretariat member, Magdalena Zielińska, they decided to move the bibliography into an existing archaeological repository: tDAR (the Digital Archaeological Record). This would help address EXARC's short-term goals: the bibliography would be stored in tDAR, freeing up server space, and resource management would be shared between Paardekooper and Reeves Eyre. It would also address EXARC's long-term goal: to add files to each bibliographic citation. There was a small amount of money in the existing EXARC budget that could be put toward tDAR and volunteer fees.

> Existing resources used for this work included:
> —current volunteer and consultant experience
> —an existing platform: tDAR
> —a small amount of money to buy space in tDAR so that we could upload the citations to the repository. Files would be added at a later date.
> —an existing collaborative network (Reeves Eyre's history as a curator with Digital Antiquity, the organization that administers tDAR).

While the manager for the EXARC website would be able to export the bibliography, we needed support from Digital Antiquity to upload the citations automatically into the repository. This is where Adam Brin, Director of Technology, and Leigh Anne Ellison came in. They helped EXARC evaluate how much technical support the organization would need to import the citations. In the end, they had enough funds to pay for technical assistance with some funds left over for uploading files at a later date. Basic additional resources included outsourcing technical support (in this case, having Digital Antiquity help the organization import the citations).

This got EXARC to the current stage of the collections development: adding value to the citations. We will return to this example when looking at our other goal categories. For now, we will end with the two additional resources that are needed to address the EXARC project's long-term goals: (1) money: to add additional files to the repository, and to pay for management of the collection; and (2) time: to manage the collection, including training and managing volunteer curators.

Well-established projects can be good candidates for integrating digital tools. The projects likely have existing resources: time is dedicated to them, workflows are established, and funding is sometimes available, etc. One example from Yezzi-Woodley et al.'s Chapter 2 is the "Archaeology on the Internet" module. What is great about this module is that it utilizes the project's existing resources, as well as existing digital cultural heritage projects while helping to develop student's critical analysis of information they find on the internet.

Lewis C. Messenger's BACAB CAAS project discussed in Chapter 4 is a long-running project that has engaged students in new ways of evaluating archaeological evidence and depicting cultures and prehistory. It is also a great example of a pedagogical program that may benefit from integrating some simple digital tools. For example, posting a selection of student papers on existing blogs or other platforms can add to the positive digital presence for students and increase the already large impact of the program.

Access is also resource dependent. Access to digital cultural heritage, and the tools to access such projects, assumes a certain amount of privilege for both the people doing the cultural heritage and the communities they wish to access. For the most part, the target audience for the EXARC Digital Experimental Archaeology Collection has consistent access to the internet, and therefore to the repository. Accessing tDAR is free, although downloading files from the repository does require a person to register. However, repositories such as tDAR may not be as accessible to communities and persons with minimal internet access or to those with limited digital literacy.

Ethics and Compliance

Ethics and compliance are an integral part of considerate cultural heritage stewardship. Approaching digital heritage stewardship in an ethical manner requires us to consider the ethical standards of our discipline, the communities whose cultural heritage is being presented, and the role of rules, laws, and regulations. Context is also closely tied to presenting cultural heritage in an ethical, thoughtful manner.

Sarah Colley's "Ethics and Digital Heritage" (2015) is an excellent introductory resource for some of the ethical challenges surrounding digital cultural heritage, and we strongly suggest you read it. We believe the main takeaways are:

—The expense of developing, implementing, and maintaining digital technology is a barrier with ethical implications. This relates directly to our goal of resources.
—An ethical approach to digital cultural heritage should consider barriers to technology that include physical ability, digital literacy, and "language and cultural attitudes" (Colley 2015, 16).
—"Framing cultural assets, including digital ones, as marketable commodities concerns ethics" (ibid., 17).
—"Different technologies may support, encourage or determine ethical, or unethical, behaviours depending on their design" (ibid., 17). For example, does a platform encourage proper citation of cultural images or allow for the protection of culturally sensitive materials?
—"Vast quantities of digital information and heritage are currently at risk due to economics of technology production, organisational constraints, digital illiteracy, lack of political will and costs of compliance with digital archiving standards" (ibid., 18). This relates to our challenge of long-term preservation.

Compliance relates both to policy and legal requirements.[3] Those of us that work within the museum and library fields will be keenly aware of how copyright can affect our ability to share and preserve materials. A valuable resource on this topic is "Copyright Issues Relevant to the Creation of a Digital Archive: A Preliminary Assessment" by June M. Besek (2003). Another valuable resource for those collaborating on digital cultural heritage projects is the "Copyright and Creator Rights in DH Projects: A Checklist" (Galina et al. 2017). This checklist will help you document and address the rights of those associated with your projects.

Cultural heritage projects funded by federal agencies also need to comply with open access policies. In 2013, the White House announced a new approach to open access in which "publications from taxpayer-funded research should be made free to read after a year's delay" (Van Noorden 2013). For readers applying for federal grants, a good place to start is DMPTool.org.

A legal analysis of federal laws and regulations relating to the long-term preservation of and access to digital archaeological information was conducted in 2012 by Cultural Heritage Partners, PLLC. This report concludes that digital archaeological data generated by federal agencies must be deposited in an appropriate repository that can preserve and make materials available to qualified users. While federal guidelines may change from administration to administration, those of us working with digital cultural heritage materials should be generally aware of best practices and how to implement them to meet and go beyond mere compliance (Cultural Heritage Partners, PLLC 2012).

Cultural heritage projects should make the information they produce as accessible as possible as long as the decision to do so is made critically, with a mind to who is affected by such an act. Ethical codes developed for indigenous cultural heritage and human remains such as those adopted by the World Archaeological Congress, particularly The Vermillion Accord on Human Remains and The Tamaki Makau-rau Accord on the Display of Human Remains and Sacred Objects, need to be consulted (World Archaeological Congress 2015). It is also important to remember that developing and implementing "[g]uidelines and policies that seek to empower traditional owners in decisions about cultural heritage do not erase colonial history and legacies of inequality" (Colley 2015, 20). Consider the ethics around the sharing and preservation of cultural heritage: consulting with communities and with experts in ethics and compliance can only strengthen your project by ensuring you develop a thoughtful approach to digital cultural heritage stewardship.

For the first stage of the EXARC Digital Experimental Archaeology Collection, the project is producing metadata, or descriptive information, about publications. This type of information is widely available, and the project is able to share it without permission from the authors or publishers. However, to add copies of the publications to the citation records, EXARC will need permission from the copyright holders. The project workflow includes identifying the copyright status of the publications and what country they were published in and citations include a message asking copyright holders to get in contact if they would like to add a copy of the publication to the repository.

In Chapter 8, Moe discusses how Project Archaeology engaged descendant communities in the development of curriculum, including adding and removing material. This is a good model to follow for any outreach program and can be key in many digital cultural heritage projects. In 2005, the Smithsonian repatriated the Killer Whale clan crest hat, or Kéet S'aaxw, to Tlingit clan leader Mark Jacobs, Jr. In 2010, Jacob's successor, Edwell John, Jr., returned the hat to the Smithsonian for a specific digitization project (Solly 2017):

> Over the next two years, the Smithsonian worked closely with John to create a copy that was both respectful of Tlingit culture and suitable for education purposes. Digitization experts laser-scanned the hat, bouncing a beam off of its surface and deriving measurements from the time it took the laser to bounce back, and also collected 3D data through an imaging technique called photogrammetry.

The Smithsonian provides an example of how to replicate cultural heritage materials: there was collaboration with the tribe both during and after the hat was scanned, the hat was debuted following Tlingit protocols, and access to the 3D scan of the hat is limited. Most importantly, there is a recognition that the replica (digital and physical) are culturally and emotionally important.

Inspiring and Maintaining Interest

While many of the chapters within this volume detail projects that take place within the education system, they each shed light on different ways of inspiring and maintaining interest that are applicable to any cultural heritage stewardship project or program. As with the graduate program documented by P. Messenger in Chapter 5, some heritage stewardship programs are designed to train people with an established interest in cultural heritage. In Chapter 1, White emphasizes the fact that in order to develop education programs that function and have impact, there needs to be a thoughtful consideration of teachers' goals and requirements.

Again, a good first step is to identify what your goals are, both short-term and long-term. Available resources and ethical concerns directly affect how you approach inspiring and maintaining interest. Do you have the resources to generate and maintain public interest? Are you letting known public interests or beliefs about cultural heritage sway how you present that material? In addition to these types of questions, you should be continually evaluating the project goals. Another key step is to identify your audience. These often go hand-in-hand. For example, your goal may be to increase interest and appreciation of a local cultural heritage site so that local government will continue to support the preservation of the site. It is likely that your audience will be local communities, and perhaps tourists, who will overlap with audiences of other local sites.

Sometimes, simply making cultural heritage accessible is a valuable goal in itself. The Center for Digital Antiquity, which manages tDAR, will often receive emails concerning reports on local sites or local historical information, as well as inquiries related to genealogical research. In these examples, people already have an interest in an aspect of cultural heritage, and the digital medium gives them access to the materials they are interested in. If you have digital cultural heritage materials, and you have the right to disseminate them, putting them in a repository, such as Archaeology Data Service (ADS), tDAR, or an institutional repository, can be a low-cost way to inspire and maintain interest, as well as make resources available for other cultural heritage projects. Depending on the repository and the quality of the digital materials, placing resources in them can also address the challenge of preservation.

Experience is an established way of increasing and maintaining interest. Traditionally these experiences related to cultural heritage include visiting archaeological and other cultural heritage sites, visiting museums and exhibits, handling artifacts, viewing or participating in reenactments, or experimenting with traditional technologies. Digital technologies can supplement and extend these experiences, providing access to related materials before and after a physical visit.

In Chapter 1, White recounts the importance of touch when it comes to engaging people in the past. Where items are fragile, inaccessible, or have been destroyed, digital cultural heritage, 3D scans and printing specifically, can help facilitate physical interaction with materials. A perfect example of integrating digital cultural heritage tools is Touching the Past: Investigating Sensory Engagement and Authenticity in the Provision of Touch Experiences in Museums Across a Range of Media, a project led by Linda Hurcombe of the University of Exeter.

In one prototype from the Touching the Past project, a 3D-printed mirrored replica was made of the twelfth-century Scottish Lewis Queen chess piece, which is displayed in a glass case at the National Museum of Scotland. Next, the replica (which mirrors the original) was placed in front of the glass case where the original is held. A black barrier was placed behind and over the replica. They applied the principle of Pepper's Ghost: this is a theater technique in which the image of an actor is projected onto a large glass pane placed between the audience and the stage. The result is a translucent image of the actor that looks like a ghost. The image of the replica is transposed right over the glass containing the original. A visitor can now reach around the side of the barrier that blocks the replica from view, while gazing at the original in the case (Dima, Hurcombe, and Wright 2014). They can touch the replica, but the reflection in the glass makes it look as though they are touching the original chess piece. "Because she sees the actual artefact (and her hands) and touches the replica she experiences the sensation that she is actually touching the artefact itself. The illusion is further strengthened by placing a cover over the replica to shield it from the user's direct gaze" (Dima et al. 2014, 6).

3D printing may seem like a financially inaccessible approach. However, many university libraries now have 3D printers for use by faculty, staff, and students. They may also extend this service to affiliates and non-affiliates. For those interested in the relationship between 3D printing and teaching and learning, *Shiny Things* by Jennifer Grayburn, Veronica Ikeshoji-Orlati, Anjum Najmi, and Jennifer Parrott (2017) may be of interest. 3D scanning and printing is a popular example of applying new approaches to cultural heritage, particularly because of its use in creating items that can be handled, and its use in creating facsimiles of lost or damaged monuments and items. However, it is only one tool among many. When incorporating 3D scanning or any other unfamiliar technologies into a cultural heritage project, an ideal step is to identify potential partners with existing expertise and technology.

Additionally, as Yezzi-Woodley et al. state in Chapter 2, we should take into account how people learn and engage with information. Hands-on experiences have an impressive impact, but access to information through the internet and social media is also standard practice. As people who value cultural heritage, we should be supplying access to resources in repositories dedicated to preservation and access, such as tDAR, and we should also consider the use of existing platforms and new technologies. Social media is the first tool that may come to mind for many people. In the beginning of this chapter we presented a vignette of a curator who tried to use social media to promote collections. Depending on your goals and aims, social media can be a key tool for raising an interest in a project, sharing the outcomes of a program, engaging people in research, etc. In "The Alchemy of Tumblr Gold," Megan Miller (2017) outlines the process employed for running Othmer Library's Tumblr, Othmeralia. We would suggest any group interested in developing a social media profile review Miller's presentation as well as Othmeralia.

Perhaps a most essential step in any cultural heritage stewardship project of program is evaluating impact. Several of the chapters in this volume discuss the implementation of surveys to document the impact of a program or project. Depending on the tools and the project, there are ways of quantitatively evaluating impact for digital cultural heritage projects. For projects using websites, social media, or online repositories, analytics are often given by the platform being used. Google analytics is perhaps the most well-known in terms of tracking page visits and views for websites, although many platforms will provide complementary information. Social media platforms also track quantitative information. Using Twitter as an example, you can track how many people are following a project account, interacting with material through likes, retweets, and comments. Qualitative information on impact may be gained from analyzing comments made on posts or websites. Many repositories will also track information on the use of resources and collections, such as downloads of files. Additionally, repositories provide citation information that may also be tracked. Still, much of this is quantitative in nature and there are considerations that need to be taken into account such as how analytics are measured, how are bots eliminated from counts, etc.

However, most digital heritage projects have a "real world" aspect to how communities interact with them. Courses, tutorials, and school programs that use digital tools can integrate questions about the impact of those tools into current course surveys to gauge impact. Observation of visitors and visitor surveys are well used methods that are still applicable.

Management, Preservation, and Stewardship

Preservation is a primary goal of heritage stewardship, and the preservation of digital materials is just as important as the preservation of buildings, objects, and intangible heritage. Preservation is also an ethical issue; we agree with Colley that we "are ethically obliged to make [our] research data publicly accessible" and that a key part of this is long-term preservation (2015, 19). So far in this chapter, we have focused on approaches that may be used for projects such as the ones described in other chapters of this volume. These projects are interested in producing digital materials, such as websites, digital images, etc., or are interested in utilizing already digitized materials. In this section we are going to shift focus and look at heritage stewardship projects that are specifically interested in digital preservation, which aims to keep digital materials, such as born digital materials or the digital files that result from digitization, accessible and available for use. While the focus may have shifted, many of the tools and techniques discussed here are applicable to any project producing digital materials.

We would like to quickly return to the UNESCO Charter on the Preservation of Digital Heritage, which highlights the importance of preservation. The charter recognizes that digital cultural heritage materials are "frequently ephemeral, and require purposeful production, maintenance and management to be retained" (2003). While the charter was written fifteen years ago, this statement is still applicable. Take a moment to think on a cultural heritage project you may have worked on in the early 2000s, whether it was a survey, an excavation, or an outreach or education program. You will likely know where any final reports are, but what about the data used in those reports? Or the original photographs and other images? Are they on a CD? Floppy disk? This chapter was primarily written on a laptop with no internal CD drive, much less a mechanism for reading a floppy disk. Hardware obsolescence is something physical and easy to understand, but there are other, less tangible issues.

Assume you are able to find the CD that has the distribution data and images made from that data. If you used a proprietary software to organize the data or produce the images, do you still have access to that software? Can the current software version open older files? This is another roadblock in preserving digital data: file format and proprietary file formats.

Another issue is file corruption. You may have found a CD drive and software to read the files, but if information on the CD has been lost or degraded over time, it may all be for nothing. Assume you are able to open the file and it works. Now you can use it in a new project or to replicate your past results if—and this is a big if—there is enough descriptive information about the file and its content.

This descriptive information, often referred to as metadata (data about data) is key. You will have no idea which data set is final if they are named final.csv, final final.csv, FINAL.xls, etc. If a code sheet or code book does not accompany the dataset, or there is no descriptive information about an image, then those files, and your past hard work, may have lost significant value.

Each of the issues above can usually be avoided if good data management and data preservation policies are put in place. While this can seem daunting, there are freely accessible resources on data management, digitization, curation, and preservation that are easily accessible. One such resource is the "Guides to Good Practice," which is available online from the Archaeology Data Service and the Center for Digital Antiquity. The guide can help to answer basic questions about managing and formatting digital cultural heritage materials, particularly when it comes to producing file formats that are appropriate for long-term curation.

For projects looking to incorporate digitization and want a file that is suitable for preservation purposes, "Technical Guidelines for Digitizing Cultural Heritage Materials" by the Still Image Working Group of the Federal Agencies Digital Guidelines Initiative (FADGI) is a good resource for best practices. The guides offer several levels of standards based on the goals of your project, from developing images for access-only to developing images that are suitable for preservation. However, understanding and meeting the "Technical Guidelines for Digitizing Cultural Heritage Materials" requires technical knowledge and access to equipment and space that many projects may not have. There are other guidelines available for digitization of cultural heritage materials that may better meet your project or institutional needs and your current level of resources. Another freely accessible resource, the "Digital Preservation Handbook," produced by the Digital Preservation Coalition, focuses primarily on preserving digital materials and includes information on developing policies and procedures.

The resources above can help organizations and programs that are at the beginning of their digital preservation journey. However, management of digital heritage materials does require consistent documentation, some knowledge of good management practices, and time to implement these practices and keep documentation up to date. These hurdles can be relatively easy to overcome in terms of time and money. Preservation can potentially be a greater challenge, depending on your project's or program's aims, institutional ties, and whether you decide to use existing, potentially external, preservation services or develop an in-house preservation system.

The EXARC Digital Experimental Archaeology Collection is primarily focused on improving access to materials through long-term preservation. To address this primary goal, they involve project members with experience in digital curation and preservation. There are some lessons that can be learned from the two examples, even if long-term digital preservation is a secondary goal for your project:

1. Identify what digital materials you are producing.
2. Identify your goals.
3. Identify whether your goals affect the format and descriptive information you need to keep with your digital materials.

For EXARC, the produced digital materials are: metadata records, born digital materials or materials digitized by a third party that are at risk of loss, and, in the future, materials selected for digitization specifically for the collection. These materials will be assessed in terms of level of risk, ownership, community and partner support, and financial support for the curation of the materials.

Reuse, Collaboration, and Increasing Impact with Digital Heritage Stewardship

The primary aim of this chapter has been to highlight accessible projects, tools, and resources for those interested in digital cultural heritage stewardship, but who do not know where to start. We have touched on some approaches to utilizing your resources, working with ethical and compliance frameworks, inspiring and maintaining interest, and issues surrounding long-term preservation of digital cultural heritage. We would like to conclude our chapter with some additional suggestions.

Evaluate your project or program resources, stakeholders, goals, and obligations. What digital tools can help you to better use resources and improve the program for current and future stakeholders? Perhaps using images published in a repository and freely available can supplement a current education program with limited resources, or digitizing artifacts can improve access for more members of the community. Simple steps can make it easier to meet project goals and obligations, and they may open up new obligations such as ensuring the right to reproduce images or making sure the digital surrogates you create are accessible to others and preserved for the long-term.

Consider using other peoples' and projects' digital workflows or building on the tools developed by another project. Many people working within digital cultural heritage are happy to share their results (and you should strive to do so too). This leads right into another suggestion: when in doubt, collaborate. For example, many university libraries are increasingly employing staff or faculty with a focus on digital humanities, digital curation, or data management. There is an active digital archaeology community on Twitter (#digiarch), as well as communities centered around collections (#AskACurator) and digital preservation.

Speaking of Twitter, when creating an outreach program, a low barrier approach is to use existing social media platforms such as Twitter, Tumblr, or Facebook. This is a great thing to do and perfectly acceptable. Communities already exist on these platforms that will be interested in cultural heritage and these platforms benefit from having thoughtful, critically evaluated content contributed to them. However, these platforms are run by for-profit businesses and do not necessarily have the concerns or rights of your stakeholders at heart. They do not prescribe to the same or similar ethical guidelines that cultural heritage professionals and organizations do. However, this is not a reason to re-invent the wheel and develop your own solutions (although you can if you like). Instead, also utilize existing platforms for dissemination of digital cultural heritage that are open and ethically focused, especially for archiving images, documents, and data.

In Article 9, the UNESCO Charter on the Preservation of Digital Heritage states that "digital heritage is inherently unlimited by time, geography, culture or format. It is culture-specific, but potentially accessible to every person in the world. Minorities may speak to majorities, the individual to a global audience" (2003). We have seen how it can preserve archives at risk of loss, make them accessible to researchers and the wider public and make it possible to experience touching unique, fragile artifacts. We have also seen how using digital tools can supplement learning experiences in new ways such as developing critical thinking skills and technical skills, and it can enable students half a world away to interact with materials new to them and that would have otherwise been inaccessible. Digital approaches to cultural heritage supplement stewardship in new and exciting ways; we encourage you to explore how your current and future projects can benefit.

Jodi Reeves Eyre, PhD, RPA, Council on Library and Information Resources.

Leigh Anne Ellison, MA, RPA, Associate Director, The Center for Digital Antiquity.

Notes

1. *Mobilizing the Past* is available, completely free, in digital format here: https://thedigitalpress.org/mobilizing-the-past-for-a-digital-future/. It is it a great text for those interested in using digital techniques to collect data in the field, and we highly recommend it.
2. This term is used interchangeably in this chapter. Digital archaeology is the more common phrase in the literature but can be exclusionary of other heritage stewardship activities. However, the tools, methods, and considerations are similar.
3. Here we focus on US policies and requirements.

References

Archaeology Data Service, and Digital Antiquity. n.d. "Guides to Good Practice." Accessed 14 September 2017. http://guides.archaeologydataservice.ac.uk/.

Besek, June M. 2003. "Copyright Issues Relevant to the Creation of a Digital Archive: A Preliminary Assessment" 112. Council on Library and Information Resources and the Library of Congress. Accessed 22 October 2018. https://www.clir.org/pubs/reports/pub112/contents.html.

Colley, Sarah. 2015. "Ethics and Digital Heritage." In *The Ethics of Cultural Heritage*, ed. Tracy Ireland and John Schofield, 13–32. Ethical Archaeologies: The Politics of Social Justice 4. New York, NY: Springer.

Cultural Heritage Partners, PLLC. 2012. "Federal Agency Responsibilities for Preservation and Access to Archaeological Records in Digital Form." Prepared for Arizona State University. Accessed 22 October 2018. https://www.digitalantiquity.org/wp-uploads/2013/05/2013-CHP-Legal-Analysis-of-Fed-Req-for-Curation-of-Dig-Arch-Docs-Data-.pdf.

Digital Preservation Coalition. "Digital Preservation Handbook," 2nd ed. Accessed 14 September 2017. http://www.dpconline.org/handbook.

Dima, Mariza, Linda Hurcombe, and Mark Wright. 2014. "Touching the Past: Haptic Augmented Reality for Museum Artefacts." In *Virtual, Augmented and Mixed Reality. Applications of Virtual and Augmented Reality*, ed. Randall Shumaker and Stephanie Lackey, 3–14. Cham, Switzerland: Springer International Publishing. https://doi.org/10.1007/978-3-319-07464-1_1.

Graves, Michael W. 2014. *Digital Archaeology: The Art and Science of Digital Forensics*. Upper Saddle River, NJ: Addison-Wesley.

Galina, Isabel, Alex Gil, Padmini Ray Murray, and Vika Zafrin. 2017. "Copyright and Creator Rights in DH Projects: A Checklist." http://dx.doi.org/10.17613/M6148V.

Grayburn, Jennifer, Veronica Ikeshoji-Orlati, Anjum Najmi, and Jennifer Parrott. 2017. "Shiny Things: 3D Printing and Pedagogy in the Library." In *A Splendid Torch: Learning and Teaching in Today's Academic Libraries*, ed. Jodi Reeves Eyre, John C. Maclachlan, and Christa Williford, 125–42. CLIR Pub 174. Washington, DC: Council on Library and Information Resources. https://www.clir.org/pubs/reports/pub174/shiny.pdf.

Kersel, Morag M. 2016. "Response: Living a Semi-digital Kinda Life." In *Mobilizing the Past for a Digital Future: The Potential of Digital Archaeology*, ed. Erin Everett, Jody Gordon, and Derek Counts. Mobilizing the Past 1. Accessed 22 October 2018. http://dc.uwm.edu/arthist_mobilizingthepast/1.

Miller, Megan. 2017. "The Alchemy of Tumblr Gold: Uses of Social Media at the Chemical Heritage Foundation." http://dx.doi.org/10.17613/M6ND52.

Richter, Ashley. 2014. "So What Is Digital Archaeology?" *Popular Archeology* (blog). Accessed 18 July 2017. http://popular-archaeology.com/blog/adventures-in-digital-archaeology/so-what-is-digital-archaeology.

Still Image Working Group of the Federal Agencies Digital Guidelines Initiative. 2016. "Technical Guidelines for Digitizing Cultural Heritage Materials: Creation of Raster Image Files," ed. Thomas Rieger. Federal Agencies Digital Guidelines Initiative. Accessed 22 October 2018. http://www.digitizationguidelines.gov/guidelines/FADGI%20Federal%20%20Agencies%20Digital%20Guidelines%20Initiative-2016%20Final_rev1.pdf.

Solly, Meilan. 2017. "This Replica of a Tlingit Killer Whale Hat Is Spurring Dialogue About Digitization." *Smithsonian*, 11 September. Accessed 22 October 2018. http://www.smithsonianmag.com/smithsonian-institution/replica-tlingit-killer-whale-hat-spurring-dialogue-about-digitization-180964483/.

UNESCO. 2003. "Charter on the Preservation of Digital Heritage." Accessed 22 October 2018. http://portal.unesco.org/en/ev.php-URL_ID=17721&URL_DO=DO_TOPIC&URL_SECTION=201.html.

van Noorden, Richard. 2013. "White House Announces New US Open-Access Policy: News Blog." *News Blog* (blog). 22 February. Accessed 22 October 2018. http://blogs.nature.com/news/2013/02/us-white-house-announces-open-access-policy.html.

World Archaeological Congress. 2015. "Code of Ethics." World Archaeology Congress, 23 May 2015. Accessed 22 October 2018. http://worldarch.org/code-of-ethics/.

Glossary

Active learning: A form of learning in which teaching strives to involve students in the learning process more directly than in other methods.
Adult and senior learners: Learners demographically identified as age fifty-five years and older, and because of life experiences, have a different approach to learning than younger students.
Adult education: Topics and courses offered through community-based education or enrichment programs that target lifelong learners outside of formal education settings.
Alternative learning center: Educational institutions, typically high schools, which provide educational services to students who have struggled in mainstream school settings.
Andragogy: The process of adult learning, using techniques that are most effective for adult education; the adult version of pedagogy.
Archaeobotany: The study of plant remains that have survived in archaeological contexts, and can include everything from macrofossils (seeds, fragments of plants themselves, stems, etc.) to microfossils such as pollen. Their presence in archaeological context helps suggest how ancient people may have cultivated and/or used them.
Archaeology education: Programs and resources that explain what archaeology is; what archaeologists do; how sites are discovered, uncovered, and interpreted; and what we know about the human past from archaeological inquiry.
Assessment: Process of ascertaining what a learner knows and understands.
Authentic data/content: Learning materials employing real data.
Authentic learning: A form of learning in which students generate knowledge, engage in disciplined inquiry, and create products (pres-

entations and performances) that they would find in the real world outside of school.

C3 Framework (C3): A curriculum framework for social studies education developed by the National Council for the Social Studies in 2013. Its full title is *The College, Career, and Civic Life (C3) Framework for Social Studies State Standards: Guidance for Enhancing the Rigor of K–12 Civics, Economics, Geography, and History*. It was designed to correlate with the Common Core State Standards.

Civic Engaged Digital Storytelling (CEDS): A method by which individuals use some form of digital media (e.g., film, pictures, blogging) to share part of their individual story for the purpose of addressing an issue of public concern.

Cognition: The mental action or process of acquiring knowledge and understanding through thought, experience, and the senses.

Common Core State Standards (CCSS): Completed in 2010, the Common Core State Standards initiative, directed by the National Governors Association (NGA) and the Council of Chief State School Officers (CCSSO), was a state-led effort to establish a shared set of academic standards for English language arts and mathematics.

Common school movement: The early nineteenth century reform movement led by Horace Mann that sought to prepare citizens in the new democratic republic to sustain democratic institutions. Other goals included the preparation of an educated workforce as well as a disciplined citizenry resistant to disorder in the face of rapid social and economic change.

Community education: Local and community-based, informal learning and development programs organized for both young and adult residents.

Constructivist learning theory: This theory of learning states that individuals construct meaning and knowledge through their own personal experiences and social interactions.

Cross-cultural empathy: Anthropologically, this term reflects a focus upon trying to empathize, or learn to understand what it is like to experience what a person from another culture—the "other"—is thinking, feeling, or doing from a first-person point of view, as closely and accurately as possible. This is a goal set, recognizing that it can never be completely actualized.

Culture wars: Conflict across an increasingly polarized ideological divide reflected in opposing positions on an array of cultural, religious, class, and policy issues, especially heated in US during the 1990s.

Decision-making: A process in which one identifies a need, lists alternative actions, identifies positive and negative consequences of each, reflects on one's values, and chooses a preferred action.

Deep content learning: A form of learning that goes beyond superficial knowledge of a topic and basic facts and delves into a greater understanding of the topic based on reflection of the student's experience with the topic.

Descendant communities: Descendants of people who occupied an archaeological site and who might have an inherent interest in that place.

Digital cultural heritage: The use of digital tools to promote public interest around cultural heritage, digital objects from cultural heritage, digital publications of cultural heritage data and information, preservation and curation of digital cultural data and information, use of digital tools to manage and visualize data, and the digital collection of data in the field.

Digital preservation: Methods used to keep digital materials, such as born digital materials or the digital files that result from digitization, accessible and available for use.

Environmental education (EE): A field of study that teaches children and adults how to learn about and investigate their environment and to make intelligent, informed decisions about how they can take care of it.

Environmental stewardship: The responsibility for environmental quality shared by all those whose actions affect the environment.

Epistemology: The study of the nature of our understanding of knowledge and its validity. More practically, it fundamentally refers to, "How do we know what we know?" This applies to virtually every aspect of our human existence (e.g., How is it that the processes employed by archaeology inform us about the ancient environmental circumstances and cultural trajectories of ancient humans?).

Experiential learning: The process of learning through experience rather than reading about it or listening to a lecture, more specifically defined as "learning through reflection on doing"; it engages the whole human sensory system (sight, hearing, touch, taste, and smell).

Experimental archaeology: An approach that generates and tests archaeological hypotheses, usually by replicating or approximating the feasibility of ancient cultures performing various tasks or feats, or the particular procedures they performed to accomplish them (i.e., producing particular kinds of edge-ware on lithics or burn marks on ceramic firing).

Formal learning: Also called structured learning, refers to organized and structured education with defined goals for knowledge acquisition led by a trained instructor using proven instructional approaches and typically occurs in a traditional classroom setting, e.g., K–12 classrooms, universities.

Ground-penetrating radar (GPR): A geophysical method for imaging a subsurface whereby a device sends electromagnetic radiation (in the microwave band of the radio spectrum) in the form of radar pulses below the surface of the ground. When this energy encounters an object that is different from the surrounding soil, radio waves diffract and a signal is reflected back toward the surface. This signal is detected by an antenna in the apparatus.

Hands-on learning: Learning by doing, where the activity mimics a scenario an individual might encounter outside of the classroom, and the learner is engaged both mentally and physically in the activity.

Heritage: An interdisciplinary concept about how people make sense of the past and use it in the present. It has qualities of engagement with multiple stories and cultures, understanding people, what they value, and how they live. It involves both tangible and intangible aspects of history and cultural heritage. In sum, heritage is whatever is of value to people today that provides some connection between the past and the present.

Heritage studies: The interdisciplinary, publicly-engaged, and community-accountable practice of historical scholarship, focusing on culture, understanding people, what they value, and how they live. Scholarship in heritage studies is practiced at the intersection of multiple fields, including archival research, archaeology, architecture and preservation, landscape studies, and other related areas.

Historic preservation: Traditionally, historic preservation has focused on preserving the physical reality of buildings, structures, objects, and places and the artifactual context of our environment. Today, preservationists are also engaged in reconsidering the meanings and uses of historic places for communities in the present. They are giving greater attention to community engagement that is necessary to identify, understand, document, and protect a fuller range of sites and practices that have cultural values associated with nature, religion, and subsistence, to name a few.

Historical empathy: An understanding of what motivated people in the past, as well as their beliefs and behaviors.

Historical narrative: A type of narrative which places the data of historical research into story form—imposing chronological order on events, suggesting causation in the sequence of events, and displaying a narrative arc with a beginning and an end.

Hypothetico-deductive approach: In archaeology, using the field as a laboratory to test hypotheses, was an idea that employed the hypothetico-deductive approach, and which was the hallmark of Louis Binford's Processual School. Archaeological excavation was done to observe and test hypotheses and thereby predict further results to be verified or not by future empirical—i.e., archaeologically derived—evidence.

Informal learning: A flexible approach to knowledge sharing which occurs outside of a traditional classroom setting (e.g., museums, science centers, archaeological sites), and often uses more interactive educational approaches. Informal learning can be used to enhance classroom learning.

Inquiry arc: A set of interrelated ideas that structure the ways students acquire social studies content knowledge. Informed inquiry requires developing questions, planning inquiries, applying disciplinary concepts and tools, evaluating sources, using evidence, communicating conclusions, and taking action as appropriate.

Inquiry-based learning: The processes of investigation employed by scientists, historians, other scholars or researchers, and students that starts by posing questions, problems, or scenarios—rather than simply presenting established facts or portraying a smooth path to knowledge.

Interdisciplinary learning: A form of learning that utilizes approaches from two or more disciplines, or fields of expertise, to address a question or explore a topic.

Intergenerational learning: A form of learning that occurs when information is shared from one generation to another.

Interpersonal learning: A form of interaction-driven learning, sometimes called social learning, where information is shared directly between the educator and the learner in real-time.

LiDAR: Stands for light detection and ranging. It is a remote sensing technology that maps bare earth below vegetation by measuring the distance laser light travels from the measuring device (typically aircraft) to the ground. This distance is calculated by recording the time it takes for the light to travel from the device to the ground and back.

Likert scale: A common approach to scaling responses in survey questionnaires, typically having five or seven levels: 1=strongly disagree; 2=disagree; 3=neither agree nor disagree; 4=agree; 5=strongly agree. Scaling helps with scoring and analysis of answers across a population.

Metadata: Data about data; descriptive information which explains the data, such as abbreviations, locations, recording techniques, or measurements.

Misconceptions: The failure to understand a certain concept correctly.

A Nation at Risk: Issued in April 1993 by a special commission under the Reagan administration, *A Nation at Risk* shined a spotlight on what they claimed was "a rising tide of mediocrity" that constituted a threat to the nation. Despite serious criticisms concerning its evidentiary base, the report gave rise to the standards movement and a plethora of education reform initiatives still influencing American education.

Non-traditional students: Students who are older than traditional college-age students (eighteen to twenty-two), who may already have careers, families, or who attend school part-time.

Open access: Refers to research, usually publications and/or data, being openly accessible with limited or no restrictions on reuse.

Paleogeography: The study of historical geography, generally physical landscapes, which includes the study of human or cultural environments. When the focus is specifically on the study of landforms, the term paleogeomorphology is sometimes used instead.

Palynology: The study of pollen collected from the air, water, or a variety of deposits. Generally, palynologists use pollen as proxy information to reconstruct past vegetational successions, and hence paleoenvironmental and paleoclimatic conditions.

Passive learning: A traditional form of learning whereby students receive information from an instructor and may engage with it in a limited way.

Pedagogy: The theories, methods, and practice of teaching; typically refers to K–12 education.

Peer-to-peer learning: A method of learning whereby students interact with other students to achieve educational objectives.

Place-based education: An immersive approach to learning that takes advantage of geography, local heritage, cultures, and landscapes to create authentic, meaningful, and engaging personalized learning for students.

Problem-based learning (PBL): A form of learning that is acquired in the effort to understand or resolve a problem.

Problem-solving: The application of a systematic method to construct an explanation or achieve a solution. Principles involve understanding the problem, constructing a plan, implementing the plan, and assessing the result.

Pro-environmental behavior: Conscious actions performed by an individual to lessen the negative impact of human activities on the environment, to enhance the quality of the environment, or to cultivate environmental consciousness.

Public history: The publicly-engaged and community-accountable practice of historical scholarship, which is practiced at the intersection of fields of study related to heritage. Key components include creating more inclusive historical narratives that represent a wide array of experiences and engaging publics in shaping historical consciousness. Public historians and community partners seek to think critically about what the past means and how sites of historical memory and monuments are interpreted, all the while making their work accessible and useful to the public. Public history takes place in historical societies, in academia, in museums, in documentaries, in living history sites, and in how people experience the landscapes of places.

Sense of place: Refers to a personal connection to a place and a sense of personal meaning based on lived experience there. A sense of place also involves a sense of the personal and ecological value of the place, an affection for and personal identification with the place, and a determination to protect the place.

Service learning: A form of learning which connects meaningful service in the school or community (community service) with academic learning and civic responsibility.

Significant life experiences (SLE): Those past experiences which were significant in founding current interests. In environmental education, SLEs are the kinds of learning experiences that produce persons who commit themselves to work actively toward the maintenance of a varied, beautiful, and resource-rich planet for future generations.

Standards-based grading (SBG): A method of grading whereby topics are divided into smaller learning targets for which students are provided feedback. Students advance to the next learning target after mastery of the first learning target.

Stewardship: The collective responsibility and effort by professionals and nonprofessionals to maintain and conserve existing archaeological sites and materials for all peoples so that we may continue to learn and expand our knowledge of human experiences in the past. As guardians, not owners, of these resources, we are ensuring that generations to come have the opportunity to contribute their voices and experiences to develop a more inclusive understanding of human history.

Student-centered learning: Also called student-directed learning, is an approach to learning that directs the educational focus on the student such that the student has agency in and responsibility for their own education and can bring their own experiences to bear on what they are learning.

Teacher buy-in: The extent to which a teacher is likely to attempt a change in pedagogy or curriculum, considering such factors as curriculum alignment, teacher adoption learning curve, ease of classroom implementation, and responsiveness to student needs and interests.

Teacher-directed learning: Also called teacher-centered learning, refers to a learning environment where the instructor is the primary focus and source of information for students.

Transfer: The ability to apply something learned in one context to another context.

Index

Note: Page numbers that appear in bold refer to the placement of the word in the glossary.

3D printing, 247–48
3D puzzles, 51–52
3D reconstructions, 8, 22, 148
3D scans, 245–48

access to
  archaeological sites and materials, 99, 175, 231
  digital information, 241, 243–48, 250–52
  educational programming, 12–13, 139
  knowledge and research materials, 164, 203, 241–46, 248–49
  media, 5–9, 204–5
  nature, 98–99
accords
  Tamaki Makau-rau Accord on the Display of Human Remains and Sacred Objects, The, 245
  Vermillion Accord on Human Remains, The, 245
active learning, 8–9, 50, 79, 216, **255**
Active Minds (program), 193–95, 197
acts (federal)
  American Revitalization and Recovery Act (ARRA), 65
  Archaeological Resources Protection Act (ARPA), 78, 138, 216, 225
  Elementary and Secondary Education Act of 1965, 76
  Every Student Succeeds Act, 76
  National Historic Preservation Act (NHPA), 225
  Native American Graves Protection and Repatriation Act (NAGPRA), 138, 197
  No Child Left Inside Act of 2013, 76
  Post-Katrina Emergency Management Reform Act (PKEMRA), 48–49
Actun Tunichil Muknal (ATM), 168
adult and senior learners, 10, **255**. *See also* adult education; andragogy
  benefits of working with, 187–90, 206
  in contrast to younger learners, 190–92, 203, 205–6
  data about, 187, 197–98
adult education, 186–92, **255**. *See also* andragogy; community education
  effective approaches to, 203–05
  examples of, 192–94
African American communities, 61
African American culture and history, 161, 221, 224, 231, 233

African American History and
Culture, National Museum of
(Washington, DC), 152
African American population
demographics, 67, 173
alternative learning center, 60–62,
255
American Indian. *See* Native
Americans
American Revitalization and
Recovery Act (ARRA), 65
Anderson, Poul (fiction author),
111
andragogy, 190–91, **255**. *See also*
adult and senior learners; adult
education
Angkor (Cambodia), 123–24
applied learning, 31, 48–49, 153,
167, 204
archaeobotany, 110, **255**
archaeological fiction, 111–12, 125,
130
archaeological heritage. *See under*
heritage
Archaeological Heritage Survey,
197–205, 207–10
Archaeological Institute of America
(AIA), 33–34, 78, 159
archaeological literacy. *See*
archaeology education
Archaeological Resources Protection
Act (ARPA), 78, 138, 216, 225
Archaeology (magazine), 6
archaeology education, **255**. *See
also* access to: educational
programming; public archaeology
benefits of, 2
developing and approaches to,
10, 12–13, 219–21, 227–29
future of, 229–233
relationship with environmental
education, 74, 78–79, 103–5
art (subject), 34, 79
artifacts
context of, 83, 168–69, 225–26
interaction and learning with,
8, 27, 59, 86, 115, 221, 226,
240–41, 247–48, 252

interpretation of, 29, 83, 127,
220–21, 225, 228
loss of, 2, 22, 174–75, 180, 196
(*see also* destruction of sites or
artifacts; illicit sales; looting)
preservation of, 168, 225
assessments, 231–32, **255**
examples of, 105–6, 131–32,
207–10
results of, 90–97, 124–27, 145,
171–80, 197–202, 225–27
tools and methods for, 88–90,
124–27, 170–71, 197–202
"at-risk" students, 61
Auel, Jean (fiction author), 112
authentic data/content, 222, 225–
226, **255**
authentic learning, 31–32, 39n3, **255**

BACAB CAAS (Bringing Ancient
Cultures Alive by Creating
Archaeologically Accountable
Stories), 109, 113
assessment, 124–27, 131–32
examples, 118–24
impacts, 127–28, 132n1
implementing, 114–18
BBC, 6
Belgrade Charter, 75–76
Belize, 157, 159–162
Belize Institute of Archaeology (IA),
157–59, 164, 167–69, 182–83
Belize National Institute of Culture
and History (NICH), 158
biology (subject), 24, 63
black market. *See* illicit sales; looting
blogs, 7–8, 200, 239, 243
Bohemian Flats (Minneapolis,
Minnesota), 146–48
Borobudur (Java), 119–122
Boston, Massachusetts
excavations at the home of
Malcom X, 35–36
time capsule, 30
Bradley Commission on History in
the Schools, 21–22
budgets for outreach projects,
59–60, 100, 241–242

Bureau of Land Management (BLM), 216–17

C3 Framework (C3), 24–25, 31, 37, **256**
chemistry (subject), 24, 65
citizenry, literate, 2–3, 75–76, 78, 103–5, 182
Civic Engaged Digital Storytelling (CEDS), 61–62, **256**
civic engagement, 37–38, 61, 103
classroom success. *See also* curriculum: alignment
   examples of, 92–93, 118
   how to achieve, 21, 24–27, 35, 217–18
climate change, 2, 199, 232–33
   coastal erosion, 2, 39
   ice melt, 2
   sea levels rising, 39
cognition, 218–221, **256**
Coliseum, or Colosseum, 27
collecting antiquities, 1, 3, 196. *See also* illicit sales; looting
College for Kids, 95–96
Common Core State Standards (CCSS), 12, 23–24, 39n1, 224, **256**. *See also* curriculum
common school movement, 22, **256**
communication (methods of), 5–10
community archaeology, 36–38, 164, 166–67. *See also* community engagement; public archaeology
community-based learning. *See* place-based education
community diversity, 66–67, 70, 109, 142, 146, 161
community education, 8–9, 13, 186–89, 193, 206, **256**. *See also* adult education
community engagement, 10–13, 55–58, 65, 146–51, 158, 164, 182–83, 224–25, 245–46, 252
community involvement. *See* community engagement
compliance, 237, 243–46
connection with the past, 8, 27–35, 77, 167, 174, 178–79, 203

conservation, 75, 90, 97–98, 100, 199, 217. *See also* heritage; stewardship
constructivist learning, 48, 219–20, 228–29, **256**. *See also* knowledge producers
Council of Chief State School Officers, 23
creative writing. *See* fiction writing
critical reflection, 48, 50, 53, 59
critical thinking, 23, 77, 225
cross-cultural empathy, 93, 96, 110, 113–14, 124, 127–30, 225–26, **256**
cultural awareness. *See* cross-cultural empathy
cultural cleansing, 39, 139. *See also* destruction of sites or artifacts
cultural heritage. *See under* heritage
cultural history, 74–75, 81–82, 99–100
culture wars, 21, **256**
curriculum
   alignment, 24–26, 33–34, 46, 58, 66, 94, 96–97, 99, 104, 217, 223–24, 227 (*see also* classroom success)
   archaeology, 24–26, 33–34, 66, 78–79, 83–88, 103, 130, 217–18, 222–25, 227–28 (*see also* archaeology education)
   challenges, 23–24, 79, 96–97
   core, 53–55, 58, 66 (*see also* Common Core State Standards)
   evaluation, 88–89, 96–97, 222, 225–27
   graduate-level, 138, 140–42
   interdisciplinary, 38, 46, 48, 58, 61, 66, 96–97, 103
   outdoor and environmental, 79–83, 96, 103 (*see also* place-based education)

data
   3D, 245
   collection, 11, 88–89, 170–71, 197–98, 231, 253n1 (*see also* question types used in assessments)

management and preservation of, 13, 239–40, 244–46, 249–52
qualitative and quantitative, 89–94, 171–80, 198–202, 221–25
decision-making, 53, 152, **257**
deep content learning, 50, **257**
descendant communities, 66–67, 115, 127–28, 147, 217–18, 223–24, 229, 245–46, **257**
destruction of sites or artifacts, 1–2, 8, 39, 162, 182, 194, 196, 200–201, 204. *See also* artifacts; cultural cleansing; illicit sales; looting
dialog. *See* communication
digital archaeology, 239–40, 252, 253n2
digital content. *See* digital media
digital cultural heritage, 237–240, 243–50, 252, **257**. *See also* heritage
digital engagement, 240–41
digital media, 7–9, 200, 205
digital preservation, **257**
digital tools, 237–40, 243, 249, 252
Discovery Channel, 129
DNR (Department of Natural Resources), 81
documentaries. *See* film and television

Elementary and Secondary Education Act of 1965, 76
elementary education. *See* K–12 education
Elgin Marbles, 196
environmental change. *See* climate change
environmental education (EE), **257**
benefits of, 103–5
examples of, 79–83
history and explanation of, 74–77
relationship with archaeology education, 74, 78–79, 103–5
Environmental Protection Agency (EPA), 65

environmental stewardship, 97–103, **257**
environmentalism, 75, 97–98. *See also* pro-environmental behavior
epistemology, 110, **257**
archaeological, 113–14
erosion, coastal, 2, 39
ethics, 243–46
evaluation. *See* assessments
Every Student Succeeds Act, 76
evidence-based interpretation, 224, 226–28
EXARC, 241–243, 245, 251
experiential learning, 48, 53, 75–77, 99–103, **257**
experimental archaeology, 110, 241–42, **257–58**. *See also* EXARC

Facebook, 8, 37, 241, 252
fiction writing, 109, 112–13, 115, 118, 124–28
file corruption, 250
film and television, 6–7, 126, 129, 189–90, 200, 239. *See also* media; *and individual television series and channels*
Florida Public Archaeology Network, 78
formal learning, 12–13, 186, 217–21, **258**
Fort Snelling (Minnesota), 148–49

games (educational), 8, 30–31
Getty Museum (Los Angeles, California), 196
GIS (Geographic Information Systems), 223
goals (learning), 26, 74, 103, 115, 129
goals (program), 140, 144–45, 158, 240–44
Gordon Parks High School (GPHS), 47, 57, 60–66
graduate program, 137, 139–42, 146, 152. *See also* curriculum
graduate students, 46, 56, 59–60, 63–64, 70, 148, 150–51, 188
Greece, 196, 200
Elgin Marbles, 196

ground penetrating radar (GPR), 64, **258**
Guantánamo Public Memory Project (GPMP), 150–51

Haffenreffer Museum of Anthropology (Providence, Rhode Island), 78
Hamline University (St. Paul, Minnesota), 109, 112, 119
hands-on learning, 32, 49–53, 63, 77, 79, **258**
hardware obsolescence, 249–250
heritage, 143–44, **258**
    archaeological, 103
    cultural, 240 (*see also* digital cultural heritage)
    inspiring appreciation for, 55–56, 69, 102–3, 173–74, 205–7, 246–49
    partnerships and collaboration, 35–38, 142–46, 162–64
    professionals, 137–39, 153
    threats to, 1–2, 12 (*see also* climate change; destruction of sites or artifacts; illicit sales; looting)
heritage education, 59, 79, 96, 194–97, 232. *See also* heritage studies; Heritage Studies and Public History program
Heritage Education Network, The (THEN), 232
heritage management, preservation, and stewardship, 21–23, 78, 97–99, 158, 243–46, 249–51. *See also* digital cultural heritage
heritage studies, 137–39, **258**. *See also* Heritage Studies and Public History program
Heritage Studies and Public History program (HSPH), 137–42
historic preservation, 34, 138–39, 141, **258–59**
historical empathy, 31, **259**
historical narrative, 27–30, 228, **259**. *See also* narrative

historical societies (partnerships with), 12–13, 62, 151–52. *See also* Minnesota Historical Society
history (subject), 21, 24–26, 29–30, 34, 78, 220–21, 224, 228, 231
Humanities Action Lab (HAL), 150–51
hypothetico-deductive approach, 112, **259**

ice melt archaeology, 2
identity, 158, 177
illicit sales, 1, 3, 196, 202. *See also* looting
inclusion (of diverse voices), 138, 151, 233. *See also* multiple stories and voices; narrative
indigenous communities, 130, 158–59
indigenous heritage and rights, 38, 158–59, 179, 245
indigenous knowledge, 114, 143
informal learning, 12, 187, 217, 231–32, **259**
InHerit: Passed to Present (initiative), 158–59
innovation in education, 26–27, 65
inquiry arc, 24, 31, 37, **259**
inquiry-based learning, 23, 31–32, 49–50, 76–77, 84–85, 95, 220–21, 224–26, 228, **259**
Instagram, 240–241
interactive learning, 5, 59. *See also* hands-on learning
interdisciplinary collaboration, 58, 137–38, 144–46, 231
interdisciplinary learning, 48–49, 58, 66, 78, **259**
intergenerational learning, 205, **259**
International Council of Museums (ICOM), 241
internet. *See also* digital media
    access, 7, 243
    repositories, 242–43, 246–48
    as a tool for learning, 7–8, 59, 175, 200
internship, 141–42, 151

interpersonal learning, 10, 56, 187, 200, 202, 204–6, **259**
interviews, 151, 154n2, 171, 178–79, 195, 226
Intrigue of the Past Archaeology Education Program, 216–17
Iowa, University of, 80–81
   Mobile Museum, 96
   Office of the State Archaeologist (OSA), 79–81, 93
   Recreational Services Outdoors Program, 79–81, 97, 99–100
Iowa City Community School District (ICCSD), 80–82
Iowa River, 81, 84, 93
Iraq, 2
   Bagdad, 196
   National Museum of, 196
ISIS (Islamic State of Iraq and Syria), 39, 194, 196

K–12 education. *See also* Common Core State Standards; curriculum
   approaches to, 32, 47–57, 82–88, 205–6, 227–28, 230
   goals of, 22–23, 38, 68, 76
K–12 students
   as citizens, 48, 61, 65, 78, 225
   learning, 25, 48–55, 77, 218–20
   needs of, 48–49, 55–56, 61–63
   program impacts on, 59–60, 80–81, 88–94, 103–4, 221, 225–27
   reaching, 27–32, 34–36, 56–57, 218
K–12 teachers
   limitations, 54, 82–83, 88–89, 92–93, 100, 217–18
   supporting and partnering with, 25–27, 35, 54–56, 60, 66, 78–79, 94–97, 227–29 (*see also* teacher buy-in)
Kennewick Man, 197
knowledge producers, 50, 53, 66. *See also* constructivist learning

landscapes, cultural, 78–79, 103

laws protecting archaeological materials, 202, 223, 225, 233, 244. *See also* Archaeological Resources Protection Act; NAGPRA; National Historic Preservation Act
lessons or lesson plans. *See* curriculum
LiDAR (Light Detection and Ranging), 65, **259–60**
lifelong learning. *See* adult education
Likert Scale (use of), 89–90, 105, 173–75, 177–78, **260**
lithics and flintknapping, 50–53, 59
looting, 2–3, 7, 196. *See also* illicit sales

Macbride Nature Recreation Area (MNRA), 80–84
magazines (learning from), 5–6, 101, 175, 200
Malcolm X, home of, 36
Maple Grove Middle School (MGMS), 46–47, 57–60, 69
Master's programs, 139–142, 153
material culture. *See* artifacts
mathematics (subject), 23–25
Maya, contemporary, 162–164, 173, 178–79
Maya, heritage and identity, 158, 161, 167, 174, 177–79, 182
Maya Area Cultural Heritage Initiative (MACHI), 158
media, traditional (audio, print, visual), 5–7, 10, 200, 204–5. *See also* access to: media; digital media; social media
memory, collective, 22, 143, 150
memory in learning situations, 50
mentors, 98–102, 142, 146, 151–52
Meskwaki Nation, 80, 85–87, 93, 103–4
   collaboration with, 82
   wickiup, 82, 85–87
metadata, 245, 250–51, **260**
Mill City Museum (Minneapolis, Minnesota), 146–48

Minnesota
  Minneapolis, 65, 67, 146–48, 193
  St. Paul, 60–61, 66–67, 109, 193
Minnesota, University of (UMN), 46–47, 59, 62, 70, 137–38, 140–41, 143–45, 148–50, 154n3, 192–93
Minnesota Historical Society (MNHS), 62, 137, 139–46, 148–52
misconceptions in archaeology, 81–82, 90–91, 95, 101–2, 219–20, 226–27, **260**
misrepresentation of groups, 127
multidisciplinary. *See* interdisciplinary learning
multiple-choice questions, 89–90, 92–93, 105–6, 171, 175–78, 197–201, 207–210
multiple stories and voices, 3, 29–30, 56, 68, 143, 151. *See also* narrative; storytelling
museums
  Getty Museum (Los Angeles, California), 196
  Haffenreffer Museum of Anthropology (Providence, Rhode Island), 78
  International Council of Museums (ICOM), 241
  National Museum of African American History and Culture (Washington, DC), 152
  National Museum of Iraq, 196
  Mill City Museum (Minneapolis, Minnesota), 146–48
  Oriental Institute (Chicago, Illinois), 10
  Peabody Museum (New Haven, Connecticut), 10
  Smithsonian (Washington, DC), 29, 146, 245–46

NAGPRA (Native American Graves Protection and Repatriation Act), 138
narrative, 27–29, 115–18, 139–40, 228. *See also* multiple stories and voices; storytelling

Nation at Risk, A, 23, **260**
National Council for the Social Studies, 24–25, 38, 223
National Endowment for the Humanities (NEH), 34
National Geographic (magazine and television), 6, 200
National Governors Association Best Practices Center, 23
National Historic Landmark, 148–49
National Historic Preservation Act (NHPA), 225
National Park Service (NPS), 34–35, 146
National Register of Historic Places (NRHP), 34–35
National Trust for Historic Preservation (NTHP), 34
Native Americans, 109, 151, 161
  Anishinaabe, Ojibwe, 67
  Dakota, Sioux, 67, 70, 151
  Crow Indians, 224–25
  incarceration, 150–51
  Meskwaki Nation, 80, 85–87, 93, 103–4
  population demographics, 67, 109, 161
  Tlingit Clan, 245–246
newspapers, 5–6, 175, 200
No Child Left Inside Act of 2013, 76
non-traditional students, **260**. *See also* adult and senior learners
North Central Association (NCA), 81
NOVA (television series), 6

Office of the State Archaeologist (OSA), 79–81, 93
Oliver H. Kelley Farm (Minnesota), 149–51
open access, 244, **260**
open-answer/ended questions, 89–90, 124, 171, 173–75, 177, 207–210
oral history and tradition, 85–86, 143, 224
Oriental Institute (Chicago, Illinois), 10

Osher Lifelong Learning Institute (OLLI), 192–95, 197
Osseo School District (Minnesota), 57, 69
outreach. *See* community engagement

paleogeography, 110, **260**
palynology, 110, **260**
Parks, Gordon (photographer), 60–61
partnerships, the value of and need for, 13, 26, 99, 232. *See also* heritage; historical societies; K–12 teachers
passive learning, 6–9, 77, 200, **260**
PBS, 6
Peabody Museum (New Haven, Connecticut), 10
pedagogy, 26, 101, 137, **260**
peer-to-peer learning, 203, 205, **261**
People and the Land (educational unit), 81–88, 91, 93–97, 100
physics (subject), 64
place-based education, 77–79, 103, **261**. *See also* curriculum: outdoor and environmental
pop culture, influence of, 101
Post-Katrina Emergency Management Reform Act (PKEMRA), 48–49
pre-existing knowledge, 48, 219–20
preservation. *See* acts; artifacts; conservation; data; digital preservation; heritage management, preservation, and stewardship; historic preservation
problem-based learning (PBL), 31, 39n2, 61, 190–91, **261**. *See also* problem-solving
problem-solving, 23, 30–32, 76–77, 102–3, 190–91, **261**. *See also* problem-based learning
pro-environmental behavior, 75, 97–98, 100–104, **261**
professional development opportunities, 35, 76, 101, 218, 227–29

program development, 10, 32–35, 58–60, 62–63, 69, 79–82, 113–14, 139–46, 187–90, 192–94, 217–18, 222–28, 241–43
Project Archaeology, 86, 97, 101, 216–18, 222–27, 230–31
public archaeology, 25–27, 37–38, 80, 157. *See also* community archaeology; community engagement
Public Education Committee (PEC), 232
public history, 138, 143, 166, **261**. *See also* heritage; Heritage Studies and Public History program

qualitative questions, 90, 93–94, 106, 197–202. *See also* interviews; open-answer/ended questions
quantifiable questions, 90–93, 171–78, 198–201. *See also* Likert Scale; multiple-choice questions
questionnaires. *See* assessments: tools and methods for
questions measuring for
    attitudes, 88–91, 173–75, 177–79, 198–200, 202
    behavior, 88–91, 175–77, 199–201
    knowledge, 88–94, 173–76, 198–99, 201
question types used in assessments (examples, discussion)
    Likert Scale, 89–90, 105, 173–75, 177–78, **260**
    multiple-choice, 89–90, 92–93, 105–6, 171, 175–78, 197–201, 207–210
    open-answer/ended, 89–90, 124, 171, 173–75, 177, 207–210
    qualitative, 90, 93–94, 106, 197–202 (*see also* interviews; open-answer/ended questions)
    quantifiable, 90–93, 171–78, 198–201 (*see also* Likert Scale; multiple-choice questions)

short answer (*see* open-answer/ended questions; qualitative questions)
true/false, 89–92, 105

race, 142
Reddit, 8
Resource Enhancement and Protection Conservation (REAP-CEP), 81, 88–89
role models. *See* mentors
Rome (Italy), 27, 29

sampling methods and sizes, 89, 127, 171, 197
scholar-practitioners, 137
School of the Wild (SoW) program, 79–83, 88–90, 94–97
science (subject) and archaeology, 24, 33, 46, 55, 58, 62, 65–66, 79, 85, 97, 110, 217–220, 224, 228, 231
Science and Social Studies Adventures (SASSA) program, 46–47, 54–57, 68–71
scientific method and inquiry, 33, 55, 78, 84–85, 226, 233
sea levels rising, 39
secondary education. *See* K–12 education
sense of place, 77, 79, 103, 223, **261**
service learning, 10, 38, 77, 186, **261**
short-answer questions. *See* open-answer/ended questions; qualitative questions
Significant Life Experiences (SLE), 75, 97–103, **261–62**
Silverberg, Robert (fiction author), 111
Smithsonian (Washington, DC), 29, 146, 245–46
social learning. *See* interpersonal learning
social media, 7–8, 182, 237, 241, 248, 252. *See also* Facebook; Instagram; Reddit; Tumblr; Twitter

social studies (subject) and archaeology, 24–26, 34, 46, 50, 55, 58, 64, 66, 97, 137, 217–18, 223–24, 228, 233
Society for American Archaeology (SAA), 34, 78, 197, 216, 230, 232
Spector, Janet, 112
stakeholders, 142, 151, 157, 252
standards-based grading (SBG), 54, **262**
STEAM (Science, Technology, Engineering, Arts, and Mathematics), 10
STEM (Science, Technology, Engineering, and Mathematics), 81
stewardship, 4, 11, 206, 222, 233, **262**
   environmental, 97–103, **257**
   heritage, 78, 97–99, 243–46, 249–51 (*see also* digital cultural heritage)
storytelling, 61, 125. *See also* multiple stories and voices; narrative
stratigraphy, 58–60, 227
structured learning. *See* formal learning
student-centered learning, 50, 190, 194, **262**
student-directed learning. *See* student-centered learning
students. *See* "at-risk" students; graduate students; K–12 students; undergraduate students
surveys. *See* assessments: tools and methods for
sustainable practices, 11, 26–27, 138, 146, 230
Syria, 2, 39. *See also* ISIS

Tamaki Makau-rau Accord on the Display of Human Remains and Sacred Objects, 245
Tbilisi Declaration, 76
tDAR (the Digital Archaeological Record), 246–47
teacher buy-in, 26–27, 45, **262**

teacher-directed learning, 190, 194–95, **262**
Teaching with Historic Places (TWHP), 34–35
technology in educational settings, 59, 64–65, 223, 248
testing in classrooms, 23–24, 54
tests, pre- and post-. *See* assessments
Tlingit Clan, 245–246
touch (sense), 9, 27–29, 63, 77, 205, 221, 247, 252
tourism and archaeology, 158, 168–70, 174–75, 177, 180, 182, 200, 202–3
transfer, 48, 219, **262**
travel. *See* tourism and archaeology
true/false questions, 89–92, 105
Tumblr, 248, 252
Twitter, 8, 241, 248, 252

undergraduate students, 46, 59–60, 112–14, 146, 148
Understanding by Design (UbD), 222, 225
UNESCO (United Nations Educational, Scientific, and Cultural Organization), 76, 239, 249, 252
universities. *See* Hamline University; Iowa, University of; Minnesota, University of
urbanization, 1, 35, 61, 75, 196
US Army Corps of Engineers, 80

value of archaeology and heritage, 3–4, 39, 55, 139, 143–44, 180, 199, 203, 248
Vermillion Accord on Human Remains, The, 245
volunteers
 in archaeology and research, 206, 230, 241–243
 in the classroom, 46, 50–51, 55–57, 59–60, 64, 68–70, 193

Wahl, Jane (fiction author), 128
war, 1–2, 196, 203–4
ways of knowing, 114, 152
wickiup, 82, 85–87

Xibun Archaeological Research Project (XARP), 157–58

www.ingramcontent.com/pod-product-compliance
Lightning Source LLC
Chambersburg PA
CBHW070913030426
42336CB00014BA/2403